Praise for
Dug Down Deep

"At the end of the day, *Dug Down Deep* is J. I. Packer's book *Knowing God* but in blue jeans with a shaved head. That is to say, it's a book of classic truth and worth, written for our day."

> —THABITI ANYABWILE, senior pastor of First Baptist
> Church of Grand Cayman

"I can probably count on one hand the number of books of which I've read every word from cover to cover in one sitting. *Dug Down Deep* is one of them. Josh describes the tremendous relevance and power of Christian truth and compels readers not only to dig their roots down deeper into biblical theology but to stir up a passion for spreading the supremacy of God in all things through Jesus Christ."

> —ADAM YOUNG of Owl City

"Via vivid autobiography, Pastor Harris takes readers on a personal journey into the biblical theology that, belatedly, he found he could not manage without. A humbling, compelling, invigorating read."

> —J. I. PACKER, author of *Knowing God*

"This is a refreshing, interesting book filled with wise insight about why our beliefs about God matter and how right beliefs can be remarkably practical in everyday life."

> —WAYNE GRUDEM, Research Professor of Theology
> and Biblical Studies

"*Dug Down Deep* is a delightful and helpful book. Joshua Harris blends basic, but much needed, theology with his own spiritual journey in such a way that theology becomes real and relevant."

> —JERRY BRIDGES, author of *The Discipline of Grace*

"If you're looking for 'that one book' that will push you farther down the road to faith than you've ever journeyed before, *Dug Down Deep* is it. I highly recommend it!"

—JONI EARECKSON TADA, author; founder and CEO,
International Disability Center, Agoura Hills, CA

"In *Dug Down Deep* my longtime friend Joshua Harris explains the basics of Christian theology in a way all of us can understand. He is a humble man and teaches humbly. If you are tired of hyped promises and want essential truth, this book is for you. As religious fads come and go, the truths in this book will last."

—DONALD MILLER, author of *Blue Like Jazz*

"When the apostle Peter says, 'Humble yourselves under the mighty hand of God…casting all your anxiety on Him,' he implies that humble people are fearless. They have the courage to stand up for truth humbly. I love the term 'humble orthodoxy.' And I love Josh Harris. When they come together (Josh and humble orthodoxy), as they do in this book, you get a humble, helpful, courageous testimony to biblical truth."

—JOHN PIPER, author of *Desiring God;* Pastor for Preaching
and Vision, Bethlehem Baptist Church, Minneapolis

"Josh has succeeded again in giving us a book that is clear, engaging, direct, solid, easy to read, sound, God centered, balanced, humorous—and it even has pictures!"

—MARK DEVER, senior pastor of Capitol Hill Baptist Church,
Washington DC

"*Dug Down Deep* is an incredible book! It's a tangible and incarnate look at theology. I would give it to any young Christian who wants to understand their faith."

—LECRAE, hip-hop artist

DUG
DOWN
DEEP

DUG
DOWN
DEEP

Building Your Life on Truths That Last

JOSHUA
HARRIS

MULTNOMAH
BOOKS

DUG DOWN DEEP
PUBLISHED BY MULTNOMAH BOOKS
12265 Oracle Boulevard, Suite 200
Colorado Springs, Colorado 80921

All Scripture quotations, unless otherwise indicated, are taken from The Holy Bible, English
Standard Version, copyright © 2001 by Crossway Bibles, a division of Good News Publishers.
Used by permission. All rights reserved. Scripture quotations marked (NASB) are taken from
the New American Standard Bible®. © Copyright The Lockman Foundation 1960, 1962,
1963, 1968, 1971, 1972, 1973, 1975, 1977, 1995. Used by permission. (www.Lockman.org).
Scripture quotations marked (NIV) are taken from the Holy Bible, New International Version®.
NIV®. Copyright © 1973, 1978, 1984 by Biblica Inc.™ Used by permission of Zondervan.
All rights reserved worldwide. www.zondervan.com.

ISBN 978-1-60142-371-9
ISBN 978-1-60142-259-0 (electronic)

Copyright © 2010, 2011 by Joshua Harris

Cover design by Mark D. Ford.

Published in the United States by WaterBrook Multnomah, an imprint of the Crown
Publishing Group, a division of Random House Inc, New York.

MULTNOMAH and its mountain colophon are registered trademarks of Random House Inc.

The Library of Congress has catalogued the hardcover edition as follows:
Harris, Joshua.
    Dug down deep : unearthing what I believe and why it matters / Joshua Harris. — 1st ed.
        p. cm.
    Includes bibliographical references.
    ISBN 978-1-60142-151-7 — ISBN 978-1-60142-259-0 (electronic) 1. Theology,
Doctrinal—Popular works. I. Title.
    BT77.H2835 2010
    230—dc22
                                    2009028885

Printed in the United States of America
2011—First Trade Paperback Edition

10 9 8 7 6 5 4 3 2 1

SPECIAL SALES
Most WaterBrook Multnomah books are available at special quantity discounts when
purchased in bulk by corporations, organizations, and special-interest groups. Custom
imprinting or excerpting can also be done to fit special needs. For information, please
e-mail SpecialMarkets@WaterBrookMultnomah.com or call 1-800-603-7051.

To Emma Grace, Joshua Quinn, and Mary Kate

Your father loves you very much. One day when you're older,
I hope you'll read this book and realize that I wrote it for you.
I have no greater hope for each of you
than to see you build your life on Jesus.

CONTENTS

INTRODUCTION

WHAT ARE YOU building your life on?

Your life is like a house. Every house has a foundation, and we're all building our lives on a foundation. It's what we trust in and hope in. It's the thing that gives life a sense of meaning and security. Some people build their lives on money, others on appearance, others on success in a career.

Jesus's teaching on this subject was radical and unsettling. He said that there is only one true and solid foundation for life. Only one that lasts.

He described the only true foundation like this: "I will show you what he is like who comes to me and hears my words and puts them into practice. He is like a man building a house, who dug down deep and laid the foundation on rock. When a flood came, the torrent struck that house but could not shake it, because it was well built" (Luke 6:47–48, NIV).

This book is the story of how I've been learning what it means to come to Jesus, to hear his words, and to put those words into practice. A fancier way to describe this is to say it's the story of how I learned that biblical theology is good and important for living life.

I share a lot of my own journey in these pages, not because I'm particularly special, but because I want to show that Christian truth is practical for real people. I've tried to keep things very simple in the hope that people who have never paid attention to theology will find it accessible (and also because simple is the only way I understand things). I hope this book will be useful as well to people who are just exploring the basics of the Christian faith.

The first two chapters describe my journey from a superficial, uninformed practice of religion to a realization of my need to truly know God. I explain terms like *theology, doctrine,* and *orthodoxy* and why they should matter to us. The next eight chapters look at the basic truths of Christianity—God, Scripture, Jesus, the Cross, salvation, sanctification, the Holy Spirit, and the church. The last chapter is called "Humble Orthodoxy," and I'll just let you read it and find out what it's about.

I've learned there is nothing more important in life than knowing God and basing my life on what he's done for me in Jesus Christ. I hope this book will draw you into the same desire to know him. Don't build your foundation on sand. Think, study, and seek Jesus. Dig deep, and build on the rock.

Joshua Harris

1

MY RUMSPRINGA

*"We're all theologians. The question is
whether what we know about God is true."*

IT'S STRANGE TO SEE an Amish girl drunk. The pairing of a bonnet and a
can of beer is awkward. If she were stumbling along with a jug of moon-
shine, it would at least match her long, dowdy dress. But right now she can't
worry about that. She is flat-out wasted.

Welcome to *rumspringa*.

———

The Amish, people who belong to a Christian religious sect with roots in
Europe, practice a radical form of separation from the modern world. They
live and dress with simplicity. Amish women wear bonnets and long, old-
fashioned dresses and never touch makeup. The men wear wide-rimmed
straw hats, sport bowl cuts, and grow chin curtains—full beards with the
mustaches shaved off.

My wife, Shannon, sometimes says she wants to be Amish, but I know
this isn't true. Shannon entertains her Amish fantasy when life feels too

1

complicated or when she's tired of doing laundry. She thinks life would be easier if she had only two dresses to choose from and both looked the same. I tell her that if she ever tried to be Amish, she would buy a pair of jeans and ditch her head covering about ten minutes into the experiment. Besides, she would never let me grow a beard like that.

Once Shannon and her girlfriend Shelley drove to Lancaster, Pennsylvania, for a weekend of furniture and quilt shopping in Amish country. They stayed at a bed-and-breakfast located next door to an Amish farm. One morning Shannon struck up a conversation with the inn's owner, who had lived among the Amish his entire life. She asked him questions, hoping for romantic details about the simple, buggy-driven life. But instead he complained about having to pick up beer cans every weekend.

Beer cans?

"Yes," he said, "the Amish kids leave them everywhere." That's when he told her about rumspringa. The Amish believe that before a young person chooses to commit to the Amish church as an adult, he or she should have the chance to freely explore the forbidden delights of the outside world. So at age sixteen everything changes for Amish teenagers. They go from milking cows and singing hymns to living like debauched rock stars.

In the Pennsylvania Dutch language, *rumspringa* literally means "running around." It's a season of doing anything and everything you want with zero rules. During this time—which can last from a few months to several years—all the restrictions of the Amish church are lifted. Teens are free to shop at malls, have sex, wear makeup, play video games, do drugs, use cell phones, dress however they want, and buy and drive cars. But what they seem to enjoy most during rumspringa is gathering at someone's barn, blasting music, and then drinking themselves into the ground. Every weekend, the man told Shannon, he had to clean up beer cans littered around his property following the raucous, all-night Amish parties.

When Shannon came home from her Lancaster weekend, her Amish aspirations had diminished considerably. The picture of cute little Amish girls binge drinking took the sheen off her idealistic vision of Amish life. We completed her disillusionment when we rented a documentary about the rite of rumspringa called *Devil's Playground.* Filmmaker Lucy Walker spent three years befriending, interviewing, and filming Amish teens as they explored the outside world. That's where we saw the drunk Amish girl tripping along at a barn party. We learned that most girls continue to dress Amish even as they party—as though their clothes are a lifeline back to safety while they explore life on the wild side.

In the documentary Faron, an outgoing, skinny eighteen-year-old sells and is addicted to the drug crystal meth. After Faron is busted by the cops, he turns in rival drug dealers. When his life is threatened, Faron moves back to his parents' home and tries to start over. The Amish faith is a good religion, he says. He wants to be Amish, but his old habits keep tugging on him.

A girl named Velda struggles with depression. During rumspringa she finds the partying empty, but after joining the church she can't imagine living the rest of her life as an Amish woman. "God talks to me in one ear, Satan in the other," Velda says. "Part of me wants to be like my parents, but the other part wants the jeans, the haircut, to do what I want to do."[1] When she fails to convince her Amish fiancé to leave the church with her, she breaks off her engagement a month before the wedding and leaves the Amish faith for good. As a result Velda is shunned by her family and the entire community. Alone but determined, she begins to attend college.

Velda's story is the exception. Eighty to 90 percent of Amish teens decide to return to the Amish church after rumspringa.[2] At one point in the film, Faron insightfully comments that rumspringa is like a vaccination for Amish teens. They binge on all the worst aspects of the modern world long enough to make themselves sick of it. Then, weary and disgusted, they turn back to the comforting, familiar, and safe world of Amish life.

But as I watched, I wondered, *What are they really going back to? Are they choosing God or just a safe and simple way of life?*

I know what it means to wrestle with questions of faith. I know what it's like for faith to be so mixed up with family tradition that it's hard to distinguish between a genuine knowledge of God and comfort in a familiar way of life.

I grew up in an evangelical Christian family. One that was on the more conservative end of the spectrum. I'm the oldest of seven children. Our parents homeschooled us, raised us without television, and believed that old-fashioned courtship was better than modern dating. Friends in our neighborhood probably thought our family was Amish, but that's only because they didn't know some of the really conservative Christian home-school families. The truth was that our family was more culturally liberal than many homeschoolers. We watched movies, could listen to rock music (as long as it was Christian or the Beatles), and were allowed to have Star Wars and Transformers toys.

But even so, during high school I bucked my parents' restrictions. That's not to say my spiritual waywardness was very shocking. I doubt Amish kids would be impressed by my teenage dabbling in worldly pleasure. I never did drugs. Never got drunk. The worst things I ever did were to steal porn magazines, sneak out of the house at night with a kid from church, and date various girls behind my parents' backs. Although my rebellion was tame in comparison, it was never virtue that held me back from sin. It was lack of opportunity. I shudder to think what I would have done with a parent-sanctioned season of rumspringa.

The bottom line is that my parents' faith wasn't really my faith. I knew how to work the system, I knew the Christian lingo, but my heart wasn't in it. My heart was set on enjoying the moment.

Recently a friend of mine met someone who knew me in early high school. "What did she remember about me?" I asked.

"She said you were girl crazy, full of yourself, and immature," my friend told me.

Yeah, she knew me, I thought. It wasn't nice to hear, but I couldn't argue. I didn't know or fear God. I didn't have any driving desire to know him.

For me, the Christian faith was more about a set of moral standards than belief and trust in Jesus Christ.

———

During my early twenties I went through a phase of blaming the church I had attended in high school for all my spiritual deficiencies. Evangelical mega-churches make good punching bags.

My reasoning went something like this: I was spiritually shallow because the pastors' teaching had been shallow. I wasn't fully engaged because they hadn't done enough to grab my attention. I was a hypocrite because everyone else had been a hypocrite. I didn't know God because they hadn't provided enough programs. Or they hadn't provided the right programs. Or maybe they'd had too many programs.

All I knew was that it was someone else's fault.

Blaming the church for our problems is second only to the popular and easy course of blaming our parents for everything that's wrong with us. But the older I get, the less I do of both. I hope that's partly due to the wisdom that comes with age. But I'm sure it's also because I am now both a parent and a pastor. Suddenly I have a lot more sympathy for my dad and mom and the pastors at my old church. Funny how that works, isn't it?

At the church where I now pastor (which I love), some young adults remind me of myself when I was in high school. They are church kids who know so much about Christian religion and yet so little about God. Some are passive, completely ambivalent toward spiritual things. Others are actively straying from their faith—ticked off about their parents' authority, bitter over a rule or guideline, and counting the minutes until they turn eighteen and can disappear. Others aren't going anywhere, but they stay just to go through the motions. For them, church is a social group.

It's strange being on the other side now. When I pray for specific young men and women who are wandering from God, when I stand to preach and feel powerless to change a single heart, when I sit and counsel people and it seems nothing I can say will draw them away from sin, I remember the pastors from my teenage years. I realize they must have felt like this too. They must have prayed and cried over me. They must have labored over sermons with students like me in mind.

I see now that they were doing the best they knew how. But a lot of the time, I wasn't listening.

———

During high school I spent most Sunday sermons doodling, passing notes, checking out girls, and wishing I were two years older and five inches taller so a redhead named Jenny would stop thinking of me as her "little brother." That never happened.

I mostly floated through grown-up church. Like a lot of teenagers in evangelical churches, I found my sense of identity and community in the parallel universe of the youth ministry. Our youth group was geared to being loud, fast paced, and fun. It was modeled on the massive and influential, seeker-sensitive Willow Creek Community Church located outside Chicago. The goal was simple: put on a show, get kids in the building, and let them see that Christians are cool, thus Jesus is cool. We had to prove that being a Christian is, contrary to popular opinion and even a few annoying passages of the Bible, loads of fun. Admittedly it's not as much fun as partying and having sex but pretty fun nonetheless.

Every Wednesday night our group of four-hundred-plus students divided into teams. We competed against each other in games and won points by bringing guests. As a homeschooler, of course I was completely worthless in the "bring friends from school" category. So I tried to make up for that by working on the drama and video team. My buddy Matt and I wrote, performed, and directed skits to complement our youth pastor's messages. Unfortunately, our idea of complementing was to deliver skits that were not even remotely connected to the message. The fact that Matt was a Brad Pitt look-alike assured that our skits were well received (at least by the girls).

The high point of my youth-group performing career came when the pastor found out I could dance and asked me to do a Michael Jackson impersonation. The album *Bad* had just come out. I bought it, learned all the dance moves, and then when I performed—how do I say this humbly?—I blew everyone away. I *was* bad (and I mean that in the good sense of the word *bad*). The crowd went absolutely nuts. The music pulsed, and girls were screaming and grabbing at me in mock adulation as I moonwalked and lip-synced my way through one of the most inane pop songs ever written. I loved every minute of it.

Looking back, I'm not real proud of that performance. I would feel better about my *bad* moment if the sermon that night had been about the depravity of man or something else that was even slightly related. But there was no connection. It had nothing to do with anything.

For me, dancing like Michael Jackson that night has come to embody my experience in a big, evangelical, seeker-oriented youth group. It was fun, it was entertaining, it was culturally savvy (at the time), and it had very little to do with God. Sad to say, I spent more time studying Michael's dance moves for that drama assignment than I was ever asked to invest in studying about God.

Of course, this was primarily my own fault. I was doing what I wanted to do. There were other kids in the youth group who were more mature and who grew more spiritually during their youth-group stint. And I don't doubt the good intentions of my youth pastor. He was trying to strike the balance between getting kids to attend and teaching them.

Maybe I wouldn't have been interested in youth group if it hadn't been packaged in fun and games and a good band. But I still wish someone had expected more of me—of all of us.

Would I have listened? I can't know. But I do know that a clear vision of God and the power of his Word and the purpose of Jesus's life, death, and resurrection were lost on me in the midst of all the flash and fun.

———

There's a story in the Bible of a young king named Josiah, who lived about 640 years before Christ. I think Josiah could have related to me—being religious but ignorant of God. Josiah's generation had lost God's Word. And I don't mean that figuratively. They *literally* lost God's Word. It sounds ridiculous, but they essentially misplaced the Bible.

If you think about it, this was a pretty big deal. We're not talking about a pair of sunglasses or a set of keys. The Creator of the universe had communicated with mankind through the prophet Moses. He gave his law. He revealed what he was like and what he wanted. He told his people what it meant for them to be his people and how they were to live. All this was dutifully recorded on a scroll. Then this scroll, which was precious beyond measure, was stored in the holy temple. But later it was misplaced. No one knows how. Maybe a clumsy priest dropped it and it rolled into a dark corner.

But here's the really sad thing: nobody noticed it was missing. No search was made. Nobody checked under the couch. It was gone and no one cared. For decades those who wore the label "God's people" actually had no communication with him.

They wore their priestly robes, they carried on their traditions in their beautiful temple, and they taught their messages that were so wise, so insightful, so inspirational.

But it was all a bunch of hot air—nothing but their own opinions. Empty ritual. Their robes were costumes, and their temple was an empty shell.

This story scares me because it shows that it's possible for a whole generation to go happily about the business of religion, all the while having lost a true knowledge of God.

———

When we talk about knowledge of God, we're talking about theology. Simply put, theology is the study of the nature of God—who he is and how he thinks and acts. But theology isn't high on many people's list of daily concerns.

My friend Curtis says that most people today think only of themselves. He calls this "me-ology." I guess that's true. I know it was true of me and still can be. It's a lot easier to be an expert on what I think and feel and want than to give myself to knowing an invisible, universe-creating God.

Others view theology as something only scholars or pastors should worry about. I used to think that way. I viewed theology as an excuse for all the intellectual types in the world to add homework to Christianity.

But I've learned that this isn't the case. Theology isn't for a certain group of people. In fact, it's impossible for anyone to escape theology. It's everywhere. All of us are constantly "doing" theology. In other words, all of us have some idea or opinion about what God is like. Oprah does theology. The person who says, "I can't believe in a God who sends people to hell" is doing theology.

We all have some level of knowledge. This knowledge can be much or little, informed or uninformed, true or false, but we all have some concept of God (even if it's that he doesn't exist). And we all base our lives on what we think God is like.

So when I was spinning around like Michael Jackson at youth group, I was a theologian. Even though I wasn't paying attention in church. Even though I wasn't very concerned with Jesus or pleasing him. Even though I was more preoccupied with my girlfriend and with being popular. Granted I was a really bad theologian—my thoughts about God were unclear and often ignorant. But I had a concept of God that directed how I lived.

I've come to learn that theology matters. And it matters not because we want a good grade on a test but because what we know about God shapes the way we think and live. What you believe about God's nature—what he is like, what he wants from you, and whether or not you will answer to him—affects every part of your life.

Theology matters, because if we get it wrong, then our whole life will be wrong.

———

I know the idea of "studying" God often rubs people the wrong way. It sounds cold and theoretical, as if God were a frog carcass to dissect in a lab or a set of ideas that we memorize like math proofs.

But studying God doesn't have to be like that. You can study him the way you study a sunset that leaves you speechless. You can study him the way a man studies the wife he passionately loves. Does anyone fault him for noting her every like and dislike? Is it clinical for him to desire to know the thoughts and longings of her heart? Or to want to hear her speak?

Knowledge doesn't have to be dry and lifeless. And when you think about it, exactly what is our alternative? Ignorance? Falsehood?

We're either building our lives on the reality of what God is truly like and what he's about, or we're basing our lives on our own imagination and misconceptions.

We're all theologians. The question is whether what we know about God is true.

———

In the days of King Josiah, theology was completely messed up. This isn't really surprising. People had lost God's words and then quickly forgot what the true God was like.

King Josiah was a contemporary of the prophet Jeremiah. People call Jeremiah the weeping prophet, and there was a lot to weep about in those days. "A horrible and shocking thing has happened in the land," Jeremiah said. "The prophets prophesy lies, the priests rule by their own authority, and my people love it this way" (Jeremiah 5:30–31, NIV).

As people learned to love their lies about God, they lost their ability to recognize his voice. "To whom can I speak and give warning?" God asked. "Who will listen to me? Their ears are closed so they cannot hear. The word of the LORD is offensive to them; they find no pleasure in it" (Jeremiah 6:10, NIV).

People forgot God. They lost their taste for his words. They forgot what he had done for them, what he commanded of them, and what he threatened if they disobeyed. So they started inventing gods for themselves. They started borrowing ideas about God from the pagan cults. Their made-up gods let them live however they wanted. It was "me-ology" masquerading as theology.

The results were not pretty.

Messed-up theology leads to messed-up living. The nation of Judah resembled one of those skanky reality television shows where a houseful of barely dressed singles sleep around, stab each other in the back, and try to win cash. Immorality and injustice were everywhere. The rich trampled the poor. People replaced the worship of God with the worship of pagan deities that demanded religious orgies and child sacrifice. Every level of society, from marriage and the legal system to religion and politics, was corrupt.

The surprising part of Josiah's story is that in the midst of all the distortion and corruption, he chose to seek and obey God. And he did this as a young man (probably no older than his late teens or early twenties). Scripture gives this description of Josiah: "He did what was right in the eyes of the LORD and walked in all the ways of his father David, not turning aside to the right or to the left" (2 Kings 22:2, NIV).

The prophet Jeremiah called people to the same straight path of true theology and humble obedience:

Thus says the LORD:
"Stand by the roads, and look,
 and ask for the ancient paths,
where the good way is; and walk in it,
 and find rest for your souls." (Jeremiah 6:16)

In Jeremiah's words you see a description of King Josiah's life. His generation was rushing past him, flooding down the easy paths of man-made religion, injustice, and immorality.

They didn't stop to look for a different path.

They didn't pause to consider where the easy path ended.

They didn't ask if there was a better way.

But Josiah stopped. He stood at a crossroads, and he looked. And then he asked for something that an entire generation had neglected, even completely forgotten. He asked for the ancient paths.

What are the ancient paths? When the Old Testament prophet Jeremiah used the phrase, he was describing obedience to the Law of Moses. But today the ancient paths have been transformed by the coming of Jesus Christ. Now we see that those ancient paths ultimately led to Jesus. We have not only truth to obey but a person to trust in—a person who perfectly obeyed the Law and who died on the cross in our place.

But just as in the days of Jeremiah, the ancient paths still represent life based on a true knowledge of God—a God who is holy, a God who is just, a God who is full of mercy toward sinners. Walking in the ancient paths still means relating to God on his terms. It still means receiving and obeying his self-revelation with humility and awe.

Just as he did with Josiah and Jeremiah and every generation after them, God calls us to the ancient paths. He beckons us to return to theology that is true. He calls us, as Jeremiah called God's people, to recommit ourselves to orthodoxy.

The word *orthodoxy* literally means "right opinion." In the context of Christian faith, orthodoxy is shorthand for getting your opinion or thoughts about God right. It is teaching and beliefs based on the established, proven, cherished truths of the faith. These are the truths that don't budge. They're clearly taught in Scripture and affirmed in the historic creeds of the Christian faith:

There is one God who created all things.

God is triune: Father, Son, and Holy Spirit.

The Bible is God's inerrant word to humanity.

Jesus is the virgin-born, eternal Son of God.

Jesus died as a substitute for sinners so they could be forgiven.

Jesus rose from the dead.

Jesus will one day return to judge the world.

Orthodox beliefs are ones that genuine followers of Jesus have acknowledged from the beginning and then handed down through the ages. Take one of them away, and you're left with something less than historic Christian belief.

———

When I watched the documentary about the Amish rite of rumspringa, what stood out to me was the way the Amish teenagers processed the decision of whether or not to join the Amish church. With few exceptions the decision seemed to have very little to do with God. They weren't searching Scripture to see if what their church taught about the world, the human heart, and salvation was true. They weren't wrestling with theology. I'm not implying that the Amish don't have a genuine faith and trust in Jesus. But for the teens in the documentary, the decision was mostly a matter of choosing a culture and a lifestyle. It gave them a sense of belonging. In some cases it gave them a steady job or allowed them to marry the person they wanted.

I wonder how many evangelical church kids are like the Amish in this regard. Many of us are not theologically informed. Truth about God doesn't define us and shape us. We have grown up in our own religious culture. And often this culture, with its own rituals and music and moral values, comes to represent Christianity far more than specific beliefs about God do.

Every new generation of Christians has to ask the question, what are we actually choosing when we choose to be Christians? Watching the stories of the Amish teenagers helped me realize that a return to orthodoxy has to be more than a return to a way of life or to cherished traditions. Of course the Christian faith leads to living in specific ways. And it does join us to a specific community. And it does involve tradition. All this is good. It's important. But it has to be more than tradition. It has to be about a person—the historical and living person of Jesus Christ.

Orthodoxy matters because the Christian faith is not just a cultural tradition or moral code. Orthodoxy is the irreducible truths about God and his work in the world. Our faith is not just a state of mind, a mystical experience, or concepts on a page. Theology, doctrine, and orthodoxy matter because God is real, and he has acted in our world, and his actions have meaning today and for all eternity.

For many people, words like *theology, doctrine,* and *orthodoxy* are almost completely meaningless. Maybe they're unappealing, even repellent.

Theology sounds stuffy.

Doctrine is something unkind people fight over.

And orthodoxy? Many Christians would have trouble saying what it is other than it calls to mind images of musty churches guarded by old men with comb-overs who hush and scold.

I can relate to that perspective. I've been there. But I've also discovered that my prejudice, my "theology allergy," was unfounded.

This book is the story of how I first glimpsed the beauty of Christian theology. These pages hold the journal entries of my own spiritual journey—a journey that led to the realization that sound doctrine is at the center of loving Jesus with passion and authenticity. I want to share how I learned that orthodoxy isn't just for old men but is for anyone who longs to behold a God who is bigger and more real and glorious than the human mind can imagine.

The irony of my story—and I suppose it often works this way—is that the very things I needed, even longed for in my relationship with God, were wrapped up in the very things I was so sure could do me no good. I didn't understand that such seemingly worn-out words as *theology, doctrine,* and *orthodoxy* were the pathway to the mysterious, awe-filled experience of truly knowing the living Jesus Christ.

They told the story of the Person I longed to know.

2

IN WHICH I
LEARN TO DIG

"Underneath was a deeper question:
what would I build my life on?"

DO YOU REMEMBER the story Jesus told about the wise and foolish builders? Simple story. The wise man dug in the ground and built his house on the rock. When storms came, his house stood firm. The foolish man built his house on the sand. When the wind and waves arrived, the house was swept away. As children we used to sing the story in Sunday school, complete with hand motions. Now that I think of it, this is really quite a traumatic concept for children to sing about—houses toppling and all. But it never really scared me because I went to church, and of course I was a "rock person."

At least that's what I thought.

Recently I reread the parable of the two builders in Luke 6:46–49 as I was sitting on a beach in Florida. I was on vacation with my family, and I'd woken up early to read my Bible and pray by the water. Doing your devotions with the sun rising behind you and an ocean at your feet makes everything you read and think seem really deep and expansive and spiritual. I wish

I could read my Bible by the beach every morning. But there is no beach in Gaithersburg, Maryland. I have a clock radio that makes ocean sounds, but it's not the same.

I've read this story about the two builders countless times. I've read it so many times that I almost don't read it anymore when I come across it in the Gospels. I skim it. I gulp down three sentences at a time because I already know what they say. I don't want to read my Bible like that, but, honestly, sometimes I do. That morning on the beach I almost skimmed right past the two builders. Almost. Maybe it was the sand between my toes. Maybe it was the soundtrack of the lapping waves. But for some reason I made myself slow down.

And as I did, I saw something I hadn't seen before. In the past I thought the point was simply that being a Christian is better than not being a Christian. And I suppose on a very rudimentary level, that is what it means. But I never thought about the specifics of what digging down to rock represents.

Jesus started his story with a piercing question. He asked, "Why do you call me Lord but don't do what I say?" That question makes me uncomfortable because I can't pretend I don't understand it. And I feel that he's talking to me, that he's talking to religious people—people who claim to belong to God, people who say that Jesus is Lord. This is interesting because it clues us in to the fact that Jesus isn't just contrasting religious and nonreligious people. He's not just saying that atheists get their houses knocked down. He's talking to people who claim to believe in God.

Jesus is calling the bluff of the religious. He says, Why play this game? Why call me Lord as if you care who I am or what I want when you don't bother really knowing me or doing what I say? And then Jesus tells the story about the builders and their two houses. The homes they build represent their lives—their beliefs, convictions, aspirations, and choices.

Jesus is telling us that there are stable and unstable foundations on which to construct our lives. Regardless of our intentions, it's possible to base our confidence and trust—the very footing of our lives—on what is insecure and faulty. On shifting sand.

It's easy to write off the man who built on sand as a know-nothing. But that's just because we see the bad outcome of his choice. The foolish builder didn't know he was foolish. At the time, building his house where he did probably made a lot of sense. An oceanfront view. Lots of sand for the kids to play in. And without the backbreaking work of digging, his construction time was cut in half.

I wonder how many years the foolish man lived in his beautiful house on the sand before the storm came. Should any of us assume we're above making his mistake? Would Jesus warn us of something obvious?

The wise builder chose a different approach. Jesus said he built his house on the rock. That involved work and strenuous effort. It took more time.

But listen to how Jesus describes what building on the rock symbolizes. This is what I had always missed. The wise builder is the one who comes to Jesus, listens to his words, and then puts them into practice. This activity—this faith-filled approach to Jesus, the acceptance of his truth and then the application of the truth—is what Jesus said is like a man who dug down deep and built on a solid foundation. When problems and trials and the storms of life came, the "house" of his life kept standing.

What hit me that morning on the beach is that digging down and building on the rock isn't a picture of being nominally religious or knowing Jesus from a distance. Being a Christian means being a person who labors to establish his beliefs, his dreams, his choices, his very view of the world on the truth of who Jesus is and what he has accomplished—a Christian who cares about truth, who cares about sound doctrine.

Doctrine is just a clunky word for truths to build our lives on—truths we'd all doubt or simply wouldn't know about without the Bible. Christian doctrine is Christian teaching about any number of subjects addressed in Scripture: God, sin, Jesus, heaven, hell, the resurrection…and on and on.

Maybe you've never thought about it in these terms, but coming to Jesus and listening to his words involves doctrine. It involves knowing and understanding what the Bible teaches about who Jesus is, why we need him, how he saves us and changes us. In other words, it involves knowing theological truth.

When Jesus talks about the person who listens to his words, he's referring to more than just the red letters in Matthew, Mark, Luke, and John. All Scripture is the Word of God. It's all Jesus speaking to us.

Studying these words and understanding what they mean involve effort. The wise builder digs. It is sweaty, salt-in-the-eyes work. Digging that involves studying. Digging that requires thinking and reading and grappling with sometimes challenging truths.

But the hardest work of all is putting the truth into practice. That's what Jesus pinpointed in his story (and it's the focus of the preceding verses in Luke 6). Truth requires action. Coming to him, calling him Lord, and knowing his words can never be enough. Church affiliation and a list of beliefs are never enough. Doctrine and theology are always meant to be applied to our lives—to shape and reshape not only a statement of faith but also the practical decisions of how we think and act. Book knowledge about building on rock has no value if we're still resting on shifting sand.

Once when my little brother Isaac was four years old, he grabbed a shovel and headed toward the woods. My mom asked what he was doing. He answered, "I'm going to dig for holes." The story has become a family favorite, and Isaac is tired of having it repeated. But it's a good description of what we do when we study and argue over beliefs without putting them into practice. We're digging for holes.

We need to dig for rock.

I know from experience that it's possible to be a Christian but live life on the surface. The surface can be empty tradition. It can be emotionalism. It can even be doctrine without application. I think I've done it all. I've spent my share of time on the sandy surface of superficial Christianity.

The first four years following high school brought good changes in my life—most notably in my spiritual life. Don't ask me to tell you when I was converted. Like a lot of church kids, I don't have a specific day when I repented, put my trust in Jesus, and was saved. For me there was no one breakthrough moment. God poked and prodded and shaped me through countless small, seemingly insignificant experiences and decisions and friend-ships. Do you know the kind of slow transformation I'm talking about? You don't really see it while it's happening. But later you look back and realize you're not the same.

I can identify a few key moments, though. When I was seventeen, I went to a Christian leadership camp in Colorado Springs. The students there were different from other Christians I'd met. They were serious, focused. That might have been the first time I was with a group of Christians who weren't simply trying to "outfun" the world. These kids wanted to outthink and out-work and outlove the world. They wanted to apply their minds to studying Scripture and gaining a Christian worldview. Many had a hunger for God and his Word that stood in stark contrast to my life.

In one session the camp director asked students to stand and recite passages of Scripture they had memorized. I misunderstood the request and at one point stood with my Bible in hand and read a passage. When I realized my mistake, I felt really dumb. I slumped back into my chair red-faced and embarrassed as others stood, one after another, and recited portions from memory. Worse than my misunderstanding was the realization that I didn't have a passage of the Bible memorized. My conscience was pricked.

Around that same time my girlfriend and I ended our two-year relationship. It was a significant moment in my spiritual life. I didn't realize till we broke up just how much our relationship, with its ongoing temptation to compromise, had been draining my spiritual passion. With the distraction and guilt of that relationship over, I began to pursue God in a way I'd never done before.

In his quiet, steady providence, God awakened in me a growing desire to know him. I just wasn't sure what to do with it. My impulse (which was a mix of godly desires and plain ambition) was to try to do something "big" for God. My hero in those days was Billy Graham, so *big* meant big crowds and big fame (all for Jesus, of course).

So at age seventeen, I followed my dad into public speaking. I also began to edit a small magazine for homeschooled teenagers. Preparing messages and writing for the magazine had a good effect on me. It drove me to dig.

Then a friend and I attended a lecture by Christian apologist Ravi Zacharias on the campus of Reed College. I was enthralled by this Indian man with his glowing white hair who was brave enough to venture onto a very secular, even anti-God campus and speak so intelligently about matters of faith. He quoted poets and philosophers as he spoke of Christian truth. He taught Scripture and built a case for the reasonableness of faith that stirred me. He asked me to think; he asked me to engage my mind with God's truth. And he did it all with a really cool accent.

I was hooked. I bought dozens of Zacharias's messages on cassette tape.

I hauled around a cardboard box of his tapes in the front seat of my car and listened to them over and over. I spent so much time with those tapes I even started pronouncing certain words with a slight Indian accent (which must have seemed very odd to people at my conferences). As I drove around listening to Zacharias, I dreamed about marrying one of his daughters and having my father-in-law train me to be the next great apologist, who could disarm atheists and skeptics with jujitsulike skill. (Of course, I wanted to marry every Christian leader's daughter in those days.)

I got hold of J. I. Packer's classic *Knowing God.* It was the first serious theological book I read. Packer taught me that it wasn't enough to know about God or know about godliness but that I needed to truly know God himself—his character and attributes. The study of these doctrines wasn't an end in itself but a means to a relationship with my Creator and Redeemer. Packer taught me that, far from being impractical or irrelevant, theology was vitally important to the living of everyday life. For the first time I began to learn theological terms such as *propitiation* and *sovereignty* and *justification.*

Unfortunately, not everything I studied was as helpful as Dr. Packer's book. Often I picked authors based on what *sounded* spiritually deep. Obscure worked too. I started reading the writings of some rather unhelpful Christian mystics. I was looking for something, anything, that was totally different from what I considered the plastic evangelical world I'd grown up in.

In terms of a church home, I found "totally different" at a large charismatic congregation that met on a hill overlooking the Columbia River. The church building itself was an architectural structure unlike any I'd ever seen—two white domes settled into the hillside. It looked as though God himself had reached down from heaven and placed two giant cereal bowls upside down.

Friends from my old church teased me about the "bubble church" with all its charismatic oddities. I didn't care what they said. I met the Holy Spirit at the bubble church, and since there were only three members of the Trinity, I thought this was fairly significant.

I loved so many things about my charismatic church. I loved the passion and emotional zeal that people had. I'd never seen people so excited about God. They raised their hands and danced during worship. They prayed for hours. They spoke about God and his Spirit with an expectation that he would break into the world at any moment. For a young man hungering for spiritual reality, this vision of God's presence and power was extremely attractive.

I wouldn't trade my time in that church for anything. I encountered God in very powerful ways and learned about the work of the Holy Spirit there. But over time the continual focus on looking for a fresh move of the Spirit began to wear thin. I couldn't shake the sense that something was missing.

I realize now that I still hadn't found what I needed most. I still hadn't uncovered the value of finding and building on bedrock. I was shuffling along the surface, poking at but not digging into sound doctrine.

If I'd been drawn to my old church for a set of friends, I began to see that in some sense my focus at the bubble church was on the latest spiritual experience. I had begun to measure my relationship with God in terms of emotional euphoria and encounters with the Spirit. I wanted to get knocked over or slain in the Spirit. I had merely gone from theology-lite, seeker-sensitive evangelicalism to theology-lite, experience-driven Pentecostalism.

———

When I turned twenty-one, my dad wrote me a letter filled with fatherly advice. One statement stood out: "Find men that you want to be like and then sit at their feet." As I launched into manhood, he was reminding me that some of the lessons I needed most wouldn't be found in a textbook; they'd be written in the heart and life of a godly man. I needed to get close enough to such a man to observe his character and to be shaped by his example. I needed a mentor.

I liked the sound of that. But finding a mentor was easier said than done. It's not as if wise, godly leaders have sign-up sheets for people to "sit at their feet." And in a lot of ways, I felt like I was doing okay. Things were going really well in my pursuit of "big" things for God. The magazine I had started had grown up to glossy, full-color splendor with more than five thousand subscribers. The teen conferences my dad had helped me start had become relatively popular. To top it off, I'd signed a contract with a Christian publisher to write a book. I was living the evangelical American dream. I was doing something big.

But big doesn't equal deep. I had a lot to learn.

One of my teen conferences was sponsored by a little church in Lancaster, Pennsylvania. In fact, that church hosted my conference two years in a row. A young woman named Debbie, who had been one of the first subscribers to my magazine, worked as the church secretary and had organized the event. After the conference I hung out with Debbie and friends from her church. They were weird, but weird in a good way. What I noticed first was the friendship and sense of community they seemed to share. The second thing was how they spoke. They talked about grace, sin, Christ's work on the cross, and sanctification with a warmth and openness that stood out to me. In their normal conversations they used some of the theological terms I'd been learning in books such as *Knowing God*. It was as if they'd taken doctrinal ideas off the high shelf, which they seemed to occupy in my mind, and put them to work in their everyday lives. I found this odd and yet appealing.

I think Debbie saw through the facade of my "success" as a young Christian speaker and writer. She saw a young man who had communication gifts but who lacked real spiritual depth. Even though she was less than a year older than I was, an almost motherly instinct kicked into gear. She was determined to help me.

Debbie's help came in the form of cassette tapes. She sent me sermons by a pastor named C. J. Mahaney, who led a church called Covenant Life in Maryland. Debbie was friends with his daughters, and C.J.'s church had helped to plant the church Debbie attended.

I had listened to dynamic, humorous preachers before, but C.J. was unique. His passion was infused with a theological depth I wasn't accustomed to. His sermons revealed his love for reading and inspired a similar love in the people he preached to. But he didn't reference the popular Christian bestsellers with which I was so impressed. Instead he quoted men like J. I. Packer, Sinclair Ferguson, John Stott, and D. A. Carson. He talked about and quoted long-since-dead pastors and theologians like Jonathan Edwards, Thomas Watson, and John Calvin as though they were still-living, personal friends. Charles Spurgeon, the nineteenth-century London pastor, whose preaching and example of gospel proclamation inspired C.J., was his "historical hero." John Owen was his tutor on the doctrine of sin.

C.J. opened up a whole universe of books and rich theology that I never knew existed. It was like finding out that the most amazing party was being held in your basement but no one had bothered to tell you. Or like a child discovering a carnival in his own backyard.

This is what I'd been longing for but had never known how to name. My soul had been craving good, solid, undiluted truth about God and the good news of his Son's life, death, and resurrection. I didn't need to be entertained. I didn't primarily need to fall over at a prayer meeting. And I didn't need lifeless information. I needed to *know* God. The authors I was discovering spoke about God in ways I'd never heard. They exulted in the God of Scripture who sovereignly ruled over the universe. He was a loving Father who saved men and women by sheer grace, all for his own praise and glory. His Son was the Savior whose atoning death rescued sinners from wrath.

And it was this message of the gospel of grace for which C.J. reserved his greatest passion. Most preachers and zealous Christians I knew got fired up over what *we* needed to do for God. But C.J.'s greatest passion was reserved for exulting in what *God* had done for us. He loved to preach about the Cross and how Christ died in our place, as our substitute.

For someone who had practically been born into church, I found this surprisingly new. The deeper I delved into Christian doctrine, the more I saw that the good news of salvation by grace alone in Jesus, who died for sin—the gospel— was the main message of the whole Bible.

I suppose it might seem completely obvious that this is the center of the Christian faith, and yet it felt new to me. I began to see orthodoxy as the treasuring of the truths that point to Jesus and his saving work. Doctrine was the living story of what Jesus did for us and what it means. Yes, caring about it involved study. Yes, it involved opening books and learning sometimes awkward words. But it was the key to truly knowing Jesus.

———

On a chilly February morning, I shoved the last few bags into my car—a worn, musty-smelling, baby blue 1988 Honda Civic hatchback. Not exactly a chick-magnet sort of car. My friends mockingly called it the grocery getter. When you're twenty-two and single, *grocery* is not a word you want associated with your vehicle. But I couldn't really argue with the description. I just hoped my homely little car would survive the trip.

I was moving to Maryland. C.J. had invited me to do an internship at his church. I was going to live in his basement and be trained as a pastor. It was still hard to believe it had all happened. But my parents thought the invitation was God's plan for me. "My son can learn things from you that I can't teach him," Dad had told C.J.

In the two years since I had first listened to a cassette tape of his sermons, C.J. and I had developed a personal friendship. I had visited his church, attended a conference he hosted for pastors, and stayed in his home. One late-night conversation at his kitchen table made a lasting impression. We talked about my speaking tour, the book I was writing, and my plans for the next few years. And then C.J. asked me, "What are you going to build with your life?" As we talked, he encouraged me to look past numbers as a measure of success and consider what it meant to build something that would last beyond a weekend conference or best-selling book.

Underneath everything he said was a deeper question that I didn't quite grasp at the time: what would I build my life *on*?

So much of my thinking and planning had been based on opportunity, on my feelings, and on the pragmatic—on what worked. C.J. was challenging me to take a radically different approach and base my choices on truth about God and what he was doing in the world.

Two days later, after the conference had ended and I was about to leave, I worked up the nerve to ask C.J. if he'd train me. "I want to learn from you," I told him. What I didn't know was that in the preceding months C.J. had felt God directing his attention to training the next generation of young pastors. My request was a confirmation of that new focus.

"I would be honored to serve you," C.J. said. "Go home, and if your parents and your pastors are supportive, we'll talk."

Less than seven months later, I packed my bags and headed east.

It took five days to drive from Oregon to Maryland. I got one ticket in

Idaho. I didn't even mind. I was glad to have proof that my dinky little Honda could actually break the speed limit.

After I got to Maryland, C.J. put me to work with a new study regimen. He gave me books by Iain H. Murray on Charles Spurgeon, including *Spurgeon v. Hyper-Calvinism* and *The Forgotten Spurgeon,* about the great pastor and his stand against the downgrading of gospel truth. He put in my hands books on practical theology, including Jerry Bridges's *The Discipline of Grace* and J. C. Ryle's *Holiness.* He assigned me messages by David Powlison, a biblical counseling expert, about progressive sanctification. I became the proud owner of Wayne Grudem's *Systematic Theology,* a textbook fatter than a phone book. And I read John Stott's *The Cross of Christ.*

It took me awhile to get used to reading meatier books about theology. Many times while reading Stott's book on the Cross, I underlined and highlighted points that I thought were good only to find at the end of the chapter that Mr. Stott had been sharing them as examples of error. I felt stupid, but I was learning.

But more than digging into the books, I studied C.J. himself. Living with C.J. and his family, I saw what he was like behind the scenes—at the end of the day when he was tired. When his four-year-old son was acting up. When people slandered him. I learned that pastoring a big church isn't glamorous. It's hard work that involves constantly carrying people on your heart— the sick, the wandering, the weak. In it all I saw C.J.'s joy—a joy always grounded in the fact that Jesus had died for his sins. I heard him confess his sin. The authenticity I witnessed in those moments made me want the knowledge of God that C.J. was building his life on.

For different reasons many Christians in my generation and older generations are leery of too much emphasis on doctrine. They have come to equate doctrine with church splits, hate mail, arrogance, and angry diatribes. They have seen how easy it is for life-giving truths to be reduced to empty formulas. No wonder that, for them, Christian doctrine can seem more hindrance than help when it comes to cultivating a vibrant relationship with Jesus.

I understand. If my heart is cold toward God, I can turn the most precious truth into an end in itself or a weapon to attack others. This is part of the reason I find the story of the wise builder so instructive. It reminds me that doctrine isn't about me or my little tribe. Jesus said that the person who digs down to the rock is the one who comes to *him*. This has to be the first and final motivation. Pursuing orthodoxy and sound doctrine has to begin with a heart drawing close to Jesus—not to a theological system, denomination, or book.

It's easy to make the mistake of thinking that since theological beliefs shouldn't be our goal, we don't need them at all. But this isn't true in knowing Jesus any more than it's true in other relationships. For example, I have a nine-year-old daughter named Emma, whom I love very much. It is absolutely true that information and facts about my daughter can never take the place of actually loving her. But this doesn't mean I should avoid knowing about her. An important part of caring for and cultivating a relationship with my little girl involves my willingness to learn her character and personality, her likes and dislikes. Details about her—the color of her hair, the music she enjoys, her gifts, fears, and dreams—are all important to me because *she* is important to me. These truths about her could be empty data, but because they describe a living person whom I love, they enrich and grow my love for her. Facts can never take her place, but I can't know her without them.

Doctrine can never take the place of Jesus himself, but we can't know him and relate to him in the right way without doctrine. This is because doctrine tells us not only what God has done but also what his actions mean to us. A theologian named J. Gresham Machen, who wrote in the early part of the twentieth century, helped me better understand all this. His explanation of Christian doctrine helped me see how it connects to the living person of Jesus. In one of his books, Machen explains that while Christians in the early church wanted to know what Jesus taught, they were primarily concerned with what Jesus had *done.* "The world was to be redeemed," Machen writes, "through the proclamation of an event."

Of course the event he's referring to is Jesus's death by crucifixion and his resurrection from the dead. The first Christians knew they had to tell people about this event. But simply telling them wasn't enough. They also had to tell them what the event meant. And this, Machen explains, is doctrine. Doctrine is the setting forth of what Jesus has done along with the meaning of the event for us.

"These two elements are always combined in the Christian message," Machen continues. "The narration of the facts is history; the narration of the facts with the meaning of the facts is doctrine. 'Suffered under Pontius Pilate, was crucified, dead and buried'—that is history. 'He loved me and gave Himself for me'—that is doctrine."[1]

Doctrine is the meaning of the story God is writing in the world. It's the explanation of what he's done and why he's done it and why it matters to you and me.

———

Jesus's story of the two builders ends with one house standing firm through storms and the other house being washed away. The sand didn't hold, and the house came crashing down. The wind and waves Jesus spoke about might represent difficulties and trials in life. They could also be a symbol of the final judgment when all mankind will stand before Jesus and give an account. I suppose it's best to think of both. Both are going to happen. Trials and suffering will touch us all eventually. And the final day, even though it seems distant, will eventually arrive.

And in both cases, knowing and living by sound doctrine are of utmost importance. Why? Because on the final day only those who have believed in Jesus Christ and lived for him will be rescued from the wrath of God. And because in the present when our lives are shaken by suffering, firsthand knowledge of God's character and love is the only thing that can hold us.

I saw this reality in the life of my younger brother Joel and his wife, Kimberly. Not long after they married, they found out they were pregnant. You've never seen a more excited dad- and mom-to-be. And then the ultrasound results came back with devastating news. Their little girl's heart was missing a chamber. After she was born, doctors discovered further complications with her heart. Baby Faith, as they named her, had a very small chance to survive. She fought hard to live, but her tiny heart worked at just half capacity. Only a heart transplant could have saved her. When it didn't come and when her strength began to fail, doctors attempted emergency heart surgery. But during the procedure the surgeon made a mistake. Her heart was punctured, and she died. Two months after she came into the world, little Faith went to be with the Lord.

I'm eight years older than Joel. Watching my little brother and his wife walk through the sadness of losing a child was gut-wrenching. To borrow the imagery of Jesus's parable, it was like watching from a distance as the home they lived in was hit by a tidal wave. The wind and waves of suffering crashed like a tsunami against their life.

But when the water cleared, the house of their life stood firm and strong.

Joel and Kimberly felt deep grief; they experienced deep anguish of the soul. But they stood firm because they were rooted in a deep knowledge of God. They had built their lives on truth.

Each day during those difficult weeks before Faith's passing, I would read what Joel and Kimberly had written on the Web page where they shared updates and prayer requests for Faith. Over and over again they wrote about the confidence and hope they had in the truth of God's sovereignty. And after Faith passed away, they never blamed the surgeon. They were never bitter. They wrote about God's providence, his sovereign control of the situation, their gratefulness for the gospel.

When I think about Joel and Kimberly, I can't bear to hear people speak of doctrine as a meaningless pursuit of facts and figures and formulas. There's nothing more important, more precious, more life securing than knowing and living by God's truth.

———

If doctrine is only words on a page, it can be perceived as a bunch of lifeless rules or formulas. But when you see orthodoxy in the vibrant colors of a person's life—when you observe that person applying it with joy and humility—you see that it's beautiful. When you see someone walking in the old paths and being led to a deeper knowledge of Jesus, it makes you want to walk in them too. When you witness the strength and security that come with being dug down into doctrinal truth, it makes you want to dig into truth yourself.

And that is the purpose of this book. I write in the hope that you'll catch a glimpse of how good and beautiful the old paths of orthodoxy are, how firm and trustworthy the solid rock of sound doctrine can be for your life.

I hope these pages will inspire you to dig into the richness of theology.

The past ten years of my life have been the story of uncovering the relevance, the joy, and the practical power that come from Christian doctrine. Doctrine isn't dry and boring. It isn't just for arguing. It's for knowing God and living life to the fullest.

The following chapters are reflections on various Christian doctrines that have particularly touched my life. This isn't a book on systematic theology proper. It's more like a mixtape of biblical truth that I've found personally significant.

Dug Down Deep is my reveling in theology in my own simple way—not too polished, sometimes awkward, less than scholarly, hopefully gracious and faithful. Even though these are deep truths, I don't pretend to be swimming in the deep end of the pool. I'm splashing in the shallow end. But if my splashing can inspire you to dive in, I will have succeeded.

A few years ago I was back in my hometown in Oregon to visit my family. While I was there, I saw Steve, the youth pastor from the church I'd grown up in (the big evangelical church where I danced like Michael Jackson). We bumped into each other in the produce section of the local grocery store. I hadn't seen him for years. He had known me when I was a cocky thirteen-year-old with Aqua Net–soaked hair. Now I was married, a father who drove a minivan, and had shaved my head as a preemptive strike against baldness.

Steve hadn't changed at all. He'd always loved to work out and was still ripped. His eyes were still bright with life. It was good to see him. We started talking about old times, and then he told me how things were going at the youth group now. A lot had changed since the days I was there, he said. He had learned so much in the past decade about what kids really needed. Now he had students studying doctrine from *Systematic Theology*, Grudem's hefty textbook that is normally used in seminaries. The students were undaunted by its size. In fact, they liked the challenge. "They're eating it up," he told me. "These kids are on fire for God like you wouldn't believe. They're sharing their faith with friends. It's incredible."

I left the grocery store that day smiling. I thought about God having mercy on a hypocritical punk of a church kid like me. He'd replaced my love for the world with a love for Jesus and his truth. I'd gone from scraping the surface of shallow Christianity to being a young pastor who loved digging into doctrine. I was learning how to build my life on the rock and to lead others in doing the same.

And I smiled as I imagined Steve with a new generation of church kids studying theology and finding that exciting. That made my day. I pictured Steve in one of his muscle shirts tearing into the ground with a big old shovel. I imagined him handing out shovels to all those kids in the youth group. Teaching them how to dig deep.

3

NEAR BUT NOT
IN MY POCKET

"God is utterly different from me.
And that is utterly wonderful."

THERE'S THIS COFFEE SHOP about ten minutes from my house where I spend a fair amount of time. I'll go there to study or work on a sermon. I usually sit at the table in the far right-hand corner, the one next to the electric outlet. If I stay long enough, the smell of roasted coffee beans soaks into my clothes. The aroma smells good while I'm there, but for some reason, after I leave, I smell like I've been chain-smoking. My wife can always tell if I've been at the coffee shop all day. When I come home, she will kiss me and say, "Hey, smoker." That always makes me smile.

One side of the coffee shop is lined with big windows that look out on a sidewalk. When I sit facing the wall of windows, I find it entertaining to watch people as they walk by, because almost every person uses the windows as a mirror. Those on the outside have to purposely focus their eyes to see inside, where the lighting is low. It's much easier just to look at their own reflections.

If you've ever watched people look at themselves in a mirror, you know how amusing this can be. I've noticed that women give themselves the once-over very quickly. Their eyes dart up and down in a millisecond. A lot of them do this funny pouty thing with their mouths. Or they purse their lips like a lipstick model. Then they tug on some part of their clothing and move on. Men are different. Some lift their heads and straighten their backs. Others tilt their heads down and narrow their eyes as if they're James Dean.

I've learned that everyone has a mirror face—that facial expression we put on when we check ourselves out in a mirror. It's the way we think we look most attractive. So we smile a certain way or arch our eyebrows or suck in our cheeks or cock our heads. The funny thing about a mirror face is that it looks ridiculous to other people. If we walked around wearing our mirror faces, our friends would laugh at us, and strangers would think we had some kind of rock-star complex.

Sitting in the coffee shop, I watch people flash their mirror faces as they pass by the windows. I find it funny that they forget people like me are inside looking out at them. They see only themselves.

People's mirror faces got me thinking about theology. But let me back up first. The study of theology encompasses many different subjects: God's church, God's plan of salvation, God's work in us to make us like Jesus, to name a few. But when we focus on God himself—who he is and what he is like—we're touching the *heart* of theology. In fact, the doctrine of God is called *theology proper,* because that's what the word *theology* means: the study of God. In this chapter we're launching into an examination of key Christian beliefs. And I think the doctrine of God, or theology proper, is a good place for us to start, because what we think about God—what we understand about his character and his attributes—shapes our understanding of every other doctrine and even life itself.

There's nothing more important than rightly knowing God and thinking true thoughts about him. But there's also nothing I find more difficult. And that's not for the reason you might assume.

You would think the hardest thing about studying the doctrine of God is that God is so immense it's impossible for our limited minds to comprehend him. And in one sense this is true. Because God is infinite and we are limited, finite creatures, we can never have a complete knowledge of him. God is incomprehensible. He is great beyond all bounds. But while we can't know God exhaustively, we can know him truly. This is only possible because God has revealed truths about himself. And while these are deep truths and God's greatness surpasses all human measurements, what God has revealed about himself in his Word is truth we can grasp.

What makes it difficult for us to see the truth about God, I think, isn't his overwhelming immensity but our overwhelming self-centeredness. Looking past ourselves is a lot harder to do than most of us realize. Many have never tried. In this way we're a lot like the people walking past the windows of the coffee shop. Instead of looking through the window of God's self-revelation and seeing him, we find it easier to admire our own reflection or to place on him the constraints of our own existence. We judge him by our standards of justice, fairness, power, and mercy. We even measure his greatness by our own ideals of greatness.

The ironic thing about these moments is that we often think we're seeing God. We think we know something about what he is like. But we're seeing mostly a reflection—a God who looks a lot like us. A God imagined in our own image.

A few years back a couple of sociologists named Christian Smith and Melinda Denton published the first results of their study on the religious beliefs of teenagers in America. I'm not really into studies or statistics. In fact, as soon as someone mentions a statistic, my eyes start to glaze over. But when I read the findings of this study, they caught my attention, because in many ways I felt they describe how I viewed and related to God in high school. And also because the findings show that most people today imagine God as they'd like him to be—a God who caters to their personal needs and desires.

In their book *Soul Searching,* Smith and Denton describe the prevalent view of God among teenagers as "moralistic therapeutic deism." Now that's a mouthful, but let me explain.

A *moralistic* outlook says if I live a moral life, do good things, and try not to do bad things, God will reward me and send me to a "better place" when I die. For most people a good life involves not killing other people or robbing old ladies and babies. The bar is not real high.

A *therapeutic* orientation to God says his primary reason for existing is to make me happy and peaceful. So God is a form of therapy, of self-help. He exists for me.

Deism says God exists but he's distant and mostly uninvolved. Or we could say *conveniently* uninvolved. He won't interrupt my plans or get in my business. He doesn't tell me what to do.

"In short," Smith and Denton write, "God is something like a combination Divine Butler and Cosmic Therapist: he is always on call, takes care of any problems that arise, professionally helps his people to feel better about themselves, and does not become too personally involved in the process."

They quote a seventeen-year-old girl from Florida who said, "God's all around you, all the time. He believes in forgiving people and whatnot and he's there to guide us, for somebody to talk to and help us through our problems. Of course, he doesn't talk back."[1]

Some of us might have a more sophisticated description of God than this seventeen-year-old. We might even have enough theological knowledge to give a very different description. But I wonder how different our functional view of God is from hers. I would never dare to call God my Divine Butler or Cosmic Therapist, but how often do I treat him as if he were? Do I live in a way that proves I have great and true thoughts of God?

"We are a modern people," writes J. I. Packer, "and modern people, though they cherish great thoughts of themselves, have as a rule small thoughts of God." He goes on to point out that just because God is personal (meaning we can speak to him, relate to him, and know him) doesn't mean he's the same sort of person that we are—"weak, inadequate, ineffective, a little pathetic." Packer says, "Our personal life is a finite thing: it is limited in every direction, in space, in time, in knowledge, in power. But God is not so limited. He is eternal, infinite and almighty. He has us in his hands; we never have him in ours. Like us, he is personal; but unlike us, he is *great*."[2]

What do I see about God when I look past my own reflection? In the Bible—the primary place God reveals himself—I behold a God who is utterly and wonderfully different from me.

I am created. *God is Creator.* I am made. God is the one who made all things, who "created the heavens and the earth" (Genesis 1:1). He spoke and created the world out of nothing.

I have a beginning. I was conceived in my mother's womb in the year 1974. Before that I didn't exist. *God is eternal.* God has no beginning and no end. He exists outside of time and space. Psalm 90:2 says, "Before the mountains were brought forth, or ever you had formed the earth and the world, from everlasting to everlasting you are God."

I am dependent. I need air to breathe, water to drink, food to eat, or my body dies. *God is self-existent.* He does not rely on anything outside of himself. He has life in himself and draws his unending energy from himself.[3] God "does not live in temples made by man, nor is he served by human hands, as though he needed anything, since he himself gives to all mankind life and breath and everything" (Acts 17:24–25).

I am limited in space. I can be in only one place at one time. *God is omnipresent.* He is everywhere always present. "God is spirit" and not limited by space (John 4:24). God says of himself, "Am I a God at hand, declares the LORD, and not a God far away? Can a man hide himself in secret places so that I cannot see him? declares the LORD. Do I not fill heaven and earth? declares the LORD" (Jeremiah 23:23–24).

I am limited in power. There are limits to how fast I can run. How much weight I can lift. How high I can jump. *God is almighty.* He is omnipotent—possessing all power. Nothing is too hard for him (Jeremiah 32:17). He can do all things, and no purpose of his can be thwarted (Job 42:2).

I am limited in knowledge. My knowledge of any subject is at best partial. No matter how much I study, it is still incomplete. I can know only what I observe, read, or am told by someone else. And my mind can forget some or all that I've learned. *God is all-knowing.* He is omniscient—he has full knowledge of all things past, present, and future. Job 37:16 tells us that God is "perfect in knowledge." And Hebrews 4:13 says, "And no creature is hidden from his sight, but all are naked and exposed to the eyes of him to whom we must give account."

God isn't a bigger, better version of me. "It is not just that we exist and God has always existed," writes Wayne Grudem, "it is also that God *necessarily* exists in an infinitely better, stronger, more excellent way. The difference between God's being and ours is more than the difference between the sun and a candle, more than the difference between the ocean and a raindrop, more than the difference between the arctic ice cap and a snowflake, more than the difference between the universe and the room we are sitting in: God's being is *qualitatively different.*"[4]

The qualitative difference of God, his "otherliness" revealed in his divine attributes, is summed up in the word *holy.* In Isaiah's vision of God on his throne, the angels covered their eyes and feet before God and cried, "Holy, holy, holy is the LORD of hosts; the whole earth is full of his glory!" (Isaiah 6:3).

I used to think of God's holiness only in terms of moral purity. But R. C. Sproul taught me that holiness primarily speaks of God being separate from his creation in his perfection and power. God's holiness means that he is transcendent—that he exceeds all limitations. That God is holy means that he is above us and beyond us.

"When the Bible calls God holy," writes Sproul, "it means primarily that God is transcendentally separate. He is so far above and beyond us that He seems almost totally foreign to us."[5]

I remember one of the first times I experienced the practical power of truth about God in my life. It wasn't long after I moved to Maryland. I was single, wanting to get married, interested in several girls (one of whom was Shannon), but unsure about when and with whom I should pursue a relationship. I was confused, impatient, and acutely aware of how little I knew about the future. I wanted God to tell me what to do. I wanted a girl's name written in the sky.

During that time I'd been studying God's attributes, in particular his sovereignty. I was learning that God had total power and authority over everything. He was sovereign over every molecule of the universe (Hebrews 1:3). Over every kingdom and earthly authority (Psalm 47:8). Over every human heart (Proverbs 21:1).

One day as I was walking and praying, I began to reflect on Romans 8:30, where Paul describes God's sovereignty in salvation: "And those whom he predestined he also called, and those whom he called he also justified, and those whom he justified he also glorified." I was overwhelmed by the thought that God knew me before I was born. The awesome implications of this truth flooded my mind. For God to see me down through time, for him to bring about my life, he had to sovereignly direct a billion countless details.

God was sovereign in the emigration of my great-grandparents from Japan. He was sovereign over the mortar in World War II that exploded near my grandfather and caused him to lose his leg, sending him to the hospital where he met my grandmother. For God to see me, he had to see both of my parents and all the moments and days of their two lives that would lead to their marriage and my birth.

The reality of God holding all human history in his hands—including my little life and my little questions—filled me with awe. God saw my past, present, and future perfectly. He had mercifully saved me. He had promised that one day I would be glorified. In light of all this, there was no reason to doubt him. I could trust him with my questions about marriage and my future.

None of my questions were answered. I still didn't know whom I was supposed to marry. I didn't know anything more about my future. But I was filled with the most amazing sense of peace as I considered the awesome God who was sovereign over all.

God's attributes are not merely a list of facts and features. They are truths that inform belief and inspire faith. God reveals truth about himself in his Word, not for the sake of knowledge, but for the sake of relationship with us. He tells us about himself so we will put our faith in him, so we will treasure and worship him and not waste ourselves on man-made idols. He wants our souls to soar in worship and communion with him—not rot in the pursuit of sin or waste away in worry and fear.

God is different from you and me. He is utterly different. And that is utterly wonderful.

There is surprising comfort in the realization that God is so unlike you and me. The fact that he's not like us is the reason we can run to him for rescue.

It's good news that God doesn't think and act the way we do. As he invites us to approach him to receive mercy and pardon, he holds out wonderful news: "For my thoughts are not your thoughts, neither are your ways my ways, declares the LORD. For as the heavens are higher than the earth, so are my ways higher than your ways and my thoughts than your thoughts" (Isaiah 55:8–9).

God is not like us. He's strong. He's unchanging. His love is steadfast (Psalm 136:1). He is full of mercy. And he does what we would never do, what we would never imagine: he dies for his enemies. "God shows his love for us in that while we were still sinners, Christ died for us" (Romans 5:8).

———

Once, as I was shopping at a mall, I noticed a woman working at a kiosk that sold beads and jewelry. She had no customers. She was leafing through a magazine. And I had a strong sense that I should talk to her about God. Trying to be bold, I walked up and said, "Excuse me, but I just felt that I was to tell you that God loves you."

She looked up from her magazine with the most bored, disinterested expression imaginable, raised one eyebrow, and said, "I know that," and immediately turned back to her magazine. I froze. I had no idea what to say next, so I turned and walked away.

I left thinking two things. First, that I stink at evangelism and that telling someone God loves them is a dumb way to start a conversation. But the second thing I realized was that, like this woman, a lot of people take lightly the idea of God loving them because they have no idea who he is.

Most people seem to assume it's God's job to love them. *Of course God loves us. What else does he have to do?* He is weak, small, and maybe even a little nerdy. He needs us. He pines for us. And if we pay him any attention—go to church, do a good deed, recycle, or maybe meditate while listening to soothing music—then we've done him a really big favor.

The love of God is wonderful news only when we understand his transcendence—when we tremble at his holiness, when we're awed by his perfection and power. God's love is perceived as amazing only when we realize that the one thing we truly deserve from him is righteous wrath and eternal punishment for our disobedience and disloyalty.

Seeing God for who he is leaves us asking with the psalmist, "What is man that you are mindful of him, and the son of man that you care for him?" (Psalm 8:4).

———

Careful study of the character and attributes of God should leave us feeling more amazed, more loved, and more secure in God's love. But this happens in the most surprising way. We become more confident of God's love for us as we understand we are not the center of the universe. God is. God is not centering himself around us and our worth. God is centered on his own eternal glory.

I remember the first time I heard someone articulate a biblical vision of a God-centered God. I was in Austin, Texas, listening to John Piper preach at Louie Giglio's Passion conference in 1998. The theme verse for the event was Isaiah 26:8: "Yes, LORD, walking in the way of your laws, we wait for you; your name and renown are the desire of our hearts" (NIV). The messages were focused on God's fame and renown.

The irony about my participation in a conference dedicated to God's glory was how consumed I was the whole time with my own glory. My first book had been released the year prior, and I found myself constantly wondering if people would recognize me, if they'd know who I was. I loved glory. But it wasn't God's glory that captured my heart. I wanted my own glory.

Piper's message was a stinging balm for my soul. He preached about God's passion for his glory. He explained how the major obstacle to glorifying God is a secular mind-set that begins with man as the starting point of life and reality. With this mind-set, he said, problems and successes are defined by us and our goals and priorities.

But the biblical mind-set, as Piper called it, is completely opposite. Here the starting point is God. His rights and goals define reality. We talk of human rights and civil rights, Piper said, but never of Creator rights. I'd never thought of that before. The implication was that what constitutes a problem in this universe is not what upsets my itsy-bitsy world of clothes, sex, food, relationships, traffic, and television. No, what constitutes a problem is anything that contradicts the goals and plans of this Creator.

Then Piper asked what the basic riddle of the universe really is. Is it the question, why is there suffering in the world? No, said Piper, not for the person with a biblical mind-set. The question for this God-centered person is, why is there any goodness for a sinner like me? How can God—a holy and righteous God—pass over the sins of man? Why doesn't he wipe us out?

I was ashamed to admit the question never kept me up at night. I had a small view of God's holiness and righteousness and an inflated view of my worth and value.

Piper continued to press the question, how can God be good and forgive sinners? He used the hypothetical illustration of a failed attempt by terrorists to destroy the White House and kill the president. If the terrorists are brought to trial and the judge forgives them, gives them a vacation, and sends them on their way, what will other nations assume about this judge? They'll think he is crazy or has been bought off. Or at least assume he has no respect for the law.

So it is with God's glory, Piper explained. If God passed over sin and brought no punishment, what else could we assume about his character except that he was less than perfect?

Then Piper pointed to the Cross. On Calvary, God displayed his justice and his love. He was glorified in the death of his Son. He loves his glory that much! And how great was the glory of the death and resurrection of the one and only Christ—the very Son of God! "The foundation of your salvation," Piper said, "is God's love for His own glory."

I'd never heard anyone speak that way about Jesus's death on the cross. I had always heard it explained in terms of my great worth. I am so valuable that God would send Jesus to die. The question Piper closed his message with deeply challenged me. "Do you love the Cross because it makes much of you?" he asked. "Or do you love it because it enables you to enjoy an eternity of making much of God?"

I left Austin with an unsettling thought that has never left me. If I love the Cross only for what it does for me, I will have reduced it to a monument to myself. But the greatest glory of the Cross is what it tells me about God. A God of justice and mercy. A God who loved helpless sinners like me so much that he came to die so we could be free to know and worship him for eternity.

In my high school youth group, we used to sing a song about how God is transcendent but also immanent and close to us. Actually, at the time I didn't know what the song was about. I didn't understand it. The words said,

> This is what the high and lofty one says,
> He who lives forever, holy is his name.
> "I dwell in a high and lofty place
> And with the lowly in spirit."

Our worship leader would have the guys and girls sing it as a round. That always sounded pretty cool. But I didn't know what it meant. Somehow I missed that the words of the song were drawn from Isaiah 57:15, which says,

> For thus says the One who is high and lifted up,
>   who inhabits eternity, whose name is Holy:
> "I dwell in the high and holy place,
>   and also with him who is of a contrite and lowly spirit,
> to revive the spirit of the lowly,
>   and to revive the heart of the contrite."

What this verse is saying, and what we used to sing about, is the incredible reality that the God who "inhabits eternity" and who is holy and transcendent—that is, totally separate and different from us—is also the God who draws close to men and women who are contrite and humble before him. God is immanent; he is near. Jesus is called Emmanuel, God with us.

I wish I'd understood the richness and wonder of the doctrine I was singing. The lofty One of heaven is also the near-at-hand One who revives the hearts of the lowly. The awesome God who transcends all creation condescends to dwell with the weak and helpless in the person of his Son. This is amazing.

We have to hold these two truths about God together. If we lose our grasp on either one, our vision of God will be distorted. If we focus only on God's transcendence, we push him out of the picture of human life. We end up acting as though God is so far away that he's nowhere to be seen. Or that, being so distant, he won't mind if we ignore him.

The opposite extreme is to bring God so close that we strip him of his "godness." These days I would guess it is the more common error. Most people I talk to aren't afraid of or even in awe of God. They think they have him figured out. So God becomes our pal, our buddy, our Divine Butler. His nearness isn't so much celebrated as it is taken for granted. He is close and familiar and commonplace. God is near, but we've made him small—so small that we can carry him around in our pocket like a good-luck charm.

To know and relate to God as we should, we must remember that God is both *transcendent* and *immanent*. God is so far above us in power and glory. But not far-off, disinterested, or disengaged. He is, as the psalmist says, at our right hand, upholding those who trust in him (Psalm 16:8).

I knew a girl who used to think the stars were tiny specks of light just over her head. I'm not kidding. And she wasn't in grade school when she believed this. She was in college. She was a really sweet, kind redhead who spoke almost perfect Spanish. She was intelligent in many ways. But one day in a conversation, she mentioned that she had just learned that stars in the night sky were actually really far away. I asked her what she meant.

She said, "You know, they're not just right up there. They're not just tiny little dots. They're really far, far away."

I was incredulous.

"What did you think they were before?" I asked.

"I thought they were, you know, just right up above us."

If you were to ask me why it matters that we study the doctrine of God, I'd say for the same reason that it's worth knowing that stars are not tiny pinpricks of light just above our heads. When we know the truth about God, it fills us with wonder. If we fail to understand his true character, we'll never be amazed by him. We'll never feel small as we stare up at him. We'll never worship him as we ought. We'll never run to him for refuge or realize the great love he's shown in bridging the measureless distance to rescue us.

There is a right way and a wrong way to approach the doctrine of God. We can study God with a microscope or a telescope. A microscope makes something very small look big. But this isn't the way we are to magnify God. When we do, we're like scientists in a sterile laboratory magnifying something miniscule for the sake of scientific categorization. But we're not bigger than God, capable of numbering and naming his parts.

Instead we should study God's attributes the way an astronomer studies a heavenly body—through a telescope. Its lenses enable us to see just how much bigger and more awesome something is than we first imagined.[6]

When we study the doctrine of God, there should be a sense of awe in our hearts. We should be like children with a telescope under a starry night sky. Then we will be filled with amazement that Someone so great—so transcendent—can be known and seen by us. We will rightly feel small and insignificant as we realize how great and powerful the God we're beholding really is.

The more you learn of who God truly is, the more incredible his invitation to know him becomes. When you know him as the infinite, almighty, holy, eternal God of heaven, the announcement that he loves you takes on a whole new meaning. It's not expected. It's not commonplace. It is cause for astonishment.

The high and lofty One offers to draw near to those who are humble. He sent his Son to die so that the One of perfect holiness could dwell among us. God is near. But we don't manage or contain him. He's not in our pockets. The almighty One is holding us in *his* hands.

4

RIPPING, BURNING, EATING

"When we read the Bible,
it opens us up. It reads us."

A. J. JACOBS MAKES a living being a human guinea pig. He puts himself through offbeat, strange life experiments, then he writes about them. Once for an article in *Esquire* called "My Outsourced Life," Jacobs hired a team of people in Bangalore, India, to live his life for him. They answered his e-mails, called his co-workers, argued with his wife, and read bedtime stories to his son. His first book was about the year he spent reading the entire *Encyclopedia Britannica* in a quest to become the smartest person in the world.

A more recent book entitled *The Year of Living Biblically* follows a similar pattern. It's the story of how Jacobs attempted to follow every rule in the Bible as literally as possible for an entire year. You should know that Jacobs is an agnostic. "I am officially Jewish," he writes, "but I'm Jewish in the same way the Olive Garden is an Italian restaurant. Which is to say: not very."[1]

Jacobs started his experiment with a visit to a Christian bookstore in midtown Manhattan. He needed to purchase a Bible and supplemental study tools. A soft-spoken salesman named Chris helped him sort through the different sizes of Bibles and linguistic options. Then he pointed out a unique Bible version for teenage girls that was designed to look exactly like a *Seventeen* magazine. "This one's good if you're on the subway and are too embarrassed to be seen reading the Bible," said Chris. "Because no one will ever know it's a Bible." Jacobs's response is one of my favorite lines in the book: "You know you're in a secular city when it's considered more acceptable for a grown man to read a teen girl's magazine than the Bible."[2]

Jacobs left the store with two shopping bags filled with Scripture. He then proceeded to read through the entire Bible in four weeks. As he read, he wrote down every rule or direction that he came across—big and small. That included obvious ones like the Ten Commandments and "love your neighbor" but also lesser known Old Testament laws for diet and ritual cleanliness. His goal was to take the Bible at face value, as literally as possible, and put it all into practice.

As you can imagine, the outcome was often hilarious.

For example, because the book of Leviticus says men should leave the edges of their beards unshaven, Jacobs stopped shaving. Within a few months he looked like a lost member of ZZ Top. He stopped wearing clothing made of mixed fibers. He played a ten-string harp. He refused to shake hands with women who might be ceremonially unclean because they were having their periods, which involved his asking every woman he knew about her monthly cycle. (Oddly enough, the women in his office were happy to supply him with their information on Excel spreadsheets.)

Possibly his most outlandish activity was his attempt to stone adulterers. He accomplished this by trying to fling tiny pebbles at strangers without their noticing. Evidently Jacobs assumed that just about any New Yorker is an adulterer.

His book is a gimmick, but it also raises serious questions about what it means to live by the Bible. Do growing a beard and playing a harp equal living biblically? More important, how should we think about the Bible? Does Scripture have the authority to tell us how to live? Or is the Bible just a bunch of archaic rules and rituals that have no meaning in our modern world?

———

In one sense I think the Bible would be easier to understand, easier to manage, if it were just a rule book about diet and facial hair and sexual behavior. I don't know if you've ever thought about this, but we humans do rule books quite well. And I don't mean just religious books. Every year a new stack of books about diet and lifestyle and time management tells us exactly what to eat, how to exercise, and how to spend our time. We dutifully buy these books and then obey them like slaves. For a month or two—till we realize we're still fat and disorganized. Then we go looking for a new book to boss us around.

Basically Jacobs approached the Bible as the ultimate rule book. But while he submitted his life to an ancient book, he didn't encounter the Person speaking through the book. He didn't know or even believe in the God of the Bible—the God who comes looking for us through his living Word.

The Bible is much more wonderful and dangerous and radically life transforming than a mere book of instructions. But you won't understand it or gain any benefit from it until you believe what the Bible claims about itself. The Bible presents itself as a living communication from a personal God to the human race—more specifically to *you*.

Stop and think about that for a moment. God speaking to you.

What an incredible claim. And yet this is what the Christian faith is built on—what it asserts without apology. God is. He exists. And as Francis Schaeffer expressed it in the title of a book, "He is not silent." God speaks. He communicates. And he has ordained that his words be recorded in the signs and symbols of our human languages—written and printed on paper in a book that we can hold in our hands.

———

When we talk about the *doctrine of Scripture*, we mean all that the Bible teaches us about itself: what the Bible is, where it comes from, what its characteristics are, and how we're to read it and obey it. Getting the doctrine of Scripture right is essential for having a solid foundation as a Christian. If you don't understand that God has spoken through the Bible, or don't trust the Bible, how can you know him or cultivate a real relationship with him?

The doctrine of Scripture is uniquely important among Christian doctrines because it touches every other Christian belief. What we know about God and salvation we know because God reveals it to us in the Bible. In other words, we only have a doctrine of God and a doctrine of the atonement if we believe that Scripture can be understood and that it's true (without error).

So Scripture is the foundation of every other Christian belief. Ephesians 2:20 tells us that the church is "built on the foundation of the apostles and prophets, Christ Jesus himself being the cornerstone." While Jesus is always the cornerstone of God's church, the church also rests on the solid foundation of the teaching and preaching of the apostles and prophets that are recorded in the Bible. God commissioned the prophets; Jesus commissioned the apostles. They were the appointed spokesmen for God. And that's why we honor their teachings. Their words written down for us in Scripture form the basis of our faith and practice as followers of Jesus Christ.

Hebrews 1:1–2 says, "Long ago, at many times and in many ways, God spoke to our fathers by the prophets, but in these last days he has spoken to us by his Son." God's communication to mankind—first through the prophets and then through Jesus—is what the Bible records. It tells us who God is and how he has acted in human history. Then it explains the meaning of his actions.

While we can learn some things about God by observing his creation (Romans 1:19–20), this knowledge is limited. We are dependent on divine revelation from God in Scripture. We need God to speak and to reveal himself to us.

This is why we have the Bible. It's not just a relic of an ancient religion. Apart from the communication of God in the Bible, apart from revelation, we could not know God or understand his activity in the world. This is called the *necessity* of Scripture, meaning that Scripture is necessary for us to know and obey God.

There is no genuine spirituality apart from God's Word. We need God's self-revelation to know what he is like. We need revelation to know who we are and why we exist. We need revelation to explain our purpose and the eternal significance of life on this planet. We need revelation to know we're sinners and deserving of judgment. And we need revelation to know the good news of salvation through faith in Jesus.

Without the Bible there is no saving knowledge of God. Without the Bible we would not know or understand the meaning of the Cross and Resurrection. Without the Bible there is nothing for us to put our faith in. Romans 10:17 says, "So faith comes from hearing, and hearing through the word of Christ."

———

My earliest memories of the Bible involve comic books. As a kid I had been given a set of three paperbacks that presented the Bible in comic-book form. I would pore over them.

I especially loved the Old Testament. Even as a kid I had a sense of it being slightly illicit. As though someone had slipped an R-rated action movie into a pile of Disney DVDs. For starters Adam and Eve were naked on the first page. I was fascinated by Eve's ability to always stand in the Garden of Eden so that a tree branch or leaf was covering her private areas like some kind of organic bikini.

But it was the Bible's murder and mayhem that really got my attention. When I started reading the real Bible, I spent most of my time in Genesis, Exodus, 1 and 2 Samuel, and 1 and 2 Kings. Talk about violent. Cain killed Abel. The Egyptians fed babies to alligators. Moses killed an Egyptian. God killed thousands of Egyptians in the Red Sea. David killed Goliath and won a girl by bringing a bag of two hundred Philistine foreskins to his future father-in-law. I couldn't believe that Mom was so happy about my spending time each morning reading about gruesome battles, prostitutes, fratricide, murder, and adultery. What a way to have a "quiet time."

While I grew up with a fairly solid grasp of Bible stories, I didn't have a clear idea of how the Bible fit together or what it was all about. I certainly didn't understand how the exciting stories of the Old Testament connected to the rather less-exciting New Testament and the story of Jesus.

This concept of the Bible as a bunch of disconnected stories sprinkled with wise advice and capped off with the inspirational life of Jesus seems fairly common among Christians. That is so unfortunate, because to see the Bible as one book with one author and all about one main character is to see it in its breathtaking beauty.

Since I started caring about theology, I've learned that an important part of being grounded in truth is not only believing that the Bible is God's Word but also understanding the story line of the Bible from start to finish. The Bible is both doctrine and narrative. It not only presents us with true principles and propositions but also uses the power of story to show us how God works and acts in human history.

I've been helped by books like Graeme Goldsworthy's *Gospel and Kingdom* and Vaughan Robert's *God's Big Picture* that unpack what is called biblical theology. Unlike systematic theology, which pulls together the teaching of Scripture on specific topics, biblical theology is concerned with what we learn about God and his plan of salvation through the story line of the Bible. Biblical theology shows us how it all connects, how God's plan unfolds from Genesis to Revelation.

Ironically, one of the most helpful books I've read on biblical theology is one for children called *The Jesus Storybook Bible* by Sally Lloyd-Jones. Here's part of the introduction from that book, which I think is beautiful:

> Now, some people think the Bible is a book of rules, telling you what you should do and shouldn't do. The Bible certainly does have some rules in it. They show you how life works best. But the Bible isn't mainly about you and what you should be doing. It's about God and what he has done.
>
> Other people think the Bible is a book of heroes, showing you people you should copy. The Bible does have some heroes in it, but (as you'll soon find out) most of the people in the Bible aren't heroes at all. They make some big mistakes (sometimes on purpose). They get afraid and run away. At times they are downright mean.
>
> No, the Bible isn't a book of rules, or a book of heroes. The Bible is most of all a Story. It's an adventure story about a young Hero who comes from a far country to win back his lost treasure. It's a love story about a brave Prince who leaves his palace, his throne—everything—

to rescue the one he loves. It's like the most wonderful of fairy tales that has come true in real life!

You see, the best thing about the Story is—it's true.

There are lots of stories in the Bible, but all the stories are telling one Big Story. The Story of how God loves his children and comes to rescue them.

It takes the whole Bible to tell this Story. And at the center of the Story, there is a baby. Every Story in the Bible whispers his name. He is like the missing piece in a puzzle—the piece that makes all the other pieces fit together, and suddenly you can see a beautiful picture.[3]

I remember the night I first read this passage to my kids. I was so moved that tears filled my eyes. My kids, of course, were bewildered. "Daddy, are you crying?" they asked. I tried to explain that I was and it was because I was overwhelmed with gratefulness for God's Word and for Jesus. I kept saying, "I wish you could understand how good this is!"

The Bible is one story—the story of God's purpose to save sinners through the sacrifice of his Son in place of those sinners. The laws and rituals of diet and cleanliness given in Leviticus, which A. J. Jacobs attempted to obey so fastidiously, were never given to save but were given to point to mankind's inability to save itself.

Only Jesus can perfectly obey. And in the Bible every page, every story whispers his name. When God tells Abraham not to sacrifice his only son, Isaac, but promises to supply the sacrifice, Jesus, "the lamb of God," is anticipated. When David defeats Goliath, it's a preview of Jesus—the ultimate Champion who will one day conquer death itself on behalf of his people.

The Bible is the story of Jesus (John 5:39–40, 46–47). And it's the truth of Jesus. All of Scripture is given to us so we can know him and love him. Revelation is for relationship.

In his book *God Has Spoken,* J. I. Packer asks why God speaks to us through his Word. "The truly staggering answer which the Bible gives to this question is that God's purpose in revelation is to *make friends* with us." He goes on to explain that God created us in his image so we could commune with him in a two-sided relationship of affection and love. This was God's purpose when he created Adam and Eve. This is his purpose in overthrowing the curse of sin—enabling us to be his children, to relate to him as Father. "God's friendship with men and women begins and grows through speech," Packer continues. "His to us in revelation, and ours to Him in prayer and praise. Though I cannot see God, He and I can yet be personal friends, because in revelation He talks to me."[4]

When God tells us truth about himself *through stories* and *through doctrine,* his purpose is relationship. The statements "God is love" and "God is holy" are propositional statements—they're doctrinal truths. But they're also deeply relational. Only by knowing truth about who God is can we have a real relationship with him. But God also uses stories to teach us and reveal himself to us. The Bible isn't limited to one or the other, and they're not at odds. Through both, God is speaking and revealing himself to us so we can truly know him.

In 2 Timothy 3:16 the apostle Paul says, "All Scripture is God-breathed" (NIV). It's hard to imagine a phrase that could more strongly communicate the connection between God and Scripture. It is not merely God-blessed or God-sanctioned. Scripture is God-breathed. "It is not a matter of God adding to what men had written," Sinclair Ferguson explains, "but of God being the origin, the source of what has been written."[5] As if when we read, he himself were speaking again, his breath rustling past us.

The process of inspiration—the way in which God directed the writing of Scripture—wasn't always the same. In some cases, as with the apostle John, God said, "Write this down" and then gave specific instructions (Revelation 21:5). But most of the time, God worked through seemingly normal means. Nehemiah wrote a first-person account. A scribe named Baruch wrote down Jeremiah's prophecies. Paul wrote letters. Luke documented eyewitness testimony in writing his gospel, then spent time traveling with Paul to write his history of the early church, found in Acts.

Yet 2 Peter 1:21 says, "For no prophecy was ever produced by the will of man, but men spoke from God as they were carried along by the Holy Spirit." God used human beings to write words, but he guided their minds and even life experiences and backgrounds to accomplish the final result. So although the human writers were very much in control of themselves, the Holy Spirit was guiding them to write the very words God wanted them to write.

Some people question the Bible because they say the church merely voted on what books to include in the New Testament. But this is a distortion of how we came to have the Bible as it is today. When the church affirmed the books that made up the Bible, they were simply acknowledging what had always been affirmed by the church from the earliest days—that the Old Testament and the writings of the apostles and their close associates whom Jesus commissioned to be his witnesses held a unique authority and were inspired. These books were acknowledged as the *canon,* a Greek word that means "staff or straight rod." *Canon* came to be used as a word for "measure" or "rule" and "came to be applied to the contents of the New Testament: together they formed the 'rule of faith and life' by which the whole Church and Christians individually governed their lives."[6]

While the ultimate affirmation of Scripture as God's Word is the testimony of Scripture itself, a second and important testimony is that of the church and individual believers down through the ages. When we read the words of Scripture in the Old and New Testaments, the Holy Spirit bears witness in our hearts that these words are unlike any others. Paul saw this effect when he preached to the Thessalonians. They received his apostolic teaching, not as the word of men, but "as what it really is, the word of God, which is at work in you believers" (1 Thessalonians 2:13). Believers everywhere can relate to this experience. Scripture speaks to our souls with a depth and intensity that is unmatched.

Hebrews 4:12–13 says, "For the word of God is living and active, sharper than any two-edged sword, piercing to the division of soul and of spirit, of joints and of marrow, and discerning the thoughts and intentions of the heart. And no creature is hidden from his sight, but all are naked and exposed to the eyes of him to whom we must give account." When we read it, the Bible opens *us* up. It reads us. It searches us in the deepest way possible. It reveals our hearts and motivations. It convicts and comforts us. When we read it, the Holy Spirit confirms in our hearts that it is not the word of men but the very Word of God himself. They are words unlike any other words on earth. They are true and eternal. Proverbs 30:5–6 says, "Every word of God proves true.... Do not add to his words, lest he rebuke you and you be found a liar."

And Jesus said, "Heaven and earth will pass away, but my words will not pass away" (Luke 21:33).

———

God honors those who revere and respect him and his Word—those who treat Scripture not as mere words on a page or human invention but as the holy, God-breathed, powerful, and authoritative words of the Almighty. God says in Isaiah 66:2, "But this is the one to whom I will look: he who is humble and contrite in spirit and trembles at my word."

My favorite story of humility before the authority of God's Word comes from the life of King Josiah. In his day the law of God had been lost—forgotten for decades. But 2 Kings 22 tells the story of the day when the lost scroll was discovered and brought before the king. Josiah was twenty-six years old. It was the defining moment of his life.

The Bible says that when Josiah heard the words of God—when he heard of God's holiness and the promises of blessing and judgment he gave to his people—he tore his royal robes. In ancient times to tear your robes was a symbol of deep anguish and grief. For the king to tear his robes was an act of humiliation—as if to say, "My position, my role mean nothing." It was a statement of sorrow and penitence. "You are God; you are right, and I am wrong."

Josiah tore his robes. And he wept.

God was watching. And the Bible says that God was pleased. God said to Josiah, "Because you humbled yourself, because you were penitent, because you wept, I have heard you." He promised to show Josiah mercy (see 2 Kings 22:18–20).

I guess all humans have wondered, *When I pray, does God hear me?* But what this story teaches is that the questions we should ask are, *Am I hearing God through his Word? Am I listening to him? Am I trembling before his Word?*

"I asked God for a sign," she told me. My fellow pastor Isaac and I were meeting with a young woman in the church who was ensnared in an immoral relationship with a non-Christian boyfriend. "I know that God brought him into my life for a reason," she kept saying.

"How do you know this?" I asked.

"I just know it," she said.

We were meeting to plead with her to turn from sin. I read three passages from the Bible that forbid sex outside of marriage, or sexual immorality (1 Corinthians 6:18; Ephesians 5:3; 1 Thessalonians 4:3). "Do you see that God says what you're doing is wrong?" I asked.

"Yes, I see that," she said. "I know it's immoral. I'm just asking God to show me what to do," she said. Earlier that week she had woken up in the middle of the night plagued with doubt about her relationship. Maybe she should break it off. "God, please give me a sign," she had prayed.

That day was their "anniversary." As she drove to work, she had the thought that her boyfriend had never sent her flowers at work. Then she walked into her office to a beautiful bouquet of roses.

"Was that a message from God?" she asked through tears. "Is that my answer?"

I found it ironic and sad that she was consumed with discovering a sign from God—an anniversary, flowers, being awake in the middle of the night—when God was speaking to her clearly in the Bible. Jesus said, "If you love me, you will keep my commandments" (John 14:15).

The doctrine of Scripture teaches us about the authority of God's Word. Scripture must be the final rule of faith and practice for our lives. Not our feelings or emotions. Not signs or prophetic words or hunches.

What more can God give us than what he's given in Scripture? The question is, will we listen? Will we obey when we don't like what the Bible has to say?

This is a moment when our belief about Scripture meets reality. What we *say* we believe makes very little difference until we act on our belief. I suppose most Christians would say that the Bible is the authoritative Word of God. But until this authority actually changes how we live—how we think and act—talk of the authority of Scripture is nothing but a bunch of religious lingo. We're treating the God-breathed Word of God like a lot of hot air.

Scripture is always meant to work in our lives. When Paul said Scripture is God-breathed, he didn't stop there. He said, "All Scripture is God-breathed and is useful for teaching, rebuking, correcting and training in righteousness, so that the man of God may be thoroughly equipped for every good work" (2 Timothy 3:16–17, NIV).

God's Word teaches us how to think. It teaches us truth. It rebukes and corrects our old, self-centered ways of thinking. It trains us in righteousness. God's Word has authority, and when we submit ourselves to it, Scripture equips us for good works. It gives us what we need to love, serve, and sacrifice.

The Bible has limited value as merely an esoteric, spiritually inspiring book of ancient wisdom. It was given to be obeyed and lived. Josiah let the Word of God *reform* him. He ripped his robes—a visual symbol that said, "I'm the one who needs to change." He didn't twist God's words to fit his agenda; he let God's words reshape his life.

I want to be like Josiah. When my life disagrees with the Word of God, I want to say, "This Word is true, and I must change."

———

How we relate to Scripture reveals how we view God himself. The Bible tells a story of a man whose regard for God was so low that he actually burned God's Word. Sadly, this man named Jehoiakim was the son of the godly King Josiah. Jehoiakim became king of Judah less than a year after his father's death. He was twenty-five and went on to reign for eleven years. Second

Kings 23:37 sums up his life by simply saying, "And he did what was evil in the sight of the LORD."

Jeremiah 36 tells the grievous tale of Jehoiakim's rejection of God's Word. A scroll with all of Jeremiah's prophecies written on it was brought to King Jehoiakim. He was staying at his winter house, and a fire was burning in a fire pot by his side. He listened as the prophecy was read, but his heart was unmoved. He didn't tremble. He despised the Word of God. As three or four columns of the prophecy were read, the king cut them off with a knife and threw them into the fire. He did this until the entire scroll was reduced to ashes. Jeremiah 36:24 states, "Yet neither the king nor any of his servants who heard all these words was afraid, nor did they tear their garments."

It's a chilling picture of blatant disregard for God and his Word. And the contrast between Josiah and his son Jehoiakim couldn't be more clear.

Josiah tore his robes. Jehoiakim cut up the words of God.

Josiah was penitent. Jehoiakim was cold-hearted.

Josiah reformed his life after hearing God's words. Jehoiakim burned God's words.

The young woman sitting in my office was burning God's Word as she heard it and refused to obey. How many times have I done the same thing? I've read God's Word, known what it called me to, but refused to turn in a new direction.

Every generation and every person can burn God's Word in their own way. Sometimes this is crass. But at other times this burning is sophisticated, nuanced, scholarly.

The most common way people cut and burn God's Word is to strip it of the qualities it claims for itself. So if I say that although Scripture is inspired, it has errors, I can claim a great regard for the Bible, but I've essentially made myself the judge over it. If it's possible for some part of it to be untrue, then I am now in the role of choosing what I will and won't listen to in Scripture.

The technical study of Scripture engaged in by academics can, when used humbly, further our understanding of God's Word. But it can also be a guise for exalting man's wisdom and opinions above the Word of God. The inerrancy of God's Word is thrown out, but the inerrancy of man's historical, textual, and scientific knowledge is assumed. Scripture is doubted, questioned, and edited until only a shell is left. The tools and words have changed since Jehoiakim's knife and fire pot, but the result is no different. God's Word is burned.

———

Can you trust what you're reading in Scripture? Is it clear enough that you can understand what God wants you to understand? Is the Bible all that you need? These aren't questions for pastors and professors; these are questions that every Christian who reads the Bible needs to answer. A handful of crucial words can help us think rightly about Scripture.

Inerrancy: The orthodox teaching of the Christian church down through the centuries has been that God's Word in its original manuscripts is inerrant. This means that it is totally true—free from error—in all it affirms. This is built on the Bible's testimony that God never lies (Titus 1:2). Proverbs 30:5 states, "Every word of God proves true; he is a shield to those who take refuge in him."

In his book *Bible Doctrine,* Wayne Grudem points out that when Jesus prays in John 17:17, he doesn't say, "Sanctify them in the truth; your words are *true.*" Instead he prays, "Sanctify them in the truth; your word is *truth.*"

"The difference is significant," writes Grudem, "for this statement encourages us to think of the Bible not simply as being 'true' in the sense that it conforms to some higher standard of truth, but rather to think of the Bible as itself the final standard of truth."[7]

Clarity: Another important quality of God's Word is its clarity. The Holy Spirit illuminates our hearts, as believers, to understand its message and apply it to our lives. It is straightforward in its meaning. And in those cases where a portion of Scripture is difficult to understand, we can test our viewpoint against other parts of Scripture. This means Scripture is self-interpreting. Psalm 19:7 says, "The testimony of the LORD is sure, making wise the simple." Though studying God's Word requires diligence and careful thought, no one can claim that it is unclear as an excuse for ignoring or disobeying it.

Sufficiency: In the Bible, God has given us all we need to know for salvation and eternal life (John 5:24). The Bible is sufficient. This doesn't mean God has told us all we could know or all that he knows; it means he has told us all *we* need to know in order to truly know him, find the forgiveness of sins, and be assured of everlasting life with our Creator and Redeemer. When Paul wrote Timothy, he said the "sacred writings" that Timothy had learned as a child "are able to make you wise for salvation through faith in Christ Jesus" (2 Timothy 3:15).

God doesn't want our view of his Word to be supported by sentimental attachment or mere emotion. He wants us to be confident in the Bible because he wants us to be confident in him. Taking time to study the doctrine of Scripture is a practical and spiritually enriching endeavor because it strengthens our trust in God's Word.[8]

Eating God's Word. It's an odd picture. Yet that's what the prophet Jeremiah describes when he says to God, "Your words were found, and I ate them, and your words became to me a joy and the delight of my heart, for I am called by your name, O LORD, God of hosts" (Jeremiah 15:16).

When I read these words, I imagine someone tearing out the crinkly, tissue-thin pages of a Bible and stuffing them in his mouth. Of course I know Jeremiah is speaking metaphorically. He's describing his wholehearted embrace of God's Word. We should have the same appetite.

That's how I want to be. But I still have a long way to go. I do love God's Word. I've tasted that it's good. But sometimes I only nibble on it. Sometimes I don't feel like eating at all. I want to delight in it the way Jeremiah describes. I want to be hungrier than I am.

Jeremiah's example is inspiring. He feeds on God's Word. He wants its truth and life *in* him. It is his joy. It is his delight. And if we didn't look more closely, we could assume that Jeremiah couldn't relate to the apathy and spiritual dryness that we lesser mortals experience.

But when we read Jeremiah's story and the context of his statement of delighting in God's Word, we make an interesting discovery. Jeremiah is in the midst of dark depression and anguished complaint. He is so discouraged, so disheartened, that he wishes he had never been born (Jeremiah 15:10). He lists all the ways he has suffered as a result of speaking God's truth. Jeremiah 15:17–18 says,

> I did not sit in the company of revelers,
>   nor did I rejoice;
> I sat alone, because your hand was upon me,
>   for you had filled me with indignation.
> Why is my pain unceasing,
>   my wound incurable,
>   refusing to be healed?
> Will you be to me like a deceitful brook,
>   like waters that fail?

It turns out that Jeremiah's spiritual life isn't one mountaintop experience after another. Instead, he's often discouraged and depressed. He's tempted to question God's goodness. At this low moment of his life, he is more aware of what he's done for God than he is of what God has done for him.

This sounds terrible, but, honestly, it encourages me. It tells me that God's Word meets us where we are. It meets us in the midst of doubt. It speaks to us in the midst of spiritual struggle. Maybe that's where you are. The teaching of a college professor has you feeling like a fool for trusting in an "outdated, flawed book." Or maybe you're just tired. Reading the Bible feels like an empty exercise.

God can meet you and me in these moments of life. The Bible isn't just for people who feel strong. I'm grateful we don't have to lead perfect lives to read God's perfect Word. Jeremiah's life teaches us this. Jeremiah suffered. He was discouraged. God's Word isn't just for the happy people of the world. We can find joy in God's Word and in the trustworthiness of his promises even when we lack joy in our hearts.

Sometimes we have to work to find delight in God's Word. Jeremiah said that when he ate God's words, they became a joy. They don't become a joy sitting on a shelf. We have to taste and receive them. The fact that this requires effort shouldn't discourage us. As we grow in our knowledge of how trustworthy and powerful Scripture is, our love for it will increase.

———

God responded to Jeremiah's complaint with a loving rebuke, telling him to stop uttering worthless words. Jeremiah was more focused on his own performance and all that he had done for God.

God understands our weakness, but he doesn't make allowance for distrust and disbelief. He gave Jeremiah this wonderful promise: "I am with you to save you and deliver you" (Jeremiah 15:20, NASB).

God saves. God delivers. It was true for Jeremiah. It was true for the people of Judah. It's true for you and me. God alone can save.

That is the central message of the Bible. And it's the key to understanding the Bible and learning to love it as God wants us to. The Bible is the story of what God has done for us. We don't come to it to receive instructions on saving ourselves. It's not a list of rules and guidelines that we must follow perfectly in order to earn our way into God's favor. The Bible is the story of what he has done. It's the story of how every man-made effort at salvation fails and only the grace of God can rescue and redeem sinners.

Too often we read the Bible the way A. J. Jacobs did when he attempted to spend a year "living biblically." We read it and look for all the things we have to do. And while there are things God commands us to do, we first need to read the Bible looking at all he has done for us. It's the story of his champion, his Son, who came to die for us.

My kids' children's Bible says it best. Every story whispers his name. Jesus came looking for us. He came to deliver us. When you understand that, reading the Bible becomes a delight.

GOD WITH A BELLYBUTTON

"Jesus is unique. And he came to accomplish
something that no one else could."

SOME DAYS AN early-morning mist settles on my backyard. It's as though a cloud loses its way and comes to rest there before floating back to the sky. On those mornings my backyard, with its two towering maple trees and flat stretch of grass, has a hazy glow. It looks mystical and enchanting.

I read my Bible and pray in a room that looks out over the backyard. One morning when the mist hung over the yard, I couldn't seem to focus on a single thing I read. My prayers were listless.

I stared out the window. The thought struck me that this quiet time would be better if Jesus would walk across my backyard and come talk to me. That would give my faith a boost. I imagined his bare feet sinking into the dew-wet grass. I don't know why I pictured him barefoot. He just was. He would walk up to the side door, right across from where I was sitting, and knock gently.

"That's what I wish would happen," I said out loud. "I wish you'd step out of that mist and sit right there." The armchair in the corner was empty. I imagined Jesus stepping into the quiet room and sitting down.

I am alive approximately 1,975 years after Jesus walked the earth. On some days that seems like a long time.

———

Once while surfing the Internet, I came across a Bible-themed video game that pitted Bible characters against each other in brutal combat. You could choose to fight as Moses, Noah, Eve, Mary, Satan, or Jesus. It was a sacrilegious version of the old Street Fighter II game we used to play at 7-Eleven. Besides basic kicking, punching, and jumping abilities, each character had his or her own special powers. Moses could hail down frogs. Eve threw apples and whipped a snake at her foes. Noah could call out a herd of animals to run over people. Jesus threw loaves and fish. I am not making this up.

The game was clever but obviously created by secular people who had little regard for the sacred. Sadly, I've heard of youth groups who celebrate the game as a way to teach teenagers the Bible. Somehow I don't think that Noah beating up Eve is the kind of Bible knowledge we need today.

While most people wouldn't feel comfortable playing this irreverent game, I wonder if it captures a common way of thinking about Jesus—as just one person in the pantheon of Bible heroes. He did miraculous things, but then so did Moses and Elijah. We know he's special, and we have a sense that we should be indebted to him for all the trouble of dying on the cross, but at the end of the day, he's just another Bible character.

———

C. S. Lewis famously said that Jesus is either the true Son of God, a demon, or else a madman.[1] The all-or-nothingness of that statement always gives me chills. Jesus is either who he claims to be—the God-man who came to redeem humanity—or he's completely insane, even sick. You can't have it somewhere in the middle. He can't be a great teacher and a wonderful moral example and at the same time a liar and a charlatan. He can't be enlightened and be a trusted source of spiritual guidance and at the same time be wrong about his identity.

This seems like an airtight argument to me, but countless people find a way to wriggle out of it. They hold on to Jesus in some form, but they deny that he is the Son of God who should be obeyed and worshiped. The intellectual gymnastics required for this remind me of pictures of people doing yoga who are able to wrap both feet around their heads and tie them in a knot. I don't know why they want to do that, and it looks painful.

I have a friend who holds to the "Jesus isn't really God, but he's still a really good thing" viewpoint. In his opinion Jesus was an enlightened and wonderful man (I would put Mr. Rogers in this same category). More than any other human, Jesus achieved a connection with what my friend calls the "Christ spirit." He thinks all the supernatural elements of the New Testament—from miracles to the resurrection—were fabricated by Jesus's followers. He believes that, while the Bible is a great work of literature and spiritual comfort, it's merely the result of human imagination and error. So he picks through the Bible as if he's at the grocery store buying green beans. He passes over what he views as the "brown and shriveled" displays of supernatural power and claims of divinity and grabs only the moral teaching, the acts of compassion, and the heroic suffering displayed in Jesus's life.

"So what do you believe was happening when Jesus died on the cross?" I asked him one day.

"I think Jesus was opposing injustice," he answered. "He was demonstrating the power of love."

I love my friend, but his beliefs befuddle me. Not because I don't understand them, but because I can't see why he bothers having them at all. To turn the old saying on its head, it's as if he's thrown out the baby but kept the bathwater. Christianity without a supernatural, divine, all-powerful Jesus seems pointless to me—less useful than old bathwater.

My question is, Why spend time figuring out a way to hold on to church attendance and Christian tradition and even Christian morality while not believing much of anything about Jesus except that he was a really great guy? I know a lot of really great guys, but I sure wouldn't spend every Sunday morning singing about them. I can find plenty of other compelling examples of suffering. I can find moving moral teaching from any number of gurus and religious teachers.

If Christianity is a tradition built on the fable of a man we know about only through reports we can't trust, why in the world would a person waste time with any part of it?

In this chapter I want to explore what theologians call the doctrine of the person and work of Christ. His *person* addresses who Jesus is, his *work,* what he has done for us. The person and work of Christ are meant to be kept together. You can't grasp the significance of either without the other. As we study both, we'll learn that Jesus is unlike anyone in the Bible or in world history. He is fully God and fully man. And he came into this world to accomplish something that no one else could.

Jesus Christ is known by some people as the founder of the Christian religion. Technically, of course, this is true. But for a Christian, who believes that Jesus is the eternal Son of God who became a man, it seems odd to call him the founder of anything. For that matter he's also the founder of the universe, having created the world and all living things.

But in strictly historical terms, the Christian faith does start with Jesus.

He claimed to be, and his followers acknowledged him to be, the fulfillment of the Jewish faith and all the promises of the Old Testament prophets. Jesus presented himself as the Messiah, the "anointed one," one who is chosen and empowered by God for a specific task. The Greek form of *messiah* is *Christ*, which explains the title Jesus is known by. For Jesus to be the Christ means that he is the specially chosen one of God, sent for a very specific purpose.

Jesus lived in Palestine during the reign of Augustus Caesar. The Jewish people were humbled and distressed by the presence of the pagan occupiers. Seeing the holy city of Jerusalem overrun with Roman soldiers grated on their souls. They longed for freedom and self-rule.

Jesus, a descendant of the great King David of old, was born in Bethlehem but raised in Nazareth. Every region has some city or town that it looks down on and considers backwoods or hick. It seems that Nazareth was on the bottom rung of that ladder in Galilee. It had no prestige or distinction. In several places in the Gospels, people snidely comment on Nazareth for its lack of sophistication, describing it as a place nothing good could come from (John 1:46).

Jesus, like his adopted father, Joseph, was a carpenter by trade. He worked in Nazareth until he was around the age of thirty. Then he started his public ministry of teaching and healing. For three years he traveled through various cities in Judea. He trained a small band of disciples. He taught in synagogues and eventually before large crowds. People mobbed him when word spread of his miraculous powers to heal sickness and cast out demons.

While Jesus gained many followers, he also made enemies. The religious leaders of the day conspired to kill him. They were jealous of his popularity, outraged by his claims to be equal with God, and offended by his rejection of their man-made traditions and laws.

Jesus was sold out by one of his closest associates, falsely accused, flogged, and executed by crucifixion at the hands of the Romans.

On the third day, in fulfillment of ancient prophecy and his own promise, Jesus rose from the dead. He appeared to his followers over the course of more than a month. He commissioned them to take the news of his death and resurrection to the world. And then he ascended into heaven.

Today, two thousand years later, a man who never traveled more than a hundred miles from his hometown has reached people in every continent of the world. The empire of Rome, under whose shadow Jesus was born and murdered, long ago crumbled to ruins. But the number of those who swear allegiance to Jesus and call him Lord has grown through every century. In the West we divide human history by his birth. Nearly two billion humans describe themselves as his followers.

Jesus Christ is the most famous, most powerful, most controversial and revolutionary figure in all human history. And he has promised to return.

The question that divides the human race is, who is Jesus? That's a question Jesus asked his own followers. It wasn't enough for them to list the ideas and opinions of other people. "Who do *you* say that I am?" he asked (Matthew 16:15, emphasis added).

During Jesus's ministry some thought he was a great teacher, others a prophet. Not surprisingly, false teaching about Jesus's nature spread easily in the early church.

One teacher named Apollinaris taught that Jesus had a human body but not a human mind or spirit. He asserted that while Jesus was a man, he had received a mind/spirit transplant of divinity. On one level this might seem like a nice way to fit Jesus together as both God and man, but church leaders saw a serious problem. Jesus had come to save the whole man—body and spirit. In order to represent us and thus fully save us, Jesus had to be fully human as Scripture claims. Scripture says Jesus was made like us in every way (Hebrews 2:17). And after his death Jesus was raised to life with a physical body; he didn't abandon it and return to spirit-only form (Luke 24:39).

Another teacher, named Nestorius, argued that Christ was made up of two separate persons. In this view the divine person and human person were like roommates sharing the same space or like Siamese twins who could argue with each other and have different agendas. But nowhere in the Bible is Jesus presented as two persons. He is always and only one person in his thoughts and actions.

A third erroneous view presented Jesus as a sort of divine-human hybrid. His divine nature came together with his human nature and morphed into a totally new nature that was neither God nor man but a mixture of both. This idea that Christ had only one nature is called Monophysitism or Eutychianism, after a man named Eutyches, who spread it. Why was this view a problem? Because it left us with a less-than-biblical Jesus who was not really God or man.

At the Council of Chalcedon in AD 451, the church fathers laid out a declaration designed to correct the false teachings and clearly delineate and protect the biblical teaching about Jesus's nature.[2] The Chalcedonian Creed stated that Jesus has two natures in one person. He is both "perfect in Godhead and also perfect in manhood; truly God and truly man" with a real human soul and body. So whatever is true of God's nature is true of Jesus's nature. And whatever is true of human nature is also true of Jesus's nature. Jesus is in every way like us in our humanity, except without sin, even as he is of the same essence as God the Father. These two natures are "to be acknowledged...inconfusedly, unchangeably, indivisibly, inseparably." In other words, Jesus's two natures are not mixed together, they're not morphing, neither one is diminished by the other, they can't be divided, and they can't be separated. Jesus is fully God and fully man in one person forever.[3]

———

Let's consider Jesus who is "truly God." Scripture points to Jesus's divine nature in many ways. The first is his virgin conception. Before Jesus was conceived, his mother, Mary, had never had sex with a man. Her first question when the angel announced her pregnancy reveals her innocence and womanly practicality: "How will this be, since I am a virgin?" (Luke 1:34).

The angel's answer leaves this miracle shrouded in mystery, but it makes one thing unmistakably certain: the child conceived in Mary's womb would be of divine, heavenly origin. "The Holy Spirit will come upon you," the angel told her. "And the power of the Most High will overshadow you; therefore the child to be born will be called holy—the Son of God" (Luke 1:35).

John the Baptist was a witness to Jesus as the Son of God (Luke 3:16). John said of Jesus, "The one who comes from above is above all; the one who is from the earth belongs to the earth, and speaks as one from the earth. The one who comes from heaven is above all" (John 3:31, NIV). And when John baptized Jesus, God spoke from heaven and said to Jesus, "You are my beloved Son; with you I am well pleased" (Luke 3:22).

Jesus also revealed his divine nature through the supernatural miracles he performed. He demonstrated his power over the human body in healing (Luke 4:40), over demonic powers (Mark 1:25), and over the natural elements. "Who is this man?" his disciples once asked themselves after he quieted a violent storm. "Even the winds and the waves obey him!" (Matthew 8:27, NIV).

Unlike any other prophet in the Bible, Jesus made claims of equality with God. He said, "I and the Father are one" (John 10:30). And once he said to the religious leaders, "I tell you the truth, before Abraham was born, I am!" (John 8:58, NIV). This was an audacious claim to divinity. Not only was Jesus saying that he existed before the patriarch Abraham, who had lived thousands of years before; he also referred to himself in a clear echo of the divine name: I AM. This was the name God had told Moses to give to the children of Israel when they asked who sent him. "Tell them I AM sent you," God instructed Moses (see Exodus 3:13–14). The point Jesus made wasn't lost on his listeners. They knew he was claiming equality with the eternal God and picked up stones to kill him.

In his book *Salvation Belongs to the Lord,* theologian John Frame points out how incredible it is that Jesus's disciples came to believe that he was God. They were all Jews who had been raised to believe that there is one God and only God should be worshiped. They were not primed to look for God in the form of a man. The idea was preposterous. "Somehow," Frame writes, "during the next three years or so, all these Jewish disciples, and many more people besides, are convinced that Jesus is God and deserves to be worshiped as God. They have known him intimately as a man, have walked and talked and eaten with him; yet, they have come to worship him. That is quite an amazing thing."[4]

Frame goes on to talk about the fact that Jesus's deity wasn't debated by Christians in the early church (although they were more than ready to argue about other theological issues). They didn't argue about it, Frame says, because the whole Christian community agreed that Jesus was God.

The apostle Paul, who encountered the risen Jesus Christ, said, "He is the image of the invisible God, the firstborn of all creation" and "in him the whole fullness of deity dwells bodily" (Colossians 1:15; 2:9).

Once when Jesus was on a mountain with Peter, James, and John, he was transfigured, or changed in form, before their eyes (Mark 9:2–13). The three disciples saw a preview of the eternal glory Jesus would possess after his resurrection. His clothes became dazzling white. Jesus stood and spoke to Moses and Elijah—the two greatest prophets of the Old Testament. When Peter beheld the sight, he was awestruck (unfortunately, not enough to refrain from speaking). He offered to set up three tents, one for each of the men. But then God the Father spoke from heaven and made something very clear: this wasn't about three great heroes of faith coming together for a reunion tour. God said, "This is my Son, whom I love. Listen to him!" (Mark 9:7, NIV).

This is my Son. Unlike any other. Greater than anyone else who has ever walked this earth. Not merely a servant or prophet of God but the one and only Son of God.

———

Jesus is "perfect in Godhead and also perfect in manhood." Have you ever taken time to reflect on the reality of Jesus's human nature? The world has had two millennia to get used to the concept of God becoming a man. But even after all that time, the idea of God being a human—a bundle of muscle, bones, and fluid—is scandalous. Hands. Arms. Feet. Body hair. Sweat glands. How can this possibly be?

This is, without question, the greatest miracle recorded in Scripture. The parting of the Red Sea is nothing in comparison. Fire from heaven that consumed Elijah's altar? No big deal. Even the raising of Lazarus from the dead takes a backseat to a moment that no human eye saw. In the womb of a virgin, a human life was conceived. But no human father was involved. The Holy Spirit, in a miracle too wonderful for the human mind to comprehend, overshadowed a young woman (Luke 1:35). And in a split second that the cosmos is still reeling from, God "incarnated." He took on our humanity.

God the Son, existing for all eternity, now became dependent, floating in the amniotic fluid of a female womb. The One by whose power the whole world is sustained, now nourished by an umbilical cord. The God-man would have a bellybutton.

And then he had to be born. He had to come out. Think about that. When the angels announced Jesus's birth to shepherds outside the town of Bethlehem, they said, "Born this day in the city of David a Savior, who is Christ the Lord" (Luke 2:11). When we read this account, we're often distracted by the fact that angels have appeared. We imagine them shining, and we picture the shepherds and sheep. But none of this is truly incredible. What is incredible is this word *born*.

God has been *born*.

Born in what sense? Carried-down-from-the-sky-by-angels, pink-and-chubby-and-wrapped-in-white-blankets born? No. Born in the painful, screaming, sweaty, pushed-out-between-the-legs-of-a-woman sense. Born in all the bloody, slimy mess of real human birth. Squeezed and prodded from the darkness of his mother's womb by the powerful, rhythmic contractions of her uterus.

And there he is, the Son of God, covered in fluid and blood. His lungs filling with oxygen for the first time. Crying. Helpless.

———

That Jesus was fully man is clearly taught in the Bible. Not only did he have a human mother; he grew and developed like any child (Luke 2:52). He was hungry (Matthew 4:2). He was thirsty (John 4:7). He experienced human emotions: he was troubled (John 12:27) and sorrowful at the death of a close friend (John 11:35). He also grew tired and needed sleep (Luke 8:23).

And beyond these examples, the response to Jesus from those who knew him was, well, normal. For years his brothers didn't believe he was the Messiah

(John 7:5). People in his hometown of Nazareth thought of him as simply "Joseph's son" and rejected him as a prophet (Matthew 13:53–58). Evidently Jesus's very normal human life and behavior had not prepared them for the idea that he could be the divine Messiah.

For thirty years Jesus lived an everyday human life in first-century Palestine. He learned the trade of a carpenter. His hands would have been calloused and rough from working with wood. He knew the salty sting of sweat in his eyes. He knew the relief of resting tired muscles after a full day of work.

Why does all this matter? The Bible tells us that Christ's full humanity is important because of the unique purpose of his mission. Jesus came to represent the human race before God. Part of his work on earth was to be our priest. In the Old Testament a priest's role was to stand before God on behalf of the people. He had to be someone from their midst—one of them—so that the sacrifices he offered before God would be counted toward his people.

Hebrews says that Jesus, who came to be our priest and representative before God, "had to be made like his brothers in every respect, so that he might become a merciful and faithful high priest in the service of God, to make propitiation for the sins of the people" (2:17).

The requirement of full humanity not only made it possible for Jesus to offer himself for our sins, but it also assures us of being cared for by a priest who understands our plight. Hebrews 4:15 says, "For we do not have a high priest who is unable to sympathize with our weaknesses, but one who in every respect has been tempted as we are, yet without sin."

Jesus is like us in every aspect of our humanity—in all the mundane, glorious, and impolite aspects of the human existence. He had all the weakness and desires that make us human; he was tempted in every respect as we are. The difference is that Jesus was without sin. And it was his sinless perfection that made it possible for him to pay for our sins.

This means we can be assured that we pray to and hope in a High Priest who knows us. He sympathizes with us. He has a friendly, personal understanding of our weaknesses. He says to us, "I've been there," and he actually means it. John Frame writes, "God, who has no body, has taken to himself a body in the person of Jesus Christ. God, who cannot suffer, has taken to himself a human nature, in which he can suffer, in Christ."[5]

———

Jesus is the center, the focal point, of the Christian faith. But it's odd how averse we Christians can be to studying and defining a clear "doctrine" of Jesus. That just doesn't seem relational. We don't want to study Jesus. We want to experience him.

I see this tendency in my own life. When I think about Jesus, I'm not inclined to ask, "What truth does the Bible tell me about Jesus? What does Jesus want me to think and believe about him?" Instead I'm more inclined to try to work my way into a certain emotional state. To "feel" a certain way about Jesus.

I'm not even sure how to describe the feeling that I believe I should have about Jesus. All I know is that I want a really deep and meaningful feeling. I want something to wash over me. I wouldn't even mind crying. Actually crying is good. The feeling I'm after definitely needs to be passionate and profound. A touch of melancholy works too. Sad and austere feel very spiritual. I want to feel like Jesus is my closest friend, like we could hang out. I want to feel that he likes me—my tastes, my sensibilities, my music, my food. I want a deep bond—the kind that doesn't even need words to communicate.

Putting all my desired "Jesus feelings" into words makes me sound like an emotional seventh-grade girl about to leave summer camp. That is not good.

I think many Christians are more interested in chasing a feeling about Jesus than pursuing Jesus himself and reviewing and thinking about the truth of who he is.

The irony of this feeling-driven approach to Jesus is that ultimately it produces the opposite of what we actually want. Deep emotion in response to Jesus isn't wrong. It can be good. But to find it, we need more than imagination and introspection.

One of the most valuable lessons C.J. has taught me about the Christian spiritual life is that if you want to feel deeply, you have to think deeply. Too often we separate the two. We assume that if we want to feel deeply, then we need to sit around and, well, *feel*.

But emotion built on emotion is empty. True emotion—emotion that is reliable and doesn't lead us astray—is always a response to reality, to truth. It's only as we study and consider truth about Jesus with our minds that our hearts will be moved by the depth of his greatness and love for us. When we engage our minds with the doctrine of his person and his work, our emotions are given something to stand on, a reason to worship and revel in the very appropriate feelings of awe and gratefulness and adoration.

Knowing Jesus and feeling right emotions about him start with thinking about the truth of who he is and what he's done. Jesus never asks us how we feel about him. He calls us to believe in him, to trust in him. The question he asked his disciples is the same one he confronts us with: "Who do you say that I am?" The real questions when it comes to Jesus are, Do you believe he is who he says he is? Do you believe he's done what he said he came to do?

———

We've been considering the person of Christ. But now let's look at how this relates to the work he came to do. During the early 1900s there was intense pressure in academic circles and in many churches to deny Jesus as a supernatural person. People emphasized his teaching and example instead. But J. Gresham Machen argued that Jesus was far more than "the fairest flower of humanity,"[6] as some presented him. True Christian faith had always involved looking to Jesus as a supernatural Person, indeed "a Person who was God."[7] Jesus did not just inspire faith; he was the *object* of faith for the apostles and the early church. He was the one in whom they put their faith.

"If Jesus was merely a man like the rest of men," Machen wrote, "then an ideal is all that we have in Him. Far more is needed by a sinful world. It is small comfort to be told that there was goodness in the world, when what we need is goodness triumphant over sin."[8]

Is Jesus just an ideal? Is he just a goal for which we're to aim? The Bible presents a very different narrative. In Scripture the story of Jesus is not the story of goodness cropping up in the world. It is the story of goodness conquering sin. It is the story of wickedness and death being pushed back, thrown down, and defeated by the supernatural man who came from heaven but was born on earth.

This is the work Jesus came to do. And it's only when we realize how big, how massive, the mission of Jesus truly is that we begin to understand how unique he is. The work he came to accomplish is nothing less than the setting right of all that is wrong—in our relationship with God, in our hearts, in creation, in the whole of the universe.

We can adopt small thoughts of Jesus if we limit our view of his work to our tiny self-interests. But to truly see the glory of God's purpose in Jesus, we have to look beyond our own front porch, our town, our country, even our lifetime. God's purpose is so much bigger. Jesus didn't come only to save me, forgive my sins, and improve my life. He does all this, but this is only a small part of a much larger picture.

In the book of Ephesians, Paul glories in the cosmic implications of Jesus and his work. He lists the spiritual blessings we have in Jesus: adoption by God as his children, redemption through his blood, the forgiveness of our sins (1:3–8). But then he explains the ultimate purpose to which they point.

What is this purpose? God's purpose, Paul says, is to unite all things in Jesus, things in heaven and things on earth (1:9–10). What does this mean, and what's the big deal?

Let me explain it this way. Let's say I ask you what the big deal is about Abraham Lincoln. Why does he get to have his picture on the penny and the five-dollar bill and have a big memorial in downtown Washington DC? What would you say? You'd most likely say that he is one of America's greatest presidents because he emancipated the slaves and preserved the union. But what if I asked, "Why is that so special?" You'd try to give me some historical perspective. You'd explain that this was extremely significant because of the terrible injustice and wickedness of slavery. You'd describe the great turmoil and division of the Civil War—how a whole country was being ripped apart, how hundreds of thousands of men died in the conflict.

The point is that people can't appreciate Lincoln and his unique gifts and accomplishments until they understand the circumstances of his presidency. In a similar way, we can't grasp the significance of God's plan to unite all things in Jesus until we understand the disunity and chasm between heaven and earth brought about by man's sin.

When man first sinned, it was an act of treason against almighty God. It was earth revolting against heaven. And it plunged humanity and the whole world into death and disarray. The result of sin was that mankind was separated from God. Our fellowship with the Creator was broken. And the division didn't stop there. Sin created division within humanity. It tore apart families. It turned man against woman. It created hatred and animosity among the races. The wars and genocide and ethnic cleansing that continue to this day are the tragic legacy of sin.

The Bible tells us that creation itself was affected by mankind's fall into sin. When we see earthquakes and hurricanes, it can seem as though creation is at war with itself. And in a very real way it is. Our world is, in a sense, cut off from God and under a curse (Genesis 3:17; Romans 8:20–21).

The questions that humans have asked for thousands of years are, How can this broken, sin-scorched, divided world be made right? Who can save us? Who can fix all this?

God always had a plan. But he took his time unveiling it. In the Old Testament he hinted at it. He gave clues. But his ultimate purpose was a mystery. It was hidden. The prophets of old searched and searched, seeking to glimpse God's plan and to determine the timing of the salvation he promised. They asked, "Who will bring harmony? How can sinful man make peace with a holy God? What sacrifice will cleanse us? Who can reconcile the nations? Who can bring lasting peace?"

The Bible tells us that, at just the right time, God enacted his plan. "But when the fullness of time had come, God sent forth his Son, born of woman, born under the law, to redeem those who were under the law, so that we might receive adoption as sons" (Galatians 4:4–5).

In Jesus, the eternal Son of God became a man. Heaven and earth came together in one person—fully God and fully man. And he came not to condemn but to save. How does he make peace? He gives himself in the place of sinners. How can he do this? Because he's one of us. But how can he face the wrath of God for millions upon millions of sinners? Because he is the eternal God. By his death he removes our guilt. He appeases the wrath of God the Father. And through his death and resurrection, he reverses death itself. Jesus's resurrection shows that God's purpose is to make all things new—not just spiritually, but also physically. The promise of a new heaven and a new earth is glimpsed in the risen, glorified human body of Jesus Christ. In the new earth that God will create, all things are remade (Revelation 21:1–5).

The unity that Jesus brings is total power over all things. Ephesians 1:21 says that God has placed Jesus "far above all rule and authority and power and dominion, and above every name that is named, not only in this age but also in the one to come." In other words, he's in charge. His enemies are crushed, the sinful are punished, and every knee bows to him (Revelation 21:8; Romans 14:11). The world is united because everyone is obeying Jesus.

When you glimpse the big-picture perspective of who Jesus is and what he has come to do, it takes your breath away. His person and work are unlike any other. Abraham was simply a servant of God. Moses was only a prophet for God. Muhammad was just a man. Buddha was just a teacher. Confucius, more a social philosopher. Joseph Smith, who founded Mormonism, and Charles Taze Russell, who founded the Jehovah's Witnesses, and L. Ron Hubbard, who founded Scientology, are flawed sinners like you and me. None of these people and none of their philosophies and ideas can save us. Just like us they're guilty before a holy God.

Only Jesus can rescue. Only Jesus offers the world outside help. And that's what our world needs. We need God to come down to earth to save us. Only Jesus claims this for himself. Only Jesus died and rose again. And only Jesus can and will unite all things in himself.

First Timothy 2:5 says, "For there is one God, and there is one mediator between God and men, the man Christ Jesus." A mediator is someone who stands between and reconciles two opposing parties. Jesus is the one mediator who can stand between God and man. Only Jesus, by his death on the cross, can reconcile heaven and earth.

Jesus said, "I am the way, and the truth, and the life. No one comes to the Father except through me" (John 14:6).

Have you ever wondered if believing in Jesus would be easier if you could somehow push your way back in time toward him? If you could be, chronologically speaking, closer?

I've had that thought. If I could just be nearer to the actual moment when God invaded our space and time, I'm sure my faith would be unbreakable. Or at least it would be really strong. Maybe.

But then I wonder how far back in time I'd have to go for it to make any real difference. Going back just a thousand years definitely wouldn't be enough. It's not as though living in the tenth century would make me feel much closer to Jesus. Besides, who wants to live in the Dark Ages?

I'm not even certain that living a few hundred years after Jesus would help. I live a little more than two hundred years after America's first president, George Washington. I handle money with his picture on it. Every night I toss into my change jar quarters imprinted with his likeness. Good grief, I live outside Washington DC, which is named after him. I can drive over to his old house at Mount Vernon anytime I want. But I can't say I feel much of a connection with George. I believe in him in the sense that I know he was here. But he still feels far removed and unreal.

So I guess I'd really be happy only if I met Jesus in person. To be someone who was healed by him or perhaps be that kid whose lunch he multiplied. That would be cool.

But even then I'm not sure this business of faith would be simple. Because those who were close to Jesus—people who camped with him, touched him, spoke to him, listened to him preach—also struggled with unbelief and doubts. The disciple Thomas, just *one day* after the resurrection, refused to believe Jesus had risen again unless he saw and touched the wounds in Jesus's hands (John 20:24–29). Some people give Thomas a hard time because of his doubts. But honestly, would any of us have done differently?

I understand how Thomas must have felt. I'd want to see and touch Jesus's hands too.

I think this says something about the makeup of the human soul. No matter how close in time we are, no matter how immediate and intimate the testimony about Jesus is, we want more. We want to remove the need for faith.

So you and I are living almost two thousand years after the historic moment when Jesus performed miracles, died, and rose back to life. We have to trust the testimony of the apostles that is recorded in the Bible. We have to trust that God enabled people to faithfully preserve and translate his words. We have to trust that the message has been accurately transmitted through time and culture. And at times it feels like that requires a lot of faith.

But think of Thomas. He didn't have to trust something he read in a book. No translation was required. No strangers were involved. No, the people he had to trust were his best friends. His closest friends were eyewitnesses of Jesus's resurrection. And they had seen him alive *yesterday.* And yet, even with all that, Thomas felt like believing required a lot of faith. More faith than he could muster at the moment.

Jesus was patient with Thomas. Just like he's patient with us. And when he appeared to Thomas, he said, "Have you believed because you have seen me? Blessed are those who have not seen and yet have believed" (John 20:29).

I like reading those words because I know Jesus is talking about me—me and you and all the other followers he has called to himself in the years since. It's as though he's saying, "I know it takes a lot of faith. I know you'd prefer to have been here. I know you'd like to be with me now. To see me. To have me walk through your backyard and sit in your chair. But I've spoken to you in my Word. I've told you about me. I've given you my Holy Spirit as a promise of what is to come. One day your faith will be sight. One day you'll see me and touch me."

In the verses right after this story of Thomas, the apostle John wrote, "Now Jesus did many other signs in the presence of the disciples, which are not written in this book; but these are written so that you may believe that Jesus is the Christ, the Son of God, and that by believing you may have life in his name" (verses 30–31).

I've never seen Jesus. But I do believe that Jesus is the Christ, the Son of God. And by grace, I know I've found life in his name.

6

A WAY TO BE GOOD AGAIN

*"For too long the news that Jesus died
for my sins had no real meaning."*

THE WEIGHT OF GUILT felt like it would press me into the ground. Crush me. Part of me wanted it to. Maybe then I wouldn't have to feel this way. I lay down on the bed. I longed for sleep—not to rest but to escape. I didn't want to be awake. I didn't want to be conscious, to have to think about what a stupid, hypocritical sinner I was.

I'd watched a pornographic video once before when I was thirteen years old. I had found the VHS tape while baby-sitting at the home of a Christian family. The parents were gone. The kid I watched was napping, and I just sat there, drinking in the defiling images that played out on the television screen. I remember going home that day feeling like I was covered head to foot with a grimy film. I wanted to take the most scalding hot shower possible, to scrub myself clean.

That was six years earlier. I felt dirty then, but this was worse. So much worse. At age thirteen I didn't care about God. I didn't pretend to want to please him. But this time I was different. I loved God. I was serious about serving him.

I'd flown all the way to San Juan, Puerto Rico, to be a volunteer at a Billy Graham Crusade. I had come to do God's work and be part of a historic moment in Christendom. The evangelistic crusade was being broadcast around the world, simultaneously translated into dozens of languages. Well-known Christians had gathered from many nations. There were training sessions for young evangelists. I got my picture taken with apologist Ravi Zacharias, Korean evangelist Billy Kim, and Billy Graham's famous music director, Cliff Barrows. I stood just a few feet from Graham himself and listened to him preach. I was on holy ground.

But one night, when the pastor I was staying with left the house for a meeting, I plopped down on his couch and turned on the television. I mindlessly channel-surfed. Then I clicked past a channel that was all static—the images blurred and hard to identify. I clicked back to it. When I did, the static cleared for several seconds, and the images sharpened. It was a pornographic cable channel.

I didn't turn it off. I could have. I kept thinking that later as I lay on my bed. *I could have turned it off.* Instead, I gave full vent to my lustful desires. I spent the next hour clicking back to the channel for five-second glimpses. For some reason that made it even worse. I hadn't just watched pornography. I had worn out my thumb on the remote control and strained my eyes to make out the vulgar images.

When I finally turned off the television and went to my room, the conviction I'd been holding at bay came rushing into my heart. I'd traveled all this way to sit in a pastor's house and watch porn. I was there to do God's work. I wanted to learn so God could use me. What a joke. I was nothing but a disgusting hypocrite. As I lay there staring at the ceiling, I couldn't even bring myself to pray. I finally slipped into a fitful sleep.

That's when I had the dream.

I don't remember most of my dreams. But I doubt I'll ever forget this one. It was the most vivid and powerful dream I've ever had—before or since.

I dreamed I was in a room filled with index card–size files. They were like the ones libraries used in the past. When I opened a file, I discovered that the cards described thoughts and actions from my life. The room was a crude catalog system of everything, good and bad, I'd ever done.

As I browsed the cards under the headings "Friends I've Betrayed," "Lies I've Told," and "Lustful Thoughts," I was overwhelmed with guilt. Long-forgotten moments of wrongdoing were described in chilling detail. Each card was in my handwriting and signed with my signature. Sadly, my misdeeds woefully outnumbered my good deeds. I tried to destroy a card, desperate to erase the memory of what I'd done. But the past couldn't be changed. I could only weep in the face of my failure and shame.

Then Jesus entered the room. He took the cards and, one by one, began signing his name on them. His name covered mine and was written with his blood.

When I woke from the dream, I was overcome with emotion. I had never been so aware of my guilt before God and, at the same time, the reality of my forgiveness by God. The dream helped me see that my failure and sin were so much worse than one lustful hour of watching pornography. But incredibly, God's grace and love toward me in Jesus were also much more powerful than I had ever realized.

On the cross Jesus took my place. He took every one of my sins upon himself. As never before, the incredible implications of the Son of God dying in *my* place for *my* sins flooded my soul.

Christians say that Jesus died for our sins. But what does this mean? Why did he have to die? What did Jesus accomplish through his death on the cross? What was happening as he hung there between heaven and earth? And what effect does his death have on you and me today? What does it change?

These questions bring us to the very heart of the Christian faith. They bring us to the awe-inspiring subject of the atonement. The word *atonement* speaks of how sinful, guilty men and women can have a restored relationship with a perfectly good and righteous God—how we can be united or "at one" with our Creator.

"Atonement means making amends," writes J. I. Packer, "blotting out the offense, and giving satisfaction for wrong done; thus reconciling to oneself the alienated other and restoring the disrupted relationship."[1]

The Bible teaches that our relationship with God has been disrupted by our disobedience. We are not only separated from him because of the vileness of our sin; we're guilty before him and worthy of his punishment.

The most confounding theological question humanity has ever faced is the question of how a truly good and righteous God could love and forgive guilty people. If God ignores human sin, then he is immoral and unjust. Or he is an amoral force with no standards at all. And yet God has promised to rescue us and accept us. How can this be? The answer is the Cross.

———

I grew up being told that Jesus died on the cross for me. But for too long this information had no real meaning. Of course it was really nice of him and everything. But it was like someone spending a lot of money on a gift you don't really want or need. It made no sense to me. Even after I chose to give my life to God, the Cross was a blurry concept in my thinking.

I have a vivid memory from this period in my life. I was a young teenager. I was walking into our brown duplex on Kane Road in Gresham, Oregon. As I opened the door from the carport to the kitchen, I had the thought, *I don't understand why Jesus had to die.* This matter-of-fact statement just ran through my mind.

It's odd to me that such a fleeting moment would be so clear in my memory. Maybe I was slightly discomforted by my confusion. Sadly, I wasn't distressed enough by my lack of understanding to do anything about it. I didn't ask anyone to explain the Cross to me. I didn't go read my Bible. And there was no sense of urgency in my heart, no sense I needed Jesus's death to occur.

I wonder how many people in churches today have the same unclear thoughts about the Cross. When you compare this modern fuzzy thinking with the sharp focus on Christ's death in the pages of Scripture, you can't help but think that something is very wrong.

Jesus anticipated the time and manner of his death (Matthew 20:17–19). He taught his followers that his death would be the climax of the earthly mission he had come to accomplish. Jesus said, "For even the Son of Man came not to be served but to serve, and to give his life as a ransom for many" (Mark 10:45).

The Cross wasn't the tragic upending of Jesus's plan; it was the fulfillment of his plan. The hour of his greatest anguish was the hour for which he had come (John 12:27). And on the night of his betrayal, Jesus instituted what we call the Lord's Supper—a ceremony he gave to the church by which we are to remember his death. When we eat the bread and drink the cup together as a reminder of his body broken and his blood poured out for us, we proclaim his death until his return (1 Corinthians 11:26). John Stott points out that this commemorative act "dramatizes neither his birth nor his life, neither his words nor his works, but only his death." Stott writes of Jesus,

"It was by his death that he wished above all else to be remembered. There is then, it is safe to say, no Christianity without the cross. If the cross is not central to our religion, ours is not the religion of Jesus."[2]

In the book *In My Place Condemned He Stood,* authors J. I. Packer and Mark Dever say that we can't understand the atonement without a grasp of three things: first, the Trinitarian nature of God; second, the holiness and justice of God; and, third, our own guilt and sin before God.

This helps me understand my confusion about the Cross and Jesus's atoning work. As a teenager, I certainly had not given careful thought to God as Trinity. And if you don't understand that God is one and yet three distinct persons in the Father, Son, and Holy Spirit, then the death of Jesus on the cross seems like nothing but a tragic example of injustice. Or even worse, it could be viewed as the ruthless action of a God who punishes his unsuspecting, somewhat clueless Son.

One of the few times I remember the Cross being clearly presented during high school youth group was when a speaker told a story about a train conductor who was responsible for lowering a bridge so a commuter train could safely pass. One day the conductor's young son came with him to work and, while playing, got trapped in the gears that lowered the bridge. As the train approached, the conductor realized his son's plight. Without enough time to rescue his son and with the train rushing toward the bridge, the conductor made the heart-wrenching decision to lower the bridge on his son so the people on the train could be saved. "And that," the speaker said, "is what God did for you." I remember thinking, *God is a jerk.*

I hated that story. I was mad at the conductor for bringing his son to work. Mad at the son for playing in the gears. And mad at the guy for telling me the stupid story. It didn't make me appreciate the Cross more. It made the Cross seem like some sort of cosmic accident that was supposed to make me feel indebted and guilty.

Many years later I learned how inaccurate and unhelpful the analogy of the conductor is for explaining the Cross. At the root of its error is an absence of the Trinitarian nature of God.

The Father is God, the Son is God, and the Spirit is God. God is one in three distinct persons. The Father, Son, and Holy Spirit have perfect communion, and they worked together to save mankind. The work of salvation on the Cross was the united work of all three persons of the Trinity. Many places in Scripture point to this teamwork. Hebrews 9:14 says, "How much more will the blood of *Christ*, who through the eternal *Spirit* offered himself without blemish to *God*, purify our conscience from dead works to serve the living God" (emphasis added).

Jesus was no victim trapped in the gears of Roman injustice. Jesus was God himself, who willingly laid down his life. God the Father was no cruel, abusive deity who lacked pity for his child. Instead, in the mystery of the Godhead, Father and Son chose together to redeem mankind through substitution. Human sin demanded a price be paid. But God would pay the price. With his own life.

The Son became sin in that he represented mankind and stood in the place of sinful humanity. God the Father administered justice. The righteous wrath and punishment that human treason and rebellion deserved was poured out on God the Son. At the Cross, God himself both delivered and received the blow.

Jesus wasn't trapped. He was in control. And he chose, because of love, to lay down his life for us. Jesus said, "For this reason the Father loves me, because I lay down my life that I may take it up again. No one takes it from me, but I lay it down of my own accord. I have authority to lay it down, and

I have authority to take it up again. This charge I have received from my Father" (John 10:17–18).

Jesus laid down his life. He loved his Father's glory. The Father loved his Son. And together, out of love for a lost world, they paid the greatest price to atone for sin.

———

To atone means to make amends for wrong that's been done. Most people can admit they've done wrong. The easiest, most common confession in the world is "I admit I'm not perfect." But the idea that our sins and "imperfections" need the gruesome death of an innocent—much less the Son of God—seems a little over the top. We've done wrong, but in most cases we don't think it's that big a deal.

We feel this way because we don't truly know God. We don't understand that he is holy and righteous, that he hates and must punish all sin and wickedness. Scripture says that God's eyes are so pure he cannot look on evil (Habakkuk 1:13).

Maybe you've noticed in the Bible that when people encounter God, their common response is to fall down as though dead (see, for example, Revelation 1:17). You never get the sense that they're being melodramatic. They are sure they are going to die. Their actions convey pure terror. Why? Because they behold a God who is not only overwhelming in his power and glory but who is also completely righteous. The Bible uses the word *holy* to describe him. We usually think of holiness in terms of moral purity, and God is holy in that sense. But the word *holy* primarily describes God's "otherness." He is completely separate from us. God is completely different and exalted above mankind. There is no sin or darkness in him. He is completely good, true, and righteous.

Do we have any concept of what it means to encounter the holy, righteous, pure God of heaven? When Isaiah beheld God, he was instantly aware of his guilt and cried, "Woe is me! For I am lost; for I am a man of unclean lips, and I dwell in the midst of a people of unclean lips; for my eyes have seen the King, the LORD of hosts!" (Isaiah 6:5). When Job heard God speak, he despised himself and his arrogant demands (Job 42:6). When Peter first met Jesus and saw his supernatural power and holiness, he fell at Jesus's knees and begged, "Depart from me, for I am a sinful man, O Lord" (Luke 5:8). In the presence of the Holy God, Peter was undone by an awareness of his own sinfulness.

If we don't feel the need for atonement, it's probably because we assume God has the same nonchalant attitude toward evil that we do. But he doesn't. God has a total, unremitting hatred for sin and injustice. His response to sin is extreme righteous anger. The Bible calls this God's wrath. Some people are repulsed by the idea of God being a God of wrath. But if you think about it, a God who doesn't hate evil is terrifying. True goodness hates evil. True righteousness and justice must stand in opposition to injustice and unrighteousness. God's wrath, writes John Stott, "is in fact his holy reaction to evil."[3]

This is hard for me to grasp. Too often I place sin and injustice on a scale. Sin is less sinful if everyone is doing it. Injustice is less a problem if it's not against me or someone I love. If I can't see it or feel the effects of it, I don't lose sleep.

God is so different from me. He sees sin for what it is—an affront to his rule and reign. All human sin—even when it's done against another person—is ultimately also a sin against God. It's a violation of his laws (Psalm 51:4). And he sees the death and destruction and sorrow that sin brings about in people's lives. You and I have no idea how connected and consequential our sin is. We see most of our sins as insignificant—a small match dropping on the grass or at worst a tiny brush fire. God sees what the small flames lead to. He sees the forest fire that devours the countryside and ravages homes and takes lives.

God sees the devastation that human sin has wrought in the world. And in his perfect justice, he has promised to punish it all.

This is the most comforting and yet the most terrifying truth in the world: because God is holy and just, no one will get away with anything in this life. At the end of time, there will be a final and perfect accounting before him (Romans 14:12). What human judges and human courts couldn't prosecute, God Almighty will prosecute. There will be no unsolved crimes. No cold cases. He will judge the living and the dead (1 Peter 4:5). All sin—from genocide and murder to gossip and slander, from rape and human trafficking to lust and immorality—will be punished.

The irony of all this is that a God of perfect justice is both the one for whom we long and the one whom we dread. We long for someone to set things right, to punish those who terrorize, molest, kill, and enslave the innocent. We want someone to judge and punish evil. We want a judge with total power and a piercing commitment to righteousness.

But when his eyes turn on us, we realize that we, too, are guilty. We, too, deserve his judgment.

The night I had my dream about the room of files, I woke up sobbing. I turned on the light, grabbed my laptop, and began to write about my dream. I wept as I wrote. At times I could barely see the screen through the tears.

I called the story "The Room" and a few months later printed it in the small magazine I published at the time.[4] Maybe you've read it before. After it was printed, the story made its way around the Internet as one of those forwarded "Read this!" e-mails that clog your in-box.

I'm still amazed at the response the dream generated. I received stories of it being read by chaplains at prisons and by pastors to their congregations and being performed as a drama. Since then it's been printed in various magazines and even turned into a short film. A few years later I included "The Room" in a chapter of my first book. That chapter was the most frequently referenced by readers who wrote to me. What has surprised me most is the reaction it elicits from non-Christians. Many have told me how moved they were by the story. Many times they've said, "I began to cry as I read it."

Why does the dream connect with so many different people on a deep level? I think the answer is that it touches on the universal theme of guilt and redemption. We all carry around some sense that we've done wrong, that we haven't measured up to the standards of others or to our own standards— much less the standards of God.

Most of us attempt to find peace from past sins by trying to forget and move on. We find comfort in the distance that comes with the passing of time. The further we are from our sins, the less we feel they mark our lives and the less guilty we feel. I can tell you the story of watching pornography fourteen years ago. But do I want to confess the sin I committed last week? And do I even remember half of the wrongs I've done? The truth is that I've conveniently forgotten most of my violations.

I read a newspaper story about a woman named Jill Price who has a rare condition doctors call "superior autobiographical memory." Jill can recall in vivid detail every day of her life since age fourteen. Experts at the University of California studied her for six years to confirm her ability. If you've ever wished you had a better memory, you might want to reconsider. Jill views it as a blessing and a curse. She has warm memories that comfort her in difficult times, but there's also a dark side. She recalls every bad decision, every insult, and every excruciating embarrassment. Over the years, Jill said, the memories have eaten her up. She feels paralyzed and assaulted by them. Peaceful sleep is rare.[5]

We all want to think of ourselves as basically good people. But we can believe that illusion only because we forget most of our past decisions and actions and thoughts. But what if we remembered them perfectly? God does.

It's an uncomfortable thought, isn't it? I guess that's why my dream about the room filled with cards has such an emotional impact on people. We all have things in our lives that we don't want to remember. Things we know should be made right. Things that should be atoned for.

The Bible teaches that sin requires death. When Adam and Eve rebelled against God, his judgment on them and all mankind was physical death (Genesis 3:19).

But even in the garden, God spoke of his plan to rescue and restore mankind (Genesis 3:15). He didn't unveil his purpose or plan. Instead over the course of centuries, God began to teach his people the principle of atonement through substitutionary death.

When God rescued his people from slavery in Egypt, he punished the pride of Pharaoh by striking down the firstborn of every Egyptian family. But he showed mercy to the people of Israel by giving them a way to escape this death. Through Moses, the Lord instructed his people to sacrifice a spotless, unblemished lamb and mark the doorpost of their homes with its blood. In Exodus 12:13 God said, "The blood shall be a sign for you, on the houses where you are. And when I see the blood, I will pass over you, and no plague will befall you to destroy you, when I strike the land of Egypt." Judgment and death passed over the homes with doorposts wet with blood, the symbol of life poured out. A lamb had already died. A substitute had been offered.

After God brought his people out of Egypt, he established an elaborate system of animal sacrifices that provided a means of forgiving and removing their sin. The sacrificial system taught them that sin is serious and can only be covered by the shedding of blood. Leviticus 17:11 says, "For the life of the flesh is in the blood, and I have given it for you on the altar to make atonement for your souls, for it is the blood that makes atonement by the life."

Blood symbolizes a person's life. To shed blood means to give up life, to die. When a lamb or bull was killed in the blood sacrifices of the Old Testament, it was a vivid, graphic portrayal of paying for sins by the sacrifice of life. An Israelite man would choose a lamb without defect and bring it before the Lord. He would lay his hands on the animal, a symbol of it bearing his guilt. Then the animal would be sacrificed and its blood sprinkled on the altar.

Besides the ongoing sacrifices prescribed in the Law, there was also a special day each year called the Day of Atonement (Leviticus 16). One ritual of this day involved two goats. The first goat was sacrificed in the normal way. But the high priest laid his hands on the second animal, confessed the sins of the nation, and then sent the goat outside the camp into the wilderness. The second goat portrayed what the sacrifice of the first goat accomplished. God had provided a way for the people's sins to be removed, carried away by the sacrifice of a substitute. This is the origin of the term *scapegoat,* which refers to someone who is blamed for the wrongs and misdeeds of others so they can escape punishment.

The two goats on the Day of Atonement and all the blood sacrifices practiced over the centuries gave God's people a language and vivid imagery for their need for atonement. God wanted them to understand that they needed to be cleansed, to be forgiven. But the sacrifice of bulls and lambs and goats was merely a foreshadowing of the only sacrifice that could truly remove guilt. These blood sacrifices pointed ahead to Jesus. They were given so that one day God's people would grasp the meaning of Jesus Christ and his bloody death on a cross.

Jesus was betrayed on the night of the Passover celebration. On that night he gave his followers a new ceremony to recount God's redeeming work (Matthew 26:17–29). They would not shed the blood of a lamb; instead they would remember Jesus's body broken and his blood poured out.

Like the scapegoat that bore the sins of the people, Jesus was taken outside the city when he was crucified. He bore our sins and carried them away. Hebrews 13:12 says, "So Jesus also suffered outside the gate in order to sanctify the people through his own blood."

And of all the names used for Christ, few are as powerful as "the Lamb of God." Why is Jesus called by this name? It isn't because Jesus was cute and adorable and fluffy. He is called the Lamb of God because he was sacrificed by God for our sins. John the Baptist said of Jesus, "Behold, the Lamb of God, who takes away the sin of the world!" (John 1:29). And in his vision of heaven, the apostle John saw Jesus being worshiped by countless multitudes. And how does Jesus appear in his glory? As a lamb, standing as though slain (Revelation 5:6).

This is a staggering thought. Why would God need a lamb? He has no sin of his own to pay for. Why would God offer a sacrifice? The answer is that God offers his Son, and his Son willingly lays down his life, to atone for mankind's sins. We can never pay for our own sins. The debt we owe to God and the guilt we carry before God are too great. Only God himself can remove the stain of guilt and shame.

In Jesus's death God provided the lamb. Instead of you and me facing the wrath and punishment our sins deserve, Jesus took our place. He is our substitute. He shed his blood, he gave his life, so that our sins are removed and God's wrath is turned away.

Khaled Hosseini's novel *The Kite Runner* is a powerful portrayal of the human longing for atonement. The book tells the story of Amir, a newly married Afghan immigrant living in California who is haunted by an act of betrayal from his childhood. When he was a young boy growing up in Kabul, he stood by as his best friend, Hassan, was beaten and raped by a vicious older boy named Assef. Instead of rushing to his friend's aid, Amir cowered in fear and watched from the shadows.

Afterward Amir was racked with guilt. His shame was compounded by Hassan's continued kindness and loyalty. Hassan, whose father worked as a servant for Amir's wealthy father, continued to selflessly serve Amir. Even though he knew of Amir's cowardice, Hassan refused to retaliate or even utter a harsh word. Eaten up by his guilt, Amir falsely accused Hassan of stealing a new watch. Eventually Amir's behavior forced Hassan and his father out of the home.

The story picks up years later when Amir is grown and living in America with his elderly father. He's a world away from the land of his childhood, but the moment in the alley still plagues him. "That was a long time ago," he says, "but it's wrong what they say about the past, I've learned, about how you can bury it. Because the past claws its way out. Looking back now, I realize I have been peeking into that deserted alley for the last twenty-six years."[6]

When one of his old friends who knew of his shameful act calls from Pakistan and asks him to visit, Amir knows it isn't just his friend on the line but his "past of unatoned sins" calling. Before the old friend hangs up, he says, "There is a way to be good again."[7]

A way to be good again. Isn't that what we all long for? We want forgiveness and cleansing—a way to make up for and cover our wrongdoings and acts of selfishness. In *The Kite Runner* Amir finds this opportunity when he eventually returns to Afghanistan to face his past. He learns that his friend Hassan is dead but that his orphaned son is alive and in need of rescue. But saving the young boy requires that Amir face the same sadistic Assef who violated Hassan so many years before.

The story finds resolution as Amir reenacts the moments from his past in which he miserably failed. This time when he faces Assef, he doesn't back down. To gain his old friend's son, he accepts a brutal beating from Assef. His ribs are broken. His jaw is crushed. He chokes on his own blood. And yet in the midst of his beating, he begins to laugh. He laughs as he is battered and bruised. He finally feels that he is paying for his wrongs.

Amir risks his life to save the son of his friend Hassan. By showing kindness to the boy and adopting him, Amir finds a way "to be good again."

But can any of us ever atone for our past wrongs like this? What if the people we've sinned against are gone? Whom do we repay? What if there's nothing we can give to make up for what we stole? What if a beating isn't enough to salve our conscience? What can we give to pay for the wrongs we've done?

The Bible teaches that for us the problem is even more serious. Our sin isn't just against our friends and family members. Ultimately, all the wrong we do is an act of hatred and disobedience toward God himself. Our sin is the breaking of his law. It is not just our conscience that needs to be satisfied; it is the holy wrath of God that demands payment. Our problem is far greater than we imagine. How can an act of rebellion against an infinitely holy God, who must by his very nature judge wickedness and remove it from his good creation, be forgiven? First Samuel 2:25 says, "If someone sins against a man, God will mediate for him, but if someone sins against the LORD, who can intercede for him?" God's anger burns against us.

Even if we could somehow revisit and repay all the wrongs we've done (which we can't), we'd still have God to deal with. How do we make peace with a God of perfect righteousness and justice?

How does God make us good again before him? How does he deal with our guilt and sin? The unimaginable message of the Bible is that God's love for us is so great that he has made a way for us to be good again through the atoning life and death of his Son.

Jesus did for us what we could not do ourselves. He came to intercede for the human race that had sinned against God. He lived and died on our behalf.

Whereas we disobeyed God's law, Jesus perfectly obeyed it. Just as Adam's sin plunged the world into guilt, Jesus's obedience makes all who trust in him righteous (Romans 5:19). This is "the righteousness from God that depends on faith" (Philippians 3:9).

Instead of abandoning us and condemning us, God came looking for us. He so loved the world that he sent his only Son to save the world (John 3:16–17). Jesus came to reconcile us to God.

How does he reconcile us? By paying the penalty for our sins. This is what theologians call *penal substitution*. On the cross Jesus became our substitute and took our penalty. Just as Jesus obeyed in our place, he also died in our place. Galatians 3:13 says that Jesus became "a curse for us." The prophet Isaiah described Jesus's substitutionary, atoning death when he wrote:

> But he was wounded for our transgressions;
>   he was crushed for our iniquities;
> upon him was the chastisement that brought us peace,
>   and with his stripes we are healed.

All we like sheep have gone astray;
> we have turned—every one—to his own way;

and the LORD has laid on him
> the iniquity of us all. (Isaiah 53:5–6)

We transgressed. We committed the iniquity. But Jesus was wounded for us. He was crushed in our place. God laid on him our guilt so we could be forgiven. Second Corinthians 5:21 says, "For our sake he made him to be sin who knew no sin, so that in him we might become the righteousness of God."

What was happening when Jesus hung between heaven and earth? First Peter 2:24 says, "He himself bore our sins in his body on the tree." Apart from the unthinkable physical suffering of crucifixion, Jesus endured the torment of God's wrath toward sin.

The result of Christ's substitution is that God's wrath is satisfied and turned away. This is called *propitiation*. Romans 3:25 says that God put Christ forward "as a propitiation by his blood." God's justice demands death for sin. Jesus's blood poured out, his life given in our place, satisfies that demand. First John 4:10 says, "In this is love, not that we have loved God but that he loved us and sent his Son to be the propitiation for our sins."

"It is God himself who in holy wrath needs to be propitiated," writes John Stott. "God himself who in holy love undertook to do the propitiating, and God himself who in the person of his Son died for the propitiation of our sins."[8]

At the cross God's wrath was satisfied. Our sins were paid for so we could be forgiven and accepted by God. First Peter 3:18 says, "For Christ also suffered once for sins, the righteous for the unrighteous, that he might bring us to God."

A few years ago I was told that there was a Muslim version of my story "The Room" on various Islamic Web sites.⁹

A girl named Jenny, who had grown up in a religious, fundamentalist Muslim family, wrote to tell me how she'd read the story of my dream at a week-long camp for Muslim girls. On the emotional final evening around the campfire, Jenny was asked to read the story of the room filled with files. But she said the Muslim version of the dream had been edited. Jesus never appeared. There was no assurance of forgiveness. It ended with this paragraph:

> And then the tears came. I began to weep. Sobs so deep that the hurt started in my stomach and shook through me. I fell on my knees and cried. I cried out of shame, from the overwhelming shame of it all. The rows of file shelves swirled in my tear-filled eyes. No one must ever, ever know of this room. I must lock it up and hide the key.

After she read the story, the other girls left the campfire crying. But the effect was much deeper for Jenny. She was consumed by a sense of desperation and hopelessness. Throughout her life she had been a devout follower of Islam. Along with her family, she memorized the Koran, prayed five times a day, and had even visited Mecca. She did her best, but she was constantly aware of her shortcomings. She was distracted during prayers. She sometimes lied.

In high school Jenny had begun to have vivid nightmares of hell. She would wake up in a cold sweat with a desperate sense of hopelessness. "I was no longer so confident in my admittance to heaven," she said.

The Muslim version of "The Room" had been read around the campfire to spur the girls to be better and live moral lives, but it left Jenny exhausted and disillusioned. *I can't try any harder,* she thought, *and I know I am not good enough.* She began to look for God outside of Islam.

Several years later, after many stories of God's mercy in her life, Jenny came to a saving faith in Jesus Christ as her Savior. After she became a Christian, someone e-mailed her the complete Christian version of "The Room." When she opened the e-mail, she immediately recognized the beginning of the story. She was curious how she would feel reading the story now that she was a Christian.

"As I got to the end of the part that I remembered, I did not feel the deep sadness that I had before," Jenny told me. But the surprise for her was that the original version had a different ending. The version she had read at camp ended with terror and fear. But in this conclusion Jesus entered the room. Jenny read the words about Jesus that had been deleted from the story:

> He looked at me with pity in His eyes. But this was a pity that didn't anger me. I dropped my head, covered my face with my hands and began to cry again. He walked over and put His arm around me. He could have said so many things. But He didn't say a word. He just cried with me.
>
> Then He got up and walked back to the wall of files. Starting at one end of the room, He took out a file and, one by one, began to sign His name over mine on each card.
>
> "No!" I shouted rushing to Him. All I could find to say was "No, no," as I pulled the card from Him. His name shouldn't be on these cards. But there it was, written in red so rich, so dark, so alive. The name of Jesus covered mine. It was written with His blood.
>
> He gently took the card back. He smiled a sad smile and began to sign the cards. I don't think I'll ever understand how He did it so quickly, but the next instant it seemed I heard Him close the last file and walk back to my side. He placed His hand on my shoulder and said, "It is finished."

I stood up, and He led me out of the room. There was no lock on its door. There were still cards to be written.

Do you see how essential the atonement is to the Christian faith? Apart from the Cross of Jesus Christ, our lives dead-end in hopelessness and terror. We stand guilty before a God we can't please. We know our best efforts are inadequate. And the gnawing guilt for our wrongs can't be shaken.

That's where man-made religion leaves us—not just Islam, but every religious system (including some that claim to be Christian) that excludes the atoning sacrifice of the Cross. Without the blood of Jesus Christ shed for sins, there is no atonement, no forgiveness, no reconciliation. No hope.

But the story doesn't end with our guilt. Isn't that incredible? Jesus enters the picture. He walks into the reality of our failure and shame and guilt. Think of the worst card in your room full of files and consider this: Jesus died so your worst moment could be covered. He took the blame so you could stand before God forgiven and accepted.

There is a way to be good again. It is to trust in Jesus and his atoning death. To receive by faith his rescue. There is nothing you and I can do to pay for our sins. Our good deeds cannot cover them. Time will not make them fade. Only the blood of the Lamb of God can cleanse us, cover us, and rescue us from judgment.

HOW JESUS SAVED GREGG EUGENE HARRIS

"How does redemption accomplished outside Jerusalem give life to a young man on a California beach?"

GREGG PLAYED THE GUITAR and sang on the beach for tips. With his tattered bell-bottom jeans, mustache, and wispy, shoulder-length brown hair, he was the quintessential hippie troubadour. Laguna Beach, California, circa 1970, was a magnet for artists and musicians. They came from every corner of the country. Peace, love, and a steady supply of drugs made the beach town an idyllic setting.

"Would you like to hear a song?" Gregg would ask people lounging in the sun. He learned to read people—their style, age, and interests—and then did his best to sing a song to match them. He sang only original songs. His music was his art, and he refused to be a human jukebox playing songs heard on the radio.

Once he played a song for José Feliciano, the blind, lightning-fingered guitarist whose song "Light My Fire" had been a big hit. Gregg didn't recognize the star, but afterward Feliciano told him to come to his concert that night. He said he wanted to buy Gregg's song.

But Gregg didn't show that evening because he couldn't "prostitute" his art. Besides, he planned to make it big with his music on his own. He didn't know that God had bigger plans for him than musical stardom.

One day on the beach, Gregg was approached by two hippies. "Hey, man, what do you know about Jesus?" one of them asked him. It was the last question Gregg expected. He'd run all the way from Ohio to get away from Jesus and the stifling religion of his childhood. He knew everything about Jesus, and he despised him.

He decided to have a little fun with the two Jesus freaks. He would use his Bible knowledge to skewer them. He'd ask them questions they couldn't answer. He'd overpower them with his arguments. So he launched into a rant right there on the beach.

But they weren't overpowered. They just listened and smiled. Then, when he was done, they talked about Jesus in a way Gregg had never heard before. They said Jesus was a king who had come to redeem a world ruined by sin. In Jesus, God himself had invaded the planet. Jesus died on the cross, not as a victim, but to conquer death itself. He had shown the real meaning of love. And one day very soon Jesus would return. He would judge the whole world and rule the nations. Today was the day to turn from sin and believe in him.

In spite of himself, Gregg listened. Their words, their answers to his questions, their description of Jesus sank into his soul and tugged on something deep within him. It was as though someone was calling him from far off.

When the conversation ended, he tried to play it cool. He didn't let on how deeply affected he was by their words. He didn't kneel and pray or even say he would think more about what they'd said. The two men said good-bye and walked off down the beach.

"Somehow," Gregg says, "I knew my life would never be the same."

If someone digs a well and taps a spring of the purest water, it's no use to anyone unless the water is channeled to dry soil and carried to parched lips. To be told that such a well exists or merely to see it from a distance will not quench your thirst. You have to drink from it yourself.

Jesus once described the salvation he offers as living water. He told a woman he met by a well that if she drank the water he could give her, she would never be thirsty again (you can read the story in John 4). Jesus said that his water would become a spring welling up inside her, giving eternal life. He was speaking of the new spiritual life that he came to bring.

Of course, she didn't understand all that at first. She thought he was talking about normal water. She liked the idea of not being thirsty and not having to break her back pulling up buckets from the well.

But eventually the woman did come to understand that the water Jesus spoke of was a metaphor for spiritual life—for knowing and believing in him. And she did drink this living water. She trusted in Jesus as the promised Savior.

The Bible tells us that Jesus died and rose again so that sinners could have their sins forgiven and be reconciled to God (1 Corinthians 15:1–4). This message is what Christians call the gospel, a word that means "good news." Many people have heard this message of good news, but obviously not all have been saved by it. It's possible to learn about the events of Jesus's life, death, and resurrection from a distance—to be told of their meaning, their power, and their hope—and yet receive no personal benefit from them.

Somehow, Jesus's great work of salvation has to reach us. Not only the news of it but the real spiritual power of it has to touch us and change us. So how does that happen?

Theologian John Murray has a helpful way of describing God's saving work. He uses the terms *redemption accomplished* and *redemption applied*. *Redemption accomplished* is what Jesus has already done for us—his life of perfect obedience, his substitutionary death on the cross, and his resurrection.

It's the second aspect of God's redemption—the applied part—that I want us to reflect on here. *Redemption applied* is how Jesus's accomplishment connects to us. How it reaches us and saves us. Another name for this is the *doctrine of salvation.*

The doctrine of salvation answers the questions "How does Jesus's saving work translate into our salvation? What does it mean to get saved? How do we go from being sinners who are spiritually dead and alienated from God to being spiritually alive, righteous children of God?"

Or, to put the question in terms that are much more personal to me, how does Jesus's redemption accomplished on a hill outside Jerusalem reach down through the centuries to the year 1970 and to a young man playing his guitar on a California beach?

There are many ways to explore the doctrine of salvation, but I'd like to consider it by sharing the story of how Jesus applied his mighty salvation to one person. His name is Gregg Harris, and he's my father.

His parents named him Gregg Eugene. His first name was spelled with two *g*'s on the end because that's how Grandma saw it on a nameplate at a doctor's office. His middle name, Eugene, was his father's name. He never liked his middle name, but for some reason he passed it on to me. I've mostly forgiven him for that.

Dad was born on October 23, 1952, in Dayton, Ohio, at the Miami Valley Hospital. He appeared to be a normal, healthy baby, but the doctor shared devastating news with Gene and Francis. "Nature forgot to finish her work," he said. Their little boy had three very serious internal birth defects. For there to be any hope of his survival, he had to undergo three major surgeries within forty-eight hours of his birth. In 1952 the procedures were dangerous, bordering on experimental. If he survived, the doctors said, he probably wouldn't make it past six years old. And if he did, he would be confined to a wheelchair and need constant care.

Grandma never stopped praying. My grandmother was a devout Christian who had given her life to Jesus when she was eight years old. Her family lived a mile from the church. She read her Bible and went to church every time the doors were open. Her father played the organ. He could make the organ talk. Every day Grandma asked God to grow her faith "daily, monthly, and yearly."

Her one major lapse in Christian faithfulness was dating and marrying Gene. My grandfather was a quiet World War II veteran who worked at the Frigidaire plant in Dayton, loved horses, and always had a pouch of Red Man chewing tobacco handy. He was born in Alabama and lived most of his life in Tennessee. Grandma knew he wasn't a genuine believer. During their courtship he went to church and feigned enough interest in the Bible to convince her to marry him. But afterward his church attendance slowly dropped off. Church just seemed to make him mad. When he did go with her, they would argue on their way home from the meeting. Finally he stopped going altogether.

But Grandma's faith sustained her in the difficult years after my dad's birth and the surgeries. They had only partially solved his problems; he couldn't pass solids normally. Grandma would spend hours each day, pumping him full of oil, trying to help him go to the bathroom.

Caring for him consumed every ounce of her energy, leaving her physically and emotionally exhausted. Worst of all she was alone in the endeavor.

Grandpa couldn't handle his son's disability. Wanting to pretend it away and looking for any excuse to get out of the house, he spent most of his free time at ball games and racetracks.

The daily stress was almost too much for Grandma to handle. She contemplated suicide. "I know that's wrong," she told God. And when she thought of little Gregg, she knew she had to keep living, if only for him. "My life is like a jigsaw puzzle that's all confused, and I can't put it together," she prayed. "God, only you can fix this."

Another major surgery was planned when Dad was seven. The doctors said it might make things worse instead of better, but they had to try something. Then on the day of the operation, while they were waiting at the hospital, he went to the bathroom by himself. This had never happened naturally before. The surgery was called off. Grandma knew it was a miracle from heaven.

But even with this progress, Dad still faced significant challenges. His childhood was shaped by his disability. For fear that a blow to his stomach could kill him, he was isolated and kept from any kind of rough play or sports. "I was treated like an egg," Dad remembers. And because most of his early years were spent with his mother, he had a warped view of his place in the world. Grandma was so intent on keeping him in good spirits that she treated him like a little prince. She made him believe that his every word was brilliant and his every joke was sidesplittingly funny.

When he got to school, the illusion was shattered. He wasn't brilliant or funny. And when the other kids didn't laugh at his jokes, Gregg just tried harder. To make matters worse, his disability led to several occasions when he soiled himself in class. In elementary school that's not the sort of thing you live down. For years he was ostracized and mocked.

A story from sixth grade epitomizes Gregg's elementary school years. One day a popular girl named Marilyn announced in the cafeteria that she was having a party at her house later that afternoon. Everyone was invited. Gregg thought "everyone" included him. After school he rushed home, flush with excitement. He put on his Sunday best—a crisp white shirt and clip-on bow tie—and marched off to Marilyn's house. She was standing at the door smiling as she welcomed all the kids. But when she saw Gregg, her smile turned to a scowl. "I don't remember inviting you," she sneered.

"I know," he quickly lied. "I was just coming here to meet a friend."

"Oh," Marilyn replied coolly. She went inside and shut the door.

Gregg stood there a moment listening to the sounds of the party in the house. Kids were talking and laughing. He was sure they were laughing at him. He turned and ran all the way back home, into his room, and threw himself on his bed. He buried his face in his pillow and screamed.

———

Throughout his childhood Gregg was a church kid. Each week Grandma dragged him and his brother and sister to First Baptist in Centerville. Looking back, Dad says that exposure to religion acted like a flu shot—it immunized him from genuine faith. He got just enough to develop a deep-rooted disdain for Christianity and the church.

But as a young child, he tried to please his mom by learning to parrot religious phrases and recite Bible facts. And he dutifully got himself "saved" dozens of times. Weekly attendance at Sunday school and Vacation Bible School every summer gave him countless opportunities to pray the sinner's prayer. He didn't mean any of it, and it didn't do anything for him. He had no real understanding of what it meant to trust in Jesus. And no real desire to get what the church offered.

Pastor Snoddy was a nice enough man, but the women really ran the place. In Gregg's eyes Jesus was just a long-haired version of Pastor Snoddy—

mild, gentle, and a bit of a pushover. The Jesus he saw in the painting on his Sunday school wall had a glowing face and doe eyes. And he was a little too pretty for comfort.

His Sunday school teachers said that Jesus loved him, that Jesus wanted to come into his heart. But that only made Jesus seem more clingy and desperate. And what did it really mean for Jesus to come into your heart?

———

You would think that something as important as how one gets saved would get more careful attention from Christians. But I think a lot of us share Dad's hazy conception of salvation. For many, getting saved is simply a matter of praying a prayer or responding to an altar call. But if you press Christians for the specifics of what our prayer means or what actually occurs inwardly when someone believes, our understanding starts to break down. Our "doctrine of salvation" is premised on a string of undefined religious clichés: God loves me. I gave my life to Jesus. I have a personal relationship with Jesus. I invited Jesus into my heart. I got saved. I became a Christian.

It seems that most Christians think of getting saved as something *we* do. We drive the action. We do the choosing. We find God. We invite Jesus in. We become Christians. In America, salvation is a lot like shopping for a new flat-screen television.

The odd thing about this "we do it" emphasis in our view of salvation is how different it is from the way the Bible talks about salvation. Scripture does command us to respond to Jesus, to turn to God in faith and repent of sin (Acts 2:38). But when the Bible speaks of the powerful, mysterious work of salvation in the human soul, it always emphasizes what God does. It always talks about God's grace and God's power.

God's grace, as Jerry Bridges defines it, is "God's kindness shown to the ill-deserving."[1] Because of our disobedience and rebellion toward God, we're not just undeserving of kindness; we're actually ill-deserving. We're guilty. The only thing we deserve is punishment. Salvation isn't something we earn or buy. Ephesians 2:8–9 says, "For by grace you have been saved through faith. And this is not your own doing; it is the gift of God, not a result of works, so that no one may boast." Salvation is not our doing. It is a gift. Only God can pay for our sins and make us worthy to relate to him. And this is what he's done through the death of his Son. This is why God's kindness toward us can be described as amazing grace.

Power is the ability to do or accomplish something. The Bible insistently denies that we have the spiritual power to save ourselves or even contribute to the process. We are not just weak; we are spiritually lifeless, dead (Ephesians 2:1). Salvation is accomplished not by our striving but by God's power. In Romans, the apostle Paul states that the work of Jesus in dying and rising again is "the power of God for salvation" for all who believe (1:16). Elsewhere Paul says that while the message of a crucified Savior seems foolish to many, for those who are saved, it is "the power of God" (1 Corinthians 1:18).

Even the analogies God uses in the Bible to describe salvation emphasize that it is his work. Look at how God describes the ways he redeems his people. Think about Israel's great rescue from Egypt, told in the book of Exodus. That mighty act of salvation from slavery foreshadowed Christ's salvation of sinners. Who made that happen? The mighty Israelites? No, the power of God working through his servant Moses.

Or consider the Old Testament prophet Ezekiel. God gave him the incredible vision of a valley filled with dry bones (Ezekiel 37:1–14). It was an open graveyard of human skeletons. The bones were dry and lifeless. God asked, "Can these bones live?" (verse 3). Then God told Ezekiel to prophesy to the bones, to speak God's word over them. Ezekiel spoke, and as he did, God's mighty word breathed life into the bones. They flew into alignment.

They were wrapped in sinew and muscle and flesh. The word of God transformed a valley of dry bones into a mighty, living army.

Dead bones brought to life. That's a picture of how God saves people. We have no life in ourselves. No human desire or effort can impart life. How can we live? Only by the bidding of God. Only by the power of the mighty Word of God breathing life into dead people.

Jonah 2:9 says, "Salvation belongs to the LORD!" It's true. Salvation is the supernatural work of God in the human soul. It is owned by God. Only he can give it. It depends solely on the power of God and the grace of God.

This perspective of salvation is incredibly humbling. If salvation isn't ultimately because of my spiritual insight, my discovery, my inner goodness, my effort, or my religious work, then I cannot save myself. It doesn't matter what family or church I've been born into. It doesn't matter how moral or religious or respected I am. In this sense the message of the gospel is very bad news for human ingenuity and pride.

But at the same time, it's very good news for people whom Jesus described as "the poor in spirit" (Matthew 5:3)—people who know they can't save themselves, people who realize their spiritual poverty and helplessness. For these people, the gospel imparts hope. Because if God is truly the central figure and actor in salvation—if his choosing, his searching, his calling, his grace, his regenerating power giving new life is what makes salvation possible—then *no one* is beyond hope.

And this is incredibly good news. It means God can save anyone.

Even me. Even you. Even my dad.

———

Things got a little better for Dad after elementary school. The family moved from Kettering to Miamisburg. More significantly, he got a guitar.

He had found some success writing poetry when he was younger. One of his poems had even been published in the newspaper. That got the girls' attention. Now he tried his hand at putting his poems to music. He learned a few chords and had a decent voice. He had finally found his niche. He had always been a loner. But now he was a loner with a guitar. It wasn't a bad mystique to possess.

The counterculture movement of the 1960s was in full swing. The Beatles had invaded America. Jefferson Airplane and Big Brother and the Holding Company with Janis Joplin were on the radio. Thousands had gathered in Haight-Ashbury for the Summer of Love. Dad started hanging out at the coffeehouse on Bigger Road. He started smoking pot. He grew his hair long. He found an identity among the freaks, the hippies. The song on the radio said, "If you're going to San Francisco, be sure to wear some flowers in your hair."[2] Dad dreamed of escaping the suffocating backwoods town of Miamisburg and heading west.

If he didn't already have enough reasons to leave Miamisburg, he got another one when he became a target of the Orchard Hill boys. This hillbilly gang was known for binge drinking, stealing, reselling car parts, and maliciously beating anyone who crossed them. Dad made the mistake of singing a song to a girl one of the Orchard Hill boys liked. After that whenever they saw him, they would jump him. One day at the county fair, a thug named Marvin Boleyn belted him from behind with a tire iron.

That was the last straw. Under the guise of taking his sister to a movie, he headed to downtown Dayton. He ditched his sister at the theater and, guitar in hand, headed to the bus station. He found a used ticket on the ground, put his thumb over the hole punched in it, and rode away. He was sixteen years old.

The bus took him to Cincinnati. From there he hitchhiked to Chicago, then St. Louis, where he made two dollars an hour loading crates for a shipping company. He wrote his parents from the road, trying to assuage his mom's fears. He was eating well. He was happy. He said that now that he didn't have anyone to tell him what to do, he felt like doing all they'd always told him to. (That was a lie.) He told his mom that he had Sundays off and would go to church. (That was a lie too.) He told his sister, Leslie, that he was sorry for leaving her stranded at the movie theater. (That was sincere.)

After he worked a few weeks in St. Louis, a trucker took him as far as Colorado Springs. That's when he saw his first mountain, Pikes Peak. A cop picked him up hitchhiking and asked, "Where you headed, son?"

"Home," Dad said.

"Where ya live?"

"Just over those mountains."

"There ain't nothin' on the other side of those mountains," the officer replied.

He was caught. They shipped him back to Ohio.

Dad ran away again a few months later. He asked to borrow the car, but his dad wouldn't let him. He was indignant. "I don't need a car to get where I want to go," he said to himself. Two days later he called his parents from Clearwater Beach, Florida.

In Clearwater he found a vibrant hippie scene down on the pier. He survived by panhandling and playing his guitar for spare change. He also stole purses. After emptying out their contents, he would bury them in the sand.

His life of petty crime in Florida was cut short when he was caught stealing at a convenience store. Dad wasn't the smartest thief. He walked into the store with money in his pocket but decided to steal a powdered sugar doughnut. The evidence of his crime wasn't hard for the store's owner to spot. The police arrived, and he was put in jail for three days.

His short stint in jail shook him up. He was surrounded by drunks and winos who snored at night and cussed and scuffled during the day. He was absolutely miserable and terrified.

A Baptist preacher visited the jail and asked where Dad was from and if his parents knew where he was. He shared the gospel with Dad, and although Dad listened, he didn't find it particularly compelling. They were the same words he had heard hundreds of times growing up. But then the preacher did something that did grab his attention. He paid Dad's fine for shoplifting, got him out of jail, and bought him a one-way plane ticket back to Dayton, Ohio.

That act of kindness had a profound effect on Dad. It made him want to be good. He was so filled with gratitude that he decided he was going to change. He was going to be a Christian—and not just any Christian. He was going to be a great Christian.

The only problem with his plan was that he could no more make himself a Christian than dry bones can will themselves to live.

Jesus said that in order to be saved, in order to be part of his kingdom, a person has to be "born again" (John 3:3).

Jesus liked to speak in ways that piqued people's curiosity, even shocked them. Two thousand years after Jesus's earthly ministry, we've worn the edges off most of his shocking statements and smoothed them like stones in a rock polisher. So now when we hear the phrase *born again,* we picture a certain type of person, or we think of a voting bloc. People who followed the news in the late 1970s might think of Jimmy Carter, a former peanut farmer from Georgia who became president and was famous for stating that he was a born-again Christian.

But when Jesus first said "born again," no one pictured Jimmy Carter or any other stereotype of a Christian. Instead they pictured the sticky mess of human birth, and then they imagined having to go through that process again.

That's how the Pharisee Nicodemus reacted when he heard Jesus talk about being born again. He asked, "How can a man be born when he is old? Can he enter a second time into his mother's womb and be born?" (John 3:4). Jesus explained that the spiritual life required to live in his kingdom is a *brand-new* life. It requires a change so radical, so transformational, that it could be described as new birth. The change is as powerful and fresh as when a child enters the world.

The new birth Jesus described is called *regeneration*. John Frame writes that regeneration is "a sovereign act of God, beginning a new spiritual life in us."[3] In regeneration God gives a person a new nature, a new heart, and new spiritual life.

Apart from regeneration, we are all dead spiritually (Ephesians 2:1–2). Not sick. Not weak. Not disabled. We are dead. Dead like dry bones. This means we are unable to know or respond to God. We don't just need a little shove, a kick-start, or resuscitation; we need spiritual resurrection and regeneration.

Paul speaks of regeneration in terms of a Christian being a "new creation" (2 Corinthians 5:17). This new life is what God foretold to the prophet Ezekiel hundreds of years before Jesus came. God said, "And I will give them one heart, and a new spirit I will put within them. I will remove the heart of stone from their flesh and give them a heart of flesh" (Ezekiel 11:19).

New birth. New creation. Heart transplant. You can't help but see the emphasis on salvation being the work of God. In fact, the point of Jesus's phrase *born again* is not only new life but new life brought about by the work of God's Spirit. In John 3:6–8 Jesus said, "That which is born of the flesh is flesh, and that which is born of the Spirit is spirit. Do not marvel that I said to you, 'You must be born again.' The wind blows where it wishes, and you hear its sound, but you do not know where it comes from or where it goes. So it is with everyone who is born of the Spirit."

Only the Holy Spirit imparts life. This isn't under our control. Like the wind, the Spirit blows where it wishes. We see its effect, we hear its sound, but we don't know where it comes from, and we can't control its direction. So the new birth, God's act of regenerating power, is solely dependent on God's will. We can't will ourselves to be born again any more than we could have willed ourselves to be born the first time. None of us had any control over the timing of our physical conception and birth. In the same way, our spiritual birth is utterly and completely a work of God's Holy Spirit. Before God does this work in us, we don't possess the inner desire to believe in him, seek him, repent of sin, or genuinely pray for salvation.

The problem with Dad's decision to make himself a "good Christian" at age sixteen was that he hadn't experienced the miracle of regeneration. He hadn't been born again. His pseudoconversion after his jail stint was an attempt at self-reform. It was an effort to be, by his own willpower, a better, more moral person.

It wasn't by the power of God; it wasn't really even about God. Dad didn't acknowledge his sin and guilt before God. He didn't repent. He didn't place his trust in Jesus, who died to absorb God's wrath for his sin. Instead, Dad simply decided to stop being bad and start being good. He was going to "do" religion like no ever had. He was going to try harder than anyone before him.

When he got home from Florida, he went back to school and started going to church. He cut his hair. He stopped smoking cigarettes and doing drugs. He stopped messing around with girls. He even started a Christian club at his school called Teens for Christ. His mom and all the ladies from church were thrilled.

It worked pretty well…for a while. Then, like one of the seeds in Jesus's parable of the soils, Dad's growth spurt was interrupted and proven to be superficial.

His Christian club hosted a talent show at school. They put it on so a Christian band in the area could play and share the gospel. Because it was a school-sponsored event, other, non-Christian bands were also invited to perform. When a few of the secular bands had some fun during the concert and gently mocked the Christian-themed event, the members of the Christian band were offended and refused to participate.

Dad was so mad, so outraged at being let down by these Christians that he decided he wanted nothing more to do with Christianity. (The timing of his outrage may have had something to do with a girl from school he'd been eyeing.) And just as he had turned his self-generated Christianity on, he turned it off.

———

After rejecting Christianity, Dad went back to his old ways. He hit the road again and hitchhiked to Florida. Most of his friends were gone, so he headed to California. On his way he spent a month in Austin, Texas, where he joined up with the antiauthoritarian Youth International Party, or Yippies, as they were called. He became instantly popular with the Yippies because he wrote and sang protest songs. He joined them when they invaded the LBJ Library, an act which got them on national television. But the weather in Austin was too hot, so he moved on.

He arrived in San Diego, then headed up the coast till he landed in Laguna Beach. The sleepy little beach town had its requisite surfers but was also known as an arts community that hosted two major arts festivals. It was populated by dancers, painters, jewelry craftsmen, singers, and poets. Dad felt like he had finally found a home with his own tribe. He got a three-dollar-a-night room at the Laguna Hotel and started working.

By this time he had an established routine. He would go to a nice restaurant and ask if he could serve as a troubadour, walking among the tables singing songs. All he wanted was a meal at the end of the night and whatever tips he made from singing. He wrote songs for children, songs for elderly couples, songs for couples. If he sang the right song, he could sometimes get a twenty-dollar tip. The money he made enabled him to buy a used Volvo P1800 and rent a room in a nice house with a friend. They even had a pool. He and a friend founded the Laguna Beach Free Poets Society, a little group that would gather at a local coffeehouse and read their poetry. He'd never been happier or experienced more success.

Then came his fateful conversation on the beach. Dad was sitting on one of his favorite rocks, working on a new song, when the two Christian hippies approached him.

Dad remembers that the way the two hippies talked about Jesus was unlike anything he had ever heard before. I don't know that what they said that day on the beach was a clearer or more powerful presentation of the gospel than he'd heard in Sunday school or from the Baptist preacher in the Florida jail cell. Maybe it was. But ultimately the eloquence or persuasiveness of the messenger doesn't save a person. It's the work of God's Spirit in a person's heart. That day on the beach, God's Spirit opened Dad's heart to listen. Through the message of the gospel, God called him. It's this "heavenly calling," as Hebrews 3:1 refers to it, that distinguishes all genuine Christians. No matter how a person hears or who tells him the message of Jesus crucified for sins and risen from the dead, behind it all is God, summoning a sinner to himself. Calling him, calling her "into the fellowship of his Son, Jesus Christ our Lord" (1 Corinthians 1:9).

Dad doesn't think he was saved that day on the beach, but as he puts it, "the hook was set." Like a fish on a line, he sensed God drawing him from that moment forward.

A few days after he heard the gospel on the beach, there was a drug bust at the home where he was living. He was gone when police raided the house and arrested several of his roommates. Even though the cops ransacked the house, they didn't find the bag of marijuana hidden underneath a trash bin in his room. But he figured they might come back and arrest him for his connection to his roommates. So he packed up his car that day and drove out of town.

The timing of the raid so soon after hearing the gospel wasn't lost on Dad. He was sure it was more than coincidence. He felt God chasing him. The question that kept ringing in his mind was, *What if it's true? What if Jesus is the Son of God?*

The songs he wrote in those days were different. They were songs filled with questions and yearning for meaning in life. One was called "There Are No Words to Say."

> What can I say to a mountain
> Can I tell it of some time it has not known
> What can I say to a mighty redwood tree
> Lest I speak to it how little I have grown
> I have so many stories
> Stories of my time as living clay
> I have so many stories, but I have no words to say

He made his way to Colorado and found a restaurant to work at in Vail, but nothing seemed to go right. In a drunken fog, his landlord threw a brick through the window of his car. Only after he reported the incident to the police did he learn that his landlord was a major contractor who had built half of the city. The next day he lost his job at the restaurant.

He kept running, traveling east. In Indianapolis he started singing and playing rhythm guitar in a band. The group needed a lead singer, and they liked the songs he wrote. They got a good gig that paid each band member $125 a night. But then Dad got a bad cold and started to lose his voice after the first set. Suddenly his band mates stopped being so friendly. They pushed him to sing. They were losing money and were unsympathetic to his plight.

That was Dad's breaking point. He and the other members of the band lived together in an old farmhouse. One night Dad went into the bathroom, the only room where you could be alone, locked the door, and did something he hadn't done in a long time. He prayed.

"God," he said, "if you're really there, I want to know. I don't want to psych myself up believing in something that's not true. But if you really are there, then you are the most important thing and the reason I'm here. I don't know if you're allowed to do this, but will you please show me?"

Dad says he was born again right there in the bathroom. "I know God doesn't always do this," he told me recently. "But when I prayed that night, it sounded like a thousand voices all started cheering, 'Surprise! Welcome home!' It was just in my head, but it was deafening. It was like I had walked into a room and there was a surprise party for me."

He began to weep. The welcome and deep sense of acceptance he felt were the extreme opposite of all the rejection he had experienced in his life. In that moment he knew the love of God for him. He believed that Jesus was the Son of God who had died for his sins. As he sat on a bathroom floor in

Indiana, God changed his heart. And in response he repented of his sin and gave his whole life to Jesus.

———

The Bible teaches that we must respond to the gospel in repentance and faith (Acts 3:19). Most of us understand the faith part. We trust that what Jesus did was for us, and we entrust our lives to him. But we often overlook the repentance part. To repent means to turn away from something, to renounce it. Genuine repentance involves a sorrow over sin as an offense against God. But this sorrow is not hopeless. It is a sorrow that turns and believes that Jesus can forgive and, by his death, cleanse us from all our guilt.

When God saved my dad that night in Indiana, Dad's view of his sin was so different from what it had been before. A few years earlier when he tried making himself a Christian, he simply wanted to be good. But now there was a real sorrow, even hatred for his rebellion. And there was a new-found humility.

For a long time he hadn't wanted to become a Christian in large part because he didn't want his mom to win. She could seem so smug in her confidence that God would one day save him. He just knew that if he ever became a Christian, she'd say, "I always knew you would." In the past the thought of her gloating drove him crazy. But now that didn't matter anymore. God had saved him. He didn't care if that made his mom right. He had been wrong. He wanted to live for Jesus. His repentance was real.

Repentance and faith are inseparable—two sides of the same coin. When people are genuinely converted, they don't simply turn away from sin and bad behavior; they turn toward the person of Jesus Christ and his lordship. They believe that his death atoned for sins. They believe that he alone can save. They turn to him as King, and in so doing they turn their back on a life of sin and self-rule.

It's easy to mistakenly think that because we're commanded to have faith, our faith saves us. But this isn't the case. Faith is not the grounds for our salvation. Salvation is always and only by grace alone (Ephesians 2:8–10). Our faith doesn't merit anything; it is simply the instrument by which God's grace flows to us. "Faith," writes Jerry Bridges, "is merely the hand that receives the gift of God, and God through His Spirit even opens our hand to receive the gift."[4]

Jesus has earned everything for us. It is his work, his obedience, his death in our place that saves us. We are called to trust him, to rest in his work, and through that trusting to receive all he has accomplished.

My father wasn't saved because he cleaned himself up morally and presented himself to God. He wasn't saved because he did acts of kindness as penance for his wrongdoing.

No, like every other sinner who is saved from destruction, my dad was saved by grace through faith. He was saved by Jesus Christ, whom he clung to. That is how God saves people. That is what it means to be a Christian, to know salvation. God saves people by joining them or uniting them with Christ. All the spiritual blessings of salvation—redemption from sin, new life, forgiveness of guilt—come through Christ and in Christ and because of Christ (Ephesians 1:3–14).

Jesus has done all the work. Salvation comes by getting in on what he's done. This is how Jesus's accomplishment of redemption gets applied to us. Through faith and the work of the Holy Spirit, we are united with Christ and receive all the saving benefits of Jesus's life, death, and resurrection.

When my dad trusted in Jesus, God viewed him as though all that Jesus had earned and accomplished belonged to my dad. God declared him righteous, because Jesus is righteous. And God adopted him as a son, because Jesus is his Son. These important aspects of God's saving work are called *justification* and *adoption*.

In justification, God gives sinners a new legal status. Because of our sin, we are guilty before God. In the courtroom of his justice, we rightly deserve punishment. We've violated his truth by lying. We've dishonored his plan for our sexuality by immorality, adultery, and homosexuality. We've ignored his commands to honor our parents. We've rejected his place as the only God by worshiping false gods. We've robbed, cheated, and abused others. Worst of all we've lived as though we were ultimate—we've substituted ourselves for him. All these acts of sin, all these violations of his law, make us guilty.

For God simply to overlook these real sins would make him unjust. Justice must be served. Someone has to pay; someone has to receive the punishment for sin.

And this is why Christ had to die. The only way we can be righteous is for God to give us a righteousness we don't possess in and of ourselves. The only way for our sins to be paid for (apart from our spending an eternity in hell) is for God himself, in Christ, to receive the punishment.

This has been called the blessed exchange. All who trust in Jesus are given Jesus's righteousness. And Jesus takes on the guilt of their sin. We are "justified by his grace as a gift, through the redemption that is in Christ Jesus, whom God put forward as a propitiation by his blood, to be received by faith" (Romans 3:24–25).

The Cross shows God to be just, in that he punishes all sin. And the Cross shows God to be the gracious "justifier" of all who have faith in Jesus (Romans 3:26).

When my father trusted in Jesus, God declared him justified. He was no longer Gregg Eugene Harris, the lying, immoral, selfish thief. He became Gregg Eugene Harris, who is united by faith to Jesus Christ—the holy One, the perfect keeper of the law, the righteous One.

———

While justification borrows the language of the courtroom to help us understand God's work of salvation, *adoption* uses the language of family to help us see that behind all of God's saving work is a deeply relational and personal motive of love. God tells us that when we trust in Jesus, God adopts us as his sons and daughters (Ephesians 1:5). More than anything else this should convince us of God's love. "See what kind of love the Father has given to us, that we should be called children of God; and so we are" (1 John 3:1).

Justification gives us a new legal status. Adoption gives us a new family and a new father. This is another expression of our union with Christ. Because Jesus is the only begotten Son of God, as we trust in him, we receive his status as a child of God. John 1:12 says that to all who receive Jesus, to all who believe in his name, "he gave the right to become children of God."

In Christ, we are not forgiven servants. We are given all the rights and privileges of natural-born children. We are adopted and welcomed into the warmth of relationship with God as our loving Father. Romans 8:15–16 describes the Holy Spirit as "the Spirit of adoption" who enables us to cry to God as our Abba—an intimate Hebrew term akin to *dad*. It combines intimacy and respect. The Holy Spirit bears witness with our spirit "that we are children of God."

"What is a Christian?" asks J. I. Packer. "The question can be answered in many ways, but the richest answer I know is that a Christian is one who has God as Father."[5] And Sinclair Ferguson writes, "You cannot open the pages of the New Testament without realizing that one of the things that makes it so 'new', in every way, is that here men and women call God 'Father'. This conviction, that we can speak to the Maker of the universe in such intimate terms, lies at the heart of the Christian faith."[6]

———

The first question Dad asked God after he was saved was, "What do you want me to do?" The unmistakable impression he sensed was, "Go home." And so Dad obeyed his new Lord.

If ever there was sure evidence that Gregg Harris was a new creation, it's that he was happy to be heading back to Miamisburg, Ohio. He began attending First Baptist Church. There was a new pastor and a new wave of young people whom God had saved. One of them was a beautiful Japanese American girl named Sono Sato. She had just been saved that summer.

Dad and Mom's first date was to go witnessing in a park together. My dad was truly transformed. He had a newfound love for the Bible. He had never been good at study, but now, even though he was still a slow reader, he couldn't get enough of Scripture. And he loved to tell others about Jesus. He even had a near run-in with the police when he and a friend stood in a crowded mall and began to preach the gospel. They were a little too effective in gathering a crowd, and the police arrived to usher the zealots away.

Mom says she fell in love with Dad because his faith in God was the most important thing in his life. Less than a year after they were married, I was born. My dad was twenty-one; my mom was twenty. They'd been saved only a short time, but they brought me into a Christian home.

———

I've often wished I could go back in time and listen in on that conversation on Laguna Beach when the two Christian hippies talked to my dad about Jesus. What I wouldn't give to hear Dad's best arguments as an amateur atheist and then to hear their presentation of the gospel. It's impossible to measure how much that moment has shaped my life.

Mostly, I'd just like to find the two men and thank them. I'd thank them for being bold that day and for telling my dad the truth even when he didn't want to hear it. The Bible says that without the proclamation of the gospel, without everyday Christians bearing witness to Jesus, people can't hear the good news; they can't believe in and can't call upon God (Romans 10:14).

I'd tell them how much God has used their faithfulness to share the gospel. I'd tell them about all the great things God has done through Dad in the years since. I'd tell them how over the years Dad has literally taught hundreds of thousands of parents about the importance of teaching their children to know and love God. I'd tell them about all the people who have told me that God used my dad to give them a vision for building a godly Christian home.

I'd tell them that everything I've been able to do as a pastor and writer is directly tied to my dad and the godly heritage he passed on to me and my six siblings. He raised us to seek and trust Jesus.

I guess that conversation will have to wait for heaven. I look forward to it.

Recently my dad, mom, and younger siblings came to Maryland. Our church hosted a conference featuring my younger brothers Alex and Brett, both of whom are skilled speakers and writers. They were challenging teens to "do hard things" for the glory of God. My brother Joel was leading the crowd in worship.

The building was packed with more than thirty-five hundred teenagers and their parents. People sat in the aisles and on the floors. I sat on the front row with Shannon and our kids. The whole time I felt as if I were about to explode with joy and gratefulness. I was so proud of my brothers. I was so thankful for God's kindness toward our family. He was letting us encourage other Christians and share truth from his Word.

And then my dad got up and spoke. He shared a simple but profound message about what it means to be saved, to truly be a Christian. He talked about how people can be saved only by the power of God giving them a new heart and a new nature. He preached like I've never heard him preach before.

And as I sat there, I couldn't help thinking how mighty God's salvation really is. I had seen its power at work in this man, my father. Over the years, like any child, I saw his weaknesses and his flaws. To be honest, we haven't always had the best relationship. Since I was the oldest child, Dad was still finding his way in the maze of parenting. By his own admission he made many mistakes. Of course, I added my sin to the relationship. I didn't honor and appreciate him the way I should have.

We've talked about those regrets, and we've forgiven each other. But more important, we both know the forgiveness of God. My dad and I are very different in many ways, and we disagree about a number of issues, but we have one thing—the most important thing—in common. We've both been saved by grace alone.

As I listened to my father preach the wonderful gospel of salvation by grace, I rejoiced in the truth that both his sins and mine had been dealt with on the Cross. The mighty work of Jesus that brought my dad to life and made him God's son is the same power that saved me.

And God's work isn't done in either of us.

My dad's story encourages me. It reminds me of God's faithfulness and goodness. Not just for my dad, but for me and every other person who looks to Jesus for salvation.

I've told you my dad's story. But his is just one story among countless millions.

Pick a believer and trace his or her story. Retell your own. And consider how much God loves us.

He chose us.

He called us.

He regenerated our hearts.

He justified us.

He adopted us.

He's sanctifying us day by day.

And one day, when Jesus returns, we'll receive glorified bodies. We will rise with him, and our lowly, feeble bodies will be transformed. And his mighty salvation will be complete.

On that day a man named Gregg Eugene Harris will rise to meet his Savior. A man born with a broken, flawed body—a man born dead in sin—will rise with a perfect, pain-free, sinless, glorified body.

He will rise as a child of God to live with his Father in heaven for eternity.

8

CHANGED, CHANGING,
TO BE CHANGED

"Sanctification is work. But it's good work—
the privilege of the redeemed."

A FRIEND E-MAILED ME, "You're on the latest episode of *This American Life.*"

My heart leaped. I couldn't believe it.

This American Life is a weekly radio show produced by Chicago Public Radio. I really like this show. Okay, it's more than that. I'm a slightly obsessed fan. One of my fantasies is to write something good enough to be featured on the show. But I seriously doubt that will ever happen. Not after this.

The show has a simple format: each week the producers choose a theme and then tell a variety of stories on that theme. The stories are real-life slices of life—sometimes humorous, sometimes tragic, but always intriguing. The writing is topnotch. The storytelling and production are brilliant. The host, a guy named Ira Glass, has a kind of geek chic aura. I don't know how to explain it. He's a nerd but in a really cool way. He wears big chunky glasses (I know this because he has a television show too). His voice is nasal, even whiny, but somehow he comes off sounding good. His delivery is so natural,

145

his cadence so nonchalant that when I'm driving around listening to him, I feel like he dropped out of the sky into the passenger seat and is chatting with me. He is low-key in the most brilliantly hip way imaginable.

As I said, I'm a fan. So when I heard I was featured on the show, I was ecstatic.

I went online to the show's Web site and began to play the newest episode. The theme was the Ten Commandments.

I knew immediately which of the commandments I was going to be a part of: thou shall not commit adultery. Two years earlier I had written a Christian book about lust and sexual temptation. That's when it hit me that being featured might not be a good thing. A feeling of dread spread through my body as I considered what part of my book would be quoted. I didn't bother listening to the beginning of the show but skipped ahead to the part on adultery.

The segment featured a guy named Dave telling his story. Dave was raised as an evangelical Christian in Tucson, Arizona. Evangelical Christians, Dave explained, believe that looking at a woman lustfully is as bad as committing adultery with her in your heart. He spoke of evangelicals as though he were narrating a *National Geographic* special and describing an exotic tribe of naked cannibals.

Dave said that, growing up, he desperately tried to please God. Since he didn't want to commit adultery, he decided as a young, hormone-infused teenager that he would try to never think a lustful thought. It didn't go so well. In fact, it nearly drove him crazy.

Dave became more and more preoccupied with sex. He began to spend hours wandering his college campus and even the local grocery store, checking out women and hoping to catch a glimpse of one leaning over so he could look down her shirt. As he put it, he was like a very timid stalker with incredibly low standards. His grades began to suffer. He finally asked his pastor for help. His pastor, very unhelpfully, sent him to a meeting of Sex Addicts Anonymous. He was twenty-two and a virgin, and none of the people there could relate to him.

My cameo in the story came when Dave began to talk about the abundance of Christian books on the topic of sex. "The first thing these books always tell you," Dave said, "is that sex is a beautiful gift from God. But even though it's a gift, they don't want you to touch it or even think about it because you're gonna ruin it with your filthy paws."[1]

I smiled at his description, knowing it was partly true. But I was having trouble enjoying Dave's story because I was bracing myself for my appearance in the story. I just knew he was going to quote something about lust from my book—a book that Dave no doubt considered silly, repressive, and the cause for many a grocery-store-wandering sex addict. Actually, it was worse than that. Dave didn't quote me. He played a clip of *me* reading from my book.

As I listened to my voice, I was sure that Dave, filled with malice, had picked the worst possible sentences to feature. I talked about controlling your eyes and looking away from women on the street. Then he cut to me talking about the temptation that clothing catalogs featuring scantily clad women can present. I said guys should get their wives or mothers to help by throwing these catalogs away when they arrive.

My tone was indignant, and without any context my words sounded so uptight and backward—like some old church lady railing against the dangers of liquor and rock 'n' roll music. And my voice sounded terrible. I remembered that I'd had a slight cold the day I recorded the book. My voice was nasal. But not nasal in a cool, Ira Glass sort of way. Just nasal.

I was on *This American Life*. My dream had come true. And it was a nightmare.

After I got over the trauma of sounding hopelessly uncool on my favorite radio show, I was able to see the humor in it all and laugh at myself. It was good for me. God knows I take myself too seriously.

Later I went back and listened to the show again. Instead of worrying about how I sounded, I just listened to Dave and his story. I thought about the questions he raised and the real struggle he faced. My heart went out to the guy. I could relate to his turmoil. He said he wanted to please God. But sadly, he didn't seem to understand the concept of grace and forgiveness. Instead he was eaten up by guilt because he couldn't stop doing "M," as he called it. He felt like a monster walking around campus, ogling the girls. He felt powerless to change. And none of the tips and tricks for being good— trying to control his thoughts, only looking at girls' faces, having a quiet time every morning—seemed to work for him. So he stopped trying. He concluded that a person could try too hard to obey God, "that you could lead yourself astray by following the Bible's rules." He eventually found a Christian counselor who told him to give himself permission to do the big M to his heart's content. So Dave went home that day with a copy of *Playboy* magazine. He said his life was forever changed. He was free. "It felt like a miracle," Dave said. "It was so fast, so life changing that it was like converting all over again."

Dave's story saddened me. I don't know what he believes about God today or whether he would still consider himself a Christian. I doubt his *Playboy*-sponsored conversion has led to lasting fulfillment; my own experience of indulging in lust is that it only leaves me dissatisfied and craving something more. I pray that Dave will one day escape the slavery of that so-called freedom.

Can you relate to Dave's story? We each have parts of our lives where obeying God seems really difficult. Have you ever wondered why you still want to sin? Or maybe you've started to think that the Bible's whole promise of change is exaggerated. Is it a bunch of hype? Does God really change people?

He absolutely does. God's Word promises it. And the life of every true believer proves it. If you're a Christian, your life proves it. Maybe you haven't noticed how God has changed you, because you're preoccupied with your weaknesses and areas of failure. Don't overlook what God has done in you. He wants to increase your faith as you see his work in you.

We live in a world that endlessly longs for personal, physical, relational, and political change. People search for change everywhere. But ultimately, only the gospel of Jesus Christ offers real hope for radical, lasting change because only through faith in Jesus can a person's *nature* be changed. Second Corinthians 5:17 says, "Therefore, if anyone is in Christ, he is a new creation. The old has passed away; behold, the new has come." All other sorts of manmade change are outward and superficial. Only God can give a man or woman a new, spiritually alive heart (Ezekiel 36:26). Only God can cause a person to be born again (John 3:3–8).

But if we're new, why do we so often act old? If we're changed by faith in Christ, why do so many parts of our lives still need renovation? Why do we still face temptation? Why do we still sin?

The questions surrounding how Christians deal with sin, obey God, and become more holy all relate to something that Scripture calls *sanctification*. That is the ongoing process of change that begins the moment a person is saved and continues until that person's last breath. Sanctification is the journey of becoming holy, becoming like God. Wayne Grudem defines sanctification as "a progressive work of God and man that make us more and more free from sin and like Christ in our actual lives."[2]

I like his phrase "actual lives." If you think about it, while there is a radical inward and spiritual change the instant a man or woman is saved, nothing in their "actual lives" has been altered. She might still be living with her boyfriend. He might still have a salty vocabulary. They will definitely still have old habits of thinking and speaking that they developed over the years. The process of sanctification doesn't end with the initial dramatic breaks we make with sin when we first believe—it continues for the rest of our lives. The process of becoming more like Jesus isn't a "one and done" deal. It is progressive. And it involves our effort. God doesn't leave us alone in this work; he empowers us and enables us by his Spirit. But it's still work.

While I believe all Christian doctrine is practical in that all of it affects the way we think and live, I think it's safe to say that no doctrine is more practical than sanctification. This is where we live and breathe. No matter how young or old we are, no matter how long we've been disciples of Jesus, if we're still alive, then we're still being sanctified.

Understanding sanctification is important because of its daily relevance. But it's also important because if we get this wrong, we can end up sidetracked by multiple problems—from laziness and apathy to self-sufficiency and legalism. And if our expectations aren't informed by Scripture, we can end up unnecessarily discouraged, even tempted to give up on our faith altogether. How many people have turned their backs on Christianity—grabbed a *Playboy* and headed off the narrow road—because they didn't understand the doctrine of sanctification? Too many.

———

I used to think that sanctification was a matter of personal style. Like some sort of spiritual hobby that certain Christians were really into. Some Christians are into holiness, while others might make evangelism or Scripture memory or potlucks their thing.

But that's not how the Bible talks about sanctification. God's Word teaches that sanctification isn't optional for believers. Hebrews 12:14 says, "Strive for...holiness without which no one will see the Lord." That verse always sobers me. It says that if there isn't some degree of holiness in our lives, there's a real question of whether we've truly experienced God's saving work. If we don't love what Jesus loves, if we don't want to be like him, then maybe we've never really met him.

This isn't to say that our good works earn our salvation—we are saved only by grace (Ephesians 2:8). But the way we live proves the reality of our salvation. If a person has truly been saved, truly been justified by grace, it shows in a new lifestyle. Every genuine Christian is being sanctified. The process might be slow, it might move ahead in fits and starts, but if we've been justified, we will also begin to be sanctified.

God's saving work through Jesus's life, death, and resurrection has practical, real-world implications for our lives. It is truth that can't be kept on a page or in a house of worship. It follows us home. To our school. To our work. To our bedrooms. It grabs hold of every detail of our lives. Our thoughts. Our sexuality. Our money. Our leisure. Our relationships. Our desires. Our dreams.

A big question a lot of us have is, Why is this process of changing so stinking hard? Why is it so painful? Why do Christians still struggle with sin?

Encountering sin as a believer can be one of the most confusing and potentially disillusioning aspects of the Christian experience. You become a Christian and are reveling in the fact that you've been reborn, transformed, forgiven, justified, and filled with God's Spirit. But then one day you wake up and realize you're still tempted to_____ (fill in the blank). Get angry. Get drunk. Look at pictures of naked people. Lie. Gossip. Sleep with your boyfriend. Swear like a sailor. Or maybe you seem morally upright on the outside, but inside you know you lack any real passion for prayer or God's Word. Or you lack compassion and genuine care for others. Your heart is filled with pride. The list of potential "old you" behaviors seems endless.

How could you still want any of that? You turned your back on the old you. In fact, you hate the old you and your empty former way of life. So why are you still enticed by what you left behind?

This paradox is why it's important to know what Scripture teaches about what does and doesn't change in people's relationship to sin after they're saved. The Bible teaches, and our experience confirms, that while Jesus's death freed us from the reign and absolute rule of sin in our lives (Romans 6:11, 14), we haven't yet been completely freed from the presence and influence of sin. James 3:2 states, "For we all stumble in many ways." And 1 John 1:8 says, "If we say we have no sin, we deceive ourselves, and the truth is not in us."

The analogy is flawed, but we're like prisoners of war who have been freed from captivity but are still behind enemy lines. In a real sense we have been rescued—we're no longer locked up and at the mercy of the enemy. But at the same time, the war isn't over. We're waiting for our captain to return and completely vanquish the enemy. The fallen world, the devil, and our own wandering hearts put us at risk. Like never before, we have to be on our guard.

In a similar sense we live between two moments in salvation history—

between the arrival of salvation through Jesus's first coming and the ultimate fulfillment of our salvation when Jesus returns and establishes his eternal kingdom. Theologians call this in-between reality the "already" and the "not yet" aspects of our salvation.

Jesus has *already* brought salvation by his substitutionary death on the cross and his resurrection. Jesus has *already* made us new creatures with new desires and the power to obey (2 Corinthians 5:17). He has *already* freed us from slavery to sin (Romans 6:6).

But we've *not yet* arrived. He has *not yet* fully vanquished sin and Satan. Jesus has *not yet* freed us from the presence and consequences of sin. He has *not yet* banished death, wiped away every tear, punished all injustice, and established everlasting peace (Revelation 21:1–7).

The *already* and *not yet* reality of our salvation helps us keep things in perspective. We shouldn't be surprised that even though we've been changed, we still have to struggle with weaknesses and imperfections. We still have to deal with the ugliness of life in a fallen world where people let us down and disappoint us and where sickness and death break our hearts. So we shouldn't despair over ongoing struggles with sin. This is part of the deal. Jesus has already brought salvation. But he's not yet taken us home.

It helps me to think about this process in three parts. First, God has *changed* us. When we believed, we were given new life, new desires, and a new identity as God's children (Ephesians 2:4–5; John 1:12). Second, right now as we live the Christian life, we're still *changing*. As we cooperate with God's Spirit, turn away from sin, and learn to obey God's Word, we're being conformed to God's image and becoming holy (Colossians 3:8–10). But we don't expect sinless perfection in this life. There's a third and final installment to God's work of change in us: Christians await Jesus's return *to be changed* fully and forever. Then we will be made like Christ with glorified bodies free from sin and all its corrupting effect. "For the trumpet will sound, and the dead will be raised imperishable, and we shall be changed" (1 Corinthians 15:52).

We've been changed. But we're still changing. And yet we're also waiting to be changed.

———

Until the final day, until we're changed and freed forever from our struggle against sin, we have to deal with the ongoing presence and influence of sin—what theologians call *indwelling* or *remaining sin*. *Indwelling sin* refers to the fact that even as Christians we can still be enticed and tempted by our old desires, what the Bible often refers to as "the flesh." Galatians 5:17 says, "For the desires of the flesh are against the Spirit, and the desires of the Spirit are against the flesh, for these are opposed to each other, to keep you from doing the things you want to do."

Romans 13:14 says, "But put on the Lord Jesus Christ, and make no provision for the flesh, to gratify its desires." Once when I was working on a sermon on Romans 13:14, I started doodling on my notepad (a habit that helps me think but that sometimes annoys other people when I'm supposed to be paying attention in a meeting). Anyway, I drew some cartoons to try to illustrate the Christian's relationship to the flesh. My kids liked the pictures, so the following is my first-grade-friendly explanation of "the flesh." (Feel free to color.)

———

1. **This is you.** Or us. We're humans made in God's image (Genesis 1:26–27). Ladies, sorry you have to identify with a little guy. And I'm not sure why he doesn't have on a shirt. That's just how I drew him.

2. **This is the flesh.** He's kind of Jabba the Hutt meets WWE wrestler. The flesh represents the sinful, corrupted desires of our hearts. It's not a reference to our bodies—our bodies are created by God and are good. And though my cartoon can't do this justice, the flesh isn't something outside us or just a part of us. It's who we are apart from Christ. The flesh represents our sinful cravings to live for ourselves and disobey God's laws and commands (Romans 7:18).

3. **Before Jesus saves us**, we all relate to the flesh this way. The Bible says we are slaves to our sinful desires (John 8:34; 2 Peter 2:19). Our flesh is boss. It controls us (Proverbs 5:22). Even the good things we do are stained by sin and selfishness.

4. **This is what happens when we trust in Jesus**. Because Jesus
   died on the cross and conquered sin and rose again, we are
   freed from the power or dominion of sin (Galatians 2:20). It
   no longer dominates us (Romans 6:22). It's no longer our boss.
   See how the chain is broken? And we get clothes, which is
   really great.

5. **But our flesh doesn't disappear.** It no longer reigns, but it's still a reality (Galatians 5:16–17). It still hangs around to entice us. After we become Christians, we're no longer slaves to sin, but the flesh can still tempt us. We can choose to give in to temptation and indulge the flesh. Jesus broke the power of sin, but until we're in heaven, we still live with the presence and influence of sinful desires. Don't think it's a stalemate. The Holy Spirit indwells believers and empowers us to say no to the flesh. He is at work in us, transforming us to be like Jesus (2 Corinthians 3:18).

6. **That's why the Bible is full of encouragement to fight our fleshly desires.** We can't live at peace with the flesh. We have to attack it and deny it and kill it (Romans 8:13; 13:12). In hindsight, I guess drawing a sword of the Spirit would have been a bit more biblical. Oh well. This is the "stick" of the Spirit.

7. **The problem is that too often Christians make friends with their flesh.** In fact, they *feed* their flesh. That's what "making provision" means (Romans 13:14). We feed our flesh when we do things that encourage or foster our old sinful desires. This is choosing to live like who we used to be. Giving in to temptation, dwelling on sinful thoughts, and spending time with people and in places that celebrate sin are like giving our flesh three well-rounded meals a day with snacks and dessert. We might think that since we've been freed by the Cross, it's okay to indulge the flesh, but that's not true (Galatians 5:13, 24). And there's a real problem. When we feed the flesh...

8. **Our flesh can grow!** And before we know it, the flesh is bigger and stronger than we are and starts to push us around (Romans 6:12). This is why even genuine Christians, who are no longer wearing the chains of sin, can feel like their flesh is bullying them (Galatians 6:7–8). That's why Paul tells us in Romans 13:14 that we need to…

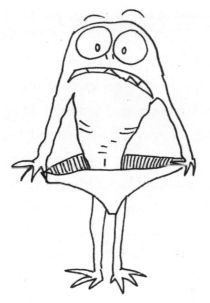

9. **Starve our flesh!** This is what we want our flesh to look like.
   We want the flesh gaunt and feeble (2 Corinthians 7:1). We
   should never expect it to be completely gone until Jesus returns and forever frees us from the presence of sin. Even a
   weak, wimpy flesh can try to trip us up (1 Corinthians 10:12).
   But when we starve the flesh, it's easier to resist temptation and
   walk in obedience.

Again, one problem with my cartoons is that they could give the impression that the flesh is an outside force attacking us. But it is called indwelling sin because it's *in* us. It resides in our hearts.

The reality of remaining sin should cause us to walk humbly, to live dependently on God, and to seek the help of other Christians. The truth is, we can be deceived. Our motives are not perfectly innocent. We need the power of the Spirit and the Word of God to search us.

I read the transcript of a television interview that Tom Brokaw did with pastor Ted Haggard several years ago.[3] At the time Haggard was at the height of his popularity and influence. His church and ministry were thriving. Brokaw insightfully asked why there was so little mention of sin in his church. Haggard said that since Jesus took care of our sin at the Cross, the church's emphasis was on fulfilling the destiny God had called them to.

Sadly, just a few years later, Haggard was forced to resign when a serious pattern of sexual immorality in his life was revealed. His casual, even flippant attitude toward sin in light of these dismaying revelations underscores the danger of neglecting the ongoing fight against sin. Yes, Jesus dealt with our sin at the Cross; those who trust in him will never face the wrath of God. But that doesn't mean we can ignore the fight against remaining sin. We ignore it to our own spiritual peril.

You and I are no better than Ted Haggard. We can be ensnared in sin just as easily. We're all susceptible to temptation. The reality of God's grace should never be an excuse to be unconcerned about holiness. The Bible says that God's grace is "training us to renounce ungodliness and worldly passions, and to live self-controlled, upright, and godly lives in the present age" (Titus 2:12). Grace doesn't lull us into indifference toward righteousness. It trains us and compels us toward self-control and godliness.

I once heard John Piper say in a sermon that sanctification isn't necessarily progressive. If we're not careful, it can be regressive. If we choose to feed our sinful desires and indulge our cravings, we make them stronger. We can backtrack in holiness.

That's why we aren't equally holy. While one Christian is not more justified than another, some Christians are more like Jesus than others. Those who hear God's Word and strive to obey it in the power of the Spirit will be more like him. Those who actively put off sin and put on the behavior of the Savior will grow in holiness. Those who give attention to communion with God through prayer and study of his Word will be more conformed to the image of Jesus Christ. We all desperately need God's help to do this. Philippians 2:12–13 urges, "Work out your own salvation with fear and trembling, for it is God who works in you, both to will and to work for his good pleasure."

I have friends who think that talking about sin and giving attention to the details of fighting sin is defeatist. I know it's possible to be morbidly introspective about sin. And that's not what I'm advocating. I think we should all be more aware of Jesus's saving work than we are of our shortcomings. Robert Murray McCheyne's advice is worth repeating: "For every one look at your sins, take ten looks at Christ."[4]

But I don't think that being aware of sin has to be an exercise in despair. In fact, though it might seem counterintuitive, I've found that facing the reality of remaining sin gives hope when connected to the gospel. First, it explains life. It explains why becoming a Christian doesn't mean we're free from temptation. It also engenders patience with other Christians. Remaining sin explains why even in the church and among Christians, we let each other down and experience relational strife. None of us has arrived. We're all still being sanctified. We all have blind spots and ways we can grow. We all need each other's mercy and patience.

Understanding what the Bible teaches about the flesh and our ongoing propensity to sin also fosters a healthy sense of humility. I don't mean a crippling sense of utter worthlessness that causes us to doubt God's love. I mean a humility that allows us to second-guess ourselves when necessary. Not to assume we're right but to listen to the constructive criticism of other people because there's a good chance we got something wrong.

If anything has turned the world off to Christianity, it's self-righteousness and arrogance that pretend our religious observance makes us better than other people. But a biblically informed view of indwelling sin and sanctification sweeps away self-righteousness. Christians who are being sanctified don't have time to be sanctimonious. They're aware of how far they have to go. They're aware of their weakness and God's ongoing grace toward them. This is what enables them to be gracious toward others.

Our pursuit of sanctification is complicated by the reality that we live in a world that has effectively pretended away sin. We've lost a clear, Bible-informed view of sin. We don't think of it as a violation of God's laws and character. We don't define it as a rejection of his rule in our lives. We don't acknowledge that sin is rebellion, a willful choice from the heart to make something besides God our ultimate concern. We don't call sin "sin." We excuse it, overlook it, and rename it.

Think about how we apologize. How rare it is, even among Christians, for a person to say, "I was wrong. I sinned, and I'm fully responsible. My sinful desires motivated me, and what I did dishonored God and hurt you. Please forgive me."

When was the last time someone asked your forgiveness with such words?

The normal approach is to talk about ourselves and our actions in sin-free categories. We like to think of ourselves as victims. We blame-shift. We add a "but…" after "I'm sorry." So we say, "I'm sorry I did that, but you made me so mad!" Or, "I'm sorry I broke our marriage vows, but I have self-esteem issues and sexual addictions." An even more subtle Christian apology is, "I'm sorry you took it that way." We like to keep the problem outside ourselves; it's someone else's fault. It's not something that needs to be repented of; it's a condition that needs to be understood and possibly medicated.

If you pretend, blame, and excuse all sin away, sanctification gets replaced by therapy. It becomes a vague, self-centered pursuit of self-improvement. And all we're left with is the hope of new drugs, new therapy, and better circumstances so our better self can emerge.

God's Word gives us a radically different picture of ourselves. It pinpoints our hearts as the source of the problem. James 1:14 says, "But each person is tempted when he is lured and enticed by his own desire." And James 4:1–2 asks, "What causes quarrels and what causes fights among you? Is it not this, that your passions are at war within you? You desire and do not have, so you murder. You covet and cannot obtain, so you fight and quarrel."

Acknowledging sin and our guilt stings our pride, but if we aren't honest enough to call sin what it is, we'll never receive the power God provides to overcome it. First John 1:8–10 says, "If we say we have no sin, we deceive ourselves, and the truth is not in us. If we confess our sins, he is faithful and just to forgive us our sins and to cleanse us from all unrighteousness. If we say we have not sinned, we make him a liar, and his word is not in us." When we think and speak as if we're only victims and never sin, we're lying to ourselves. And we're missing out on the cleansing grace of God that is available daily.

Martin Luther said that the "whole life of believers should be repentance."[5] Repentance isn't just for getting saved. It should be a normal, even daily part of the Christian's life. We're going to sin in a multitude of ways every day. Repentance is simply agreeing with God about sin, turning away from it, and accepting the redeeming grace of God through the Cross.

When you know God's cleansing grace, repentance doesn't have to be a traumatic thing. The author Tim Keller notes that some people view admitting they're wrong as an earth-shattering experience.[6] That shouldn't be the case for Christians. We already admitted we were wrong when we trusted in Jesus and acknowledged that we had no means by which to save ourselves. So it shouldn't be too hard to do this day by day as we become more like Jesus.

What do we do when Christians disagree about what obedience looks like? All around us are different opinions and standards, and they can be a significant diversion from sanctification.

I learned as a child that Christians had different standards for any number of issues. For example, some of our more conservative Christian friends thought all movies were wicked. When I was around them, I was supposed to refrain from mentioning that our family watched movies. I had to act as if I'd never heard of Darth Vader or Indiana Jones.

Other Christian friends were on the opposite end of the spectrum. They watched everything—even the bad movies I was never allowed to see. When

I was with them, I was supposed to refrain from mentioning that they were a bunch of filthy pagans dangling over the fires of hell.

I think a lot of Christians look around, see the diversity of standards, and assume that since nobody agrees, maybe it doesn't really matter. So they do whatever works for them. Sadly, few check in with God.

Other people just adopt the standards and practices of the Christians around them. This can give the appearance of holiness and growth, but it's superficial and can lead to bigger problems later. They can get sidetracked in their faith because they never took the time to cultivate personal convictions about Christian obedience. They never took the time to search God's Word for themselves. At some point, following a rule without real reference to God becomes an unwanted burden, and they start to chafe under the restriction. Obedience becomes joyless and wearying.

They know the rules but don't really know God. It's possible to know the restrictions of righteousness but never learn to appreciate the beauty and goodness of righteousness. Of course the problem is that their obedience is not motivated by a desire to please God. They're not being guided by his Word. They're just conforming to someone else's practice. As God describes in Isaiah 29:13, this brand of worship is "made up only of rules taught by men" (NIV).

Eventually people practicing rules taught by men get fed up and overreact by throwing out all restraint. I know a lot of people who were so burned by what they call their fundamentalist upbringing that they spend their life bucking every rule they can find. They start seeing legalists under every rock. If they once had blinders to all that Scripture says about grace and freedom, they have exchanged them for blinders that shut out all the Bible says about the danger of sin and the priority of holiness.

Any attitude that causes us either to *add to* our Bibles or *edit* our Bibles and live in reaction to someone besides God is unhealthy. Christian growth can't be defined by whom we don't want to be like. It has to be defined by becoming like Jesus. It has to be rooted in relationship to him. And it has to be built on real, Bible-rooted conviction.

When I use the word *conviction,* I'm talking about a heart-level, settled belief before God that doesn't change with our environment. A conviction is something we believe, not because someone is making us, not because we have to, but because we are convinced it's what *God* would have us believe.

Compliance isn't conviction. Conformity to other people's standards isn't conviction. Adapting to a church culture isn't conviction. Biblical conviction is the result of the study of Scripture, careful thought, discussion, and the search for wisdom. It requires work. It requires the humility to test the results of our choices and change our actions when necessary. Most important it requires a laser focus on God.

The solution here isn't to throw out all rules. It's to embrace God's rules and obey them out of a desire to honor him. If there's a rule in your life that you obey solely because of someone else and that person's opinion, take the time to study Scripture for yourself. See if your rule is really biblical. Sometimes you'll find that it is—either because Scripture directly commands it or because biblical principles convince you of its wisdom. But other times you might find that it's man-made and you could leave it behind.

———

Sometimes I make my relationship with God more about the sin I need to avoid than the good I'm called to pursue. Recently I wrote Galatians 5:22–23 in the front page of my journal: "But the fruit of the Spirit is love, joy, peace, patience, kindness, goodness, faithfulness, gentleness, self-control."

I wrote the words in big bold letters. These are the words that are to define and mark my life. I want them to call out to me every time I commune with God. This is who he's called me to be. This is what his Spirit wants to produce in me. I want to spend as much time seeking to be defined by love, joy, and peace as I do seeking to rid my life of anger, lust, and complaints.

Becoming like Jesus isn't just a matter of not doing wrong. It's a matter of actively "doing" righteousness. It's pursuing obedience. Romans 13:14 (the passage I cartooned earlier) tells us to avoid feeding the flesh, but it starts by telling us to "put on the Lord Jesus Christ." The New International Version says, "Rather, clothe yourselves with the Lord Jesus Christ." Paul is saying that the Christian life is about constant trust and dependence and identification with Jesus Christ. Just as the clothing we wear may identify our job or nationality, so our behavior shows our identification with Jesus. We're to "put on" righteous behavior that matches his. We're to live in a way that identifies us as his disciples. The Christian life is about putting on new behavior, clothing ourselves with Jesus himself.

Recently I've been learning how important it is for sanctification to be fueled by my status as God's child. Ephesians 5:1 says, "Therefore be imitators of God, as beloved children." Sanctification is all about imitating our Father. It's not conforming to a group or a religious culture. It's about modeling our lives and actions after the character of our heavenly Father and Jesus our brother and coheir (Romans 8:17).

When God saves us, he doesn't merely forgive us or ransom us from sin; he adopts us (Ephesians 1:4–5). In love, he makes us his children. He grants us all the rights and privileges of natural-born children. The apostle John viewed this truth as one of the greatest proofs of God's profound love for his people. He wrote, "See what kind of love the Father has given to us, that we should be called children of God; and so we are" (1 John 3:1).

Once my fellow pastor Mark pointed out that when I prayed, I rarely addressed God as Father. "I've noticed that you usually say 'Lord' or 'God' when you pray," he told me. At first I thought Mark had joined the prayer police or something. I wasn't sure why he was nitpicking words. But as we talked, and as I've learned since, it's not a matter of quibbling over words. Jesus himself taught us to pray to God as Father (Matthew 6:9). What we call God reveals how we think about him. And how we think about him shapes how we relate to him. And how we relate to him determines how we interpret his work in us and his purpose for us.

Knowing God as Father matters because he wants us to know how much he truly loves us. And that his love for us isn't the changing, professional, or skittish variety. It is real and deep and familial.

All the imagery God uses about salvation is designed to assure us how real his love for us is, how comprehensive his restoration of us is. So when we feel overwhelmed by guilt, God uses the legal language of the court and tells us that through Christ we're justified, declared completely righteous before him (Romans 5:8–9). When we feel enslaved and unworthy, he uses the language of the marketplace and tells us that he has bought us, ransomed us from sin (1 Peter 1:18–19).

And God uses the language of adoption to encourage us in the hard, ongoing work of learning to obey and follow Jesus as we wait for his return. God doesn't just point back to his love in forgiving us and redeeming us in the past. He uses the language of the family to say, "I love you *right now.* You have a relationship with me that isn't changed by your performance. I am your dad. You are my son. You are my daughter. Nothing can change that. I love you. I am always your Father."

This is the truth we need when we fall down. When we mess up again. When we do for the millionth time what we said we wouldn't do again.

Living in the present reality of God as Father will radically change your view of the Christian life. I'm in process on this. I can't say I've completely got it. But I'm learning to view my obedience and my struggle with sin through the lens of being a child of God. I have a Father in heaven who has promised to give me his Holy Spirit (Luke 11:11–13). He's promised to provide me with all the power I need to obey him (2 Peter 1:3).

Holiness is just not a list of rules. It's about imitating my Father (1 Peter 1:15–16). He is loving, he is kind, he is pure, he is truthful, he is patient, and he is gentle. And because I'm his kid, I want to look like him and please him.

Turning away from sin isn't about what I'm not allowed to do. I don't want what displeases my Father. I want to love what he loves. How can I take joy in what grieves the One who has loved me with an everlasting love (Jeremiah 31:3)?

Righteousness in relationship is what pleases my Father. I'm not trying to live up to some church standard or self-imposed standard. I want to grow in honoring and knowing and blessing the heart of my Father.

The truth of God's adopting love for me means I'm not obeying to get into his family or even to stay in the club. I obey because I'm already in. Because of Jesus, I'm family. There's incredible safety in that.

Jesus said, "If you love me, you will keep my commandments" (John 14:15). Those words always bring me back to the simplicity of sanctification. This is why I obey. This is to be my motivation. People who love Jesus do what he says. They learn to obey him in the big and small parts of their lives.

Dave, the guy on the radio show, decided you could try to obey God too much. Maybe that's true if you're chasing perfection or obeying rules taught by men. But if obeying is really about loving Jesus, can you love him too much? When we finally see Jesus face to face, will any of us regret the times we said no to our own desires and said yes to him?

I know I'll never obey God perfectly this side of heaven. Even though I've been changed, I'm still changing. I have a long way to go. I'll fail many times along the way. I'll need to repent and seek my Father's gracious forgiveness countless times between today and the final day—the day when I'm ultimately and forever changed by the power of God.

I'm really looking forward to that day.

Until then, I've got work to do. Yes, sanctification is work. But it's good work. It's work enabled by the Holy Spirit. It's the privilege of the redeemed. It's the great honor of God's adopted children to work to be like their Father.

I BELIEVE IN THE HOLY SPIRIT

"I longed to know that God was present,
that I was doing more than singing songs to the ceiling."

I WAS SEVENTEEN when I learned about my parents' secret life: they were closet charismatics. I suppose it could have been worse. I've heard of people who discovered that their parents were Nazis or in the Mafia. Still it surprised me. It wasn't what I expected to hear the night I came home from the church I'd been visiting and boldly announced that I was now a Spirit-filled, tongue-talking charismatic.

I considered this shocking news. I expected sparks to fly. I imagined their eyes widening, jaws dropping. Maybe a lip trembling. I realize now that this was immature. But at the time, I had a mischievous delight in feeling that I was living on the edge spiritually and that my new "Holy Spirit experience" would slightly scandalize my comfortably evangelical dad and mom. Since I was a good, Christian, homeschooled kid, this was the closest I would ever come to announcing that I'd joined a biker gang and gotten a skull tattooed across my chest.

But Dad and Mom just smiled and said, "Oh, honey, that's wonderful."

Then they told me the story of their own involvement in the charismatic movement as young Christians and the work of the Spirit in their lives ever since. My dreams of creating panic fizzled. It was as if Dad and Mom lifted their shirt sleeves to show off their own tattoos and told me they had two Harleys hidden in the garage.

———

I've come a long way in my beliefs about the Holy Spirit since the night I burst through the door and made my dramatic announcement. I hope my motivation has matured and my understanding has deepened. Some people might say I'm less charismatic. But I believe I've become more passionate about and more grateful for the person and work of the Holy Spirit.

In case you're feeling nervous about where I'm headed, let me assure you that I'm no longer interested in shocking people when it comes to discussing the Holy Spirit. In fact, I'm going to do my best to skirt the controversial issues associated with him. My goal isn't to prove or disprove the ongoing function of spiritual gifts; I don't want to argue about prophecy or speaking in tongues. So whether you think the miraculous gifts ended with the last apostles (referred to as the *cessationist* position) or you think the miraculous gifts continue today (sometimes called the *continuationist* viewpoint), I want to focus on our common ground.

That common ground begins with the historical, orthodox Christian belief that there is, in fact, a Holy Spirit. One line of the Apostles' Creed states, "I believe in the Holy Spirit." All orthodox Christians can affirm this statement. But what comes next? Doesn't it follow that it's important to know who the Holy Spirit is? To know what he's doing and how we're to relate to him? Jesus said in John 14:16 that the Spirit would be our "Helper." Shouldn't we understand how he wants to help us?

The reason my parents turned their backs on their charismatic roots is an interesting story. They were both saved during the Jesus movement in the early 1970s. Back then thousands of hippies across America were coming to faith in Jesus. Around the same time many Christians were experiencing a dramatic renewal of interest in the work of the Holy Spirit. Beliefs that had once been confined to Pentecostal churches—the idea of a second experience "baptism of the Spirit" and present-day manifestations of the Spirit in prophecy, tongues, and healing—began to sweep through other Christian denominations. This became known as the charismatic movement (the term *charismatic* is based on the Greek word *charisma* and refers to the "grace gifts" of the Spirit).

Many people saw the charismatic movement as a genuine and much-needed renewal of mainline denominations that were dead, formal, and lacking zeal in worship and evangelism. Skeptics saw it as unbiblical, out-of-control emotionalism and possibly the lingering effects of all those drugs. Looking back, I think both sides were partially right. Like many revivals in church history, this one had a mix of good and bad.

What isn't in question is that there was a good deal of controversy. Some churches left their denominations over the issue. Other churches split. Charismatics claimed they were teaching the "full gospel" and described themselves as "Spirit-filled." The implication was clear: Christians who didn't adopt their beliefs about the Holy Spirit had a "partial gospel" and were "Spirit-empty." Not the best way to win friends.

On the other hand, noncharismatics often judged all charismatics by the worst, most extreme examples of excess in the movement. To them it was all a chaotic mess. In their opinion, the gifts of the Spirit were imagined or faked at best, the work of demons at worst.

My dad and mom met in a Baptist church that fully embraced the charismatic renewal. The church became a magnet for young people. Many young men, my dad among them, sensed a call to full-time ministry. The church started a small Bible college, and Dad was in the first class.

But as time went by, Dad and Mom became disillusioned with certain unbiblical aspects of the church. They watched as "spiritual gifts" were used to manipulate people. At times the emphasis on gifts and anointing was used to shut down questions or concerns about the character of leaders. Then a woman in the church was diagnosed with cancer, and the pastor promised the congregation that she would be healed. When she wasn't, he publicly blamed the woman's husband, implying that there was sin or a lack of faith in the home.[1] Not long afterward the church split, and my parents left.

I don't think there was a moment when my parents changed their beliefs about the Holy Spirit. But they edged further and further away from the charismatic practice they'd seen in those early years. While they continued to depend and rely on the Spirit in their personal lives, they shed the label of charismatic and avoided churches that made the Holy Spirit and the spiritual gifts their calling card. By the time I was a teenager, they had edged so far away from that aspect of their spiritual heritage that I had no idea it had ever been part of our family history.

I tell my parents' story because it's a narrative shared by many. To one degree or another, a lot of us have had bad experiences or run-ins with "charismaniacs." This could be as involved as growing up in a charismatic or Pentecostal church or as limited as having a friend who was charismatic and who weirded us out. Maybe your bad experience was just watching a few minutes of an oily-haired televangelist wearing pancake makeup who broke into tongues and claimed to heal people over the airwaves (for a small donation).

Let's face it: the Holy Spirit has gotten a lot of bad press. A good bit of tacky, strange, and just plain wrong things have been done in his name. Of course the same could be said about Jesus. But I think it's easier to sort through the good and bad with Jesus. The Holy Spirit is a little more complicated. Maybe because he is a Spirit, it's easier to blame weird stuff on him. Or maybe because not enough is said about him outside charismatic circles, some people are left with mainly negative impressions.

This isn't a healthy state of affairs. Whenever we live some part of our faith in reaction to anything other than God's Word, we become unbalanced and misguided. We shouldn't neglect the person and work of the Holy Spirit just because other people have misrepresented him.

Making the decision to give careful thought and attention to the Holy Spirit isn't a decision to become a charismatic. It's a decision to be a faithful disciple of Jesus Christ and a student of God's Word.

———

Thinking rightly about the Holy Spirit begins with right thoughts about the Trinitarian nature of God. John Frame writes, "The Holy Spirit is God, and he is a person of the Trinity, distinct from the Father and Son."[2] The Holy Spirit is not merely a ministering angel that God sends on missions. He is not mere power from God. The Holy Spirit *is* God.

The Bible reveals that the Holy Spirit is God in passages such as Acts 5:3–4, where Peter equates lying to the Spirit with lying to God. First Corinthians 2:10–11 states that the Spirit comprehends and knows the thoughts of God. The Spirit's equality with the Father and Son is expressed in various benedictions in Scripture, including 2 Corinthians 13:14, which says, "The grace of the Lord Jesus Christ and the love of God and the fellowship of the Holy Spirit be with you all." It's also evident in Jesus's instruction that his followers be baptized in the triune name of God—"in the name of the Father and of the Son and of the Holy Spirit" (Matthew 28:19).

Like the Father and Son, the Holy Spirit is a person. Members of the Jehovah's Witnesses cult deny the Holy Spirit's personhood (they think he's a force like electricity). But ask them how they know the *Father* is a person. How do we determine personhood? The answer is that persons are those who do personal actions (speak, hear, think, feel, etc.). The Bible reveals that the Spirit engages in these personal actions. He speaks (Acts 13:2). He has a mind (Romans 8:27). He can be grieved by our sin (Ephesians 4:30). So the Holy Spirit is not an impersonal force or power. The Holy Spirit is a "he" not an "it" (John 14:17; 1 Corinthians 12:11).

And just as there could be no salvation apart from the ministry of the Father and Son, there would be no salvation apart from the work of the Holy Spirit in our lives. In perfect fellowship and unity, the members of the Godhead partner in the great work of salvation. Though equal in power and deity, each plays a unique role. What the Father planned, and the Son purchased by his death, the Holy Spirit activates or applies in our lives. It is the Holy Spirit who gives us a new spiritual heart (John 3:5–8; Romans 8:9–11). It is through the Holy Spirit that we are washed, sanctified, and justified (1 Corinthians 6:11). It is the Holy Spirit who empowers us to become like Jesus (Romans 8:14; Galatians 5:16–18).

I don't remember the charismatic church my parents attended when I was a child. That's probably a good thing. But the downside of my parents' leaving that church tradition behind was that by the time I graduated from high school, I had next to no concept of who the Holy Spirit was or why he mattered.

Then when I was seventeen, I visited a big charismatic church in Portland. The passion I saw in the people kept drawing me back. There was an emotional reality to the way people talked about God. They spoke about him as if he were *right there*—like right next to them.

And the singing! Worship was a full-body experience. I'd grown up in churches where you sang with your hands by your side or in your pockets. These people not only raised their hands; they moved their whole bodies. They danced. I remember the first time I saw the whole congregation, including the pastors in their suits, begin to hop, jump, and two-step everywhere in the auditorium. They were dancing in church! It felt like the whole building was shaking.

On one level I guess it looked silly. But that's not how it struck me. I felt like everyone around me was saying, "This is how excited we are about God! He is so real, so good that we can't hold in our joy!"

I remember the day I finally joined in the dancing. I shut my eyes tight and just started jumping in place with total abandon. For the first time I didn't care how I looked or what anyone around me thought. My heart was bursting with an awareness of how worthy God was of all the passion of my life. God felt more real and nearer than he ever had before. For a long time I'd been aching for a sense that God was present and active in my life. I wanted to know that my faith was more than just reading a book. That I was doing more than singing songs to the ceiling.

After a few months of visiting the church, I approached Bob, the youth pastor. He was a short, stocky man who looked like Fred Flintstone in a suit. He was quick to smile and was always very kind to me.

"I hear you guys talk about the Holy Spirit and being filled with the Spirit," I told Bob. "But what does that mean? How do I get that?"

I was half expecting (and hoping) that Bob would put his hand on my forehead and shout a fiery prayer over me. But he didn't.

"Do you have a pen?" he asked. Then as I scribbled furiously, he rattled off a list of references from the Old and New Testaments. "Those are passages that talk about the Holy Spirit," Bob told me. "Go read them. Pray over them. Then come talk to me in a few weeks."

I went home and began to read the passages Bob had pointed me to. I read how the Spirit equipped Joseph, Moses, and David for leadership (Genesis 41:38; Numbers 11:17; 1 Samuel 16:13). How he gave Joshua wisdom and Gideon courage (Deuteronomy 34:9; Judges 6:34). How the Spirit instructed and taught God's people (Nehemiah 9:20).

In the New Testament I read Jesus's promise to send another Helper, whom he called the "Spirit of truth" (John 14:15–17). I read Acts 2 about the Day of Pentecost when the Holy Spirit came like a wind on the men and women waiting and praying in the upper room. I saw Peter transformed from a man who cowered before a servant girl to a man of courage who stood boldly before a crowd of thousands to preach about Jesus.

I spent the next two weeks reading those scriptures and praying for God to give me what the men and women I read about had. I remember praying at night in the hallway outside the bedroom I shared with my younger brother. I would kneel in front of the window and reach my hands up toward the night sky. "God, give me your Holy Spirit!" I would pray over and over. I wasn't even sure what that meant, but I had an overwhelming sense that I needed God's Spirit. I kept praying and waiting for something, anything, to happen.

Since then I've come to believe that I already had what I was asking for. As I've studied God's Word, I've become convinced that all Christians are indwelt by the Holy Spirit when they first believe (1 Corinthians 2:12). So I don't think there is a "baptism in the Spirit" separate from regeneration.

Instead, I believe God invites us to continually seek to be filled with the Spirit. We should all desire more of the Spirit's presence and influence in our hearts and lives. Ephesians 5:18 tells us to "be filled with the Spirit." I see now that God was stirring in me a good desire to be filled. God's Spirit was working in me, illuminating his Word and showing me my need for more of his work. Those weeks of studying Scripture and seeking God in prayer were very important for me as my sense of need and dependence grew.

Not long afterward Pastor Bob and a guy named Quinn took time to pray for me after a meeting. I had what you could describe as a dramatic spiritual experience in which I spoke in tongues. That was the night I drove home and told my parents about my Holy Spirit encounter.

J. I. Packer says that for many charismatics their experience is better than their theology.[3] I think that was true of me. My experience the night Pastor Bob prayed for me and my experiences in the years that followed were real. As I continued to attend the charismatic church, God moved in my life and empowered me to serve him in specific ways. But often my experience outpaced my biblical understanding.

Today, in hindsight, I'd say that I had a very narrow understanding of how and why the Holy Spirit works in people's lives. I basically confined him to a certain emotional experience in church meetings. In my view the Holy Spirit was moving when I felt a surge of emotion while we sang or when I had a dramatic experience during times of prayer. While I believe the Spirit can move in those ways, confining his work to those moments is sort of like thinking that a fork can be used only to eat peas. It's not that my knowledge about the Holy Spirit was false; it was just woefully incomplete.

A few years after I joined the church, it was abuzz with word that a special "move of the Spirit" had started in a church in another city. People from our church flew out for special meetings with them and claimed to come back with some of whatever they had there. A few zealous but not always wise people began to steer meetings in strange directions that had less and less rooting in Scripture. The work of the Spirit became more about odd manifestations—uncontrollable laughter and extended times of prayer where half the people would be laid out on the ground "under the influence."

At first it seemed exciting. Then after a while, I started to feel like we were chasing our tails—seeking emotion and experience for their own sake. It became increasingly less clear to me what the point of it all was. People appeared to be measuring their relationship with God by how dramatic or odd their encounters with the Holy Spirit were.

Part of my spiritual journey has involved sorting through the good and the not-so-good of those days. This has taken time. I'm not willing to discount all that happened during my years at the church, nor am I willing to endorse it all as biblical. It's been a process of learning to define my ideas about the Holy Spirit by God's Word, not my good or bad experiences.

———

These days I find myself less interested in the labels of charismatic and non-charismatic, less interested in arguing about whether there is a distinct "baptism of the Spirit" or only ongoing fillings of the Spirit throughout a Christian's life, less interested in whether gifts like tongues and prophecy still function today.

Personally, I do speak in tongues. And I've been encouraged by it. But it's not the apex of my relationship with God. I know a lot of Christians (my wife among them) who have never received the gift of tongues, and they're doing just fine.

I believe in the gift of prophecy (carefully defined), but it is clearly not to be equated with Scripture or prophecy in the Bible. It's not God speaking infallibly as he did through the prophets in the Old Testament or through the apostles. So no one is adding to Holy Scripture today. The canon of Scripture is closed. I'd rather have two words of Scripture than a hundred words of prophecy. Only Scripture is perfect and authoritative (Proverbs 30:5–6).

I don't feel comfortable with people who are anxious to claim a prophetic gift or who place too much emphasis on its importance. In our church we discourage people from sharing prophetic words that are predictive or directive. It's just too easy for people's own ideas and thoughts to get mixed up in prophecy.

That being said, I've seen this gift used to edify others. And I've been encouraged by it personally. Most of the times I see prophecy function, it serves to remind people of truths and promises from God's Word. It's not revealing the future or imparting fresh revelation but affirming and applying God's already-revealed truth to specific people and situations. When prophecy is genuine, it points people to Jesus, reminds them of his faithfulness, and directs them to his priorities. True prophecy always confirms and accords with God's Word.

In a similar way, while I believe God still heals, I'm less concerned about identifying a particular person as having a gift of healing. Even the apostles didn't have a gift that ensured healing on every occasion. I believe God can and does heal and that he is glorified when we ask him to heal (James 5:13–15). But we shouldn't do this as a demand or think that a lack of healing reveals a lack of faith.

When people ask me how to discover their spiritual gifts, I say, "Just serve." Don't overspiritualize spiritual gifts. There's a good chance the gifts God has given you to serve your church are the same ones you use in your daily work. Don't worry about whether or not you have a gift that appears in one of the lists of spiritual gifts in the Bible. (See Romans 12:6–8; 1 Corinthians 12:7–10, 28; Ephesians 4:11.) Those lists aren't exhaustive. Instead, just look around you for needs, and then try to meet them. If what you do is helpful and other people are encouraged by your service, maybe you have a gift. But you don't need a badge to be useful. Just serve. It's not about you and your gift; it's about serving the needs of others and glorifying Jesus through your life.

I've come to see that you can limit God in different ways. You can limit him by thinking he can *never* work in spectacular ways. But you can also limit him by thinking that *only* the spectacular is meaningful.

The Spirit's power and work are much broader, much more multifaceted than we often think. And it's all meaningful.

What's the biggest thing you've ever asked God for? Think of all the outrageous pleas you've prayed. Have you ever stopped to realize that by giving you his Holy Spirit, your Father in heaven has presented you a gift that infinitely surpasses your greatest request? To be indwelt by the Spirit of the living, eternal God is a greater gift, a more overwhelming honor than any position, any possession, any amount of wealth, or any human achievement.

There is no greater gift that God bestows than the gift of his Spirit. Are you aware of how he is working in you?

The Holy Spirit is presently at work in the life of every Christian, reshaping and reforming us to be like Christ (2 Thessalonians 2:13; Titus 3:5). We're called to cooperate and welcome this work by obeying Jesus, treasuring his Word, and doing the things that honor him. This is what the Bible describes when it says, "If we live by the Spirit, let us also walk by the Spirit"

(Galatians 5:25). It calls qualities like love, joy, peace, patience, goodness, and self-control the "fruit of the Spirit" (Galatians 5:22–23).

The Bible also tells us that the Spirit empowers us with boldness to share the truth about Jesus with others. Before Jesus ascended to heaven, he told his disciples, "You will receive power when the Holy Spirit has come upon you, and you will be my witnesses in Jerusalem and in all Judea and Samaria, and to the end of the earth" (Acts 1:8). Repeatedly in the book of Acts, whenever the Spirit fills believers in a pronounced way, the result is their courageous witness to others about Jesus's death and resurrection (see, for example, Acts 2; 4:31).

The Spirit also gives grace gifts to believers so we can serve and build up the church of Jesus. These gifts are diverse and, oftentimes, seemingly common. And yet Scripture informs us that the Spirit empowers Christians to use them for the good of other believers. "Now there are varieties of gifts, but the same Spirit; and there are varieties of service, but the same Lord; and there are varieties of activities, but it is the same God who empowers them all in everyone. To each is given the manifestation of the Spirit for the common good" (1 Corinthians 12:4–7).

When the Holy Spirit is working in our lives, there will be a dynamic quality of holiness, evangelistic boldness, and an otherworldly willingness to play the role of a servant to others.

I'm not arguing against the supernatural and spectacular. But I think we need to broaden our definition of both. The truth is that there is no such thing as normal or nonsupernatural Christian living. Every day of faith is a day of the supernatural work of the Spirit in our lives. Every time we're filled with love for God, every time we become aware of how glorious Jesus is, every time we read God's Word and understand and believe it, every time we choose to obey God and turn away from sin, every time we selflessly use our abilities to serve others—the Holy Spirit is powerfully working in us.

Ironically, one of the most compelling pieces I've read about the Holy Spirit is an essay written by a noncharismatic New Testament professor from Dallas Theological Seminary named Dan Wallace.

In some ways Dan's story is a lot like my parents'. As a young Christian he came into contact with a charismatic church. It was a time of intense passion for the Lord, expressed in fervent prayer, study of Scripture, and a boldness in evangelism that was uncharacteristic of his normally shy disposition.

But he noticed practices in his charismatic church that didn't line up with Scripture and eventually left. He went to a Christian college and then to a seminary that took a strong stand against the gifts of the Spirit. Over time Dan slipped away from his early vibrant contact with God. While his understanding of Scripture was heightened, he says his walk with God slowed to a crawl.

Then his eight-year-old son was diagnosed with a rare and deadly form of cancer. The boy lost weight. His hair fell out. He was so weak he had to be carried everywhere, even to the bathroom. The months of watching his son suffer and waste away during chemotherapy treatments shook Dan to the core of his being. He was in an emotional wasteland. He was angry. God seemed distant.

For the first time Dan realized that all the restrictions he had placed on the Spirit were suffocating his faith. He writes:

> I needed God in a personal way—not as an object of my study, but as friend, guide, comforter. I needed an existential experience of the Holy One.... I found the scriptures to be helpful—even authoritatively helpful—as a guide. But without *feeling* God, the Bible gave

me little solace.… I found a longing to get closer to God, but found myself unable to do so through my normal means: exegesis, scripture reading, more exegesis. I believe that I had depersonalized God so much that when I really needed him I didn't know how to relate.[4]

Mercifully, Dan's son recovered from his cancer. But the lessons Dan learned about his relationship with God during that excruciating time stayed with him.

He decided to radically rethink his attitude and perspective on the Holy Spirit. While he still believed the miraculous or sign gifts had died in the first century, he realized he needed to acknowledge that the Holy Spirit had not. What could he affirm that the Holy Spirit was doing today?

Dan began to consider what it meant when Jesus said, "My sheep listen to my voice" (John 10:27, NIV). "I am increasingly convinced," Dan writes, "that although God does not communicate in a way that opposes the scriptures, he often communicates in a non-verbal manner to his children, giving them assurance, bringing them comfort, guiding them through life's rough waters. To deny that God speaks verbally to us today apart from the scriptures is not to deny that he communicates to us apart from the scriptures."[5]

Dan realized that a Christian can depersonalize God by making him the object of investigation rather than the Lord to whom we are subject. The vitality of our faith gets sucked out when our stance toward God changes from "I trust in" to "I believe that."

He acknowledged that part of his own motivation for depersonalizing God was a craving for control. "What I despised most about charismatics was their loss of control, their emotionalism," he says. "But should we not have a reckless abandon in our devotion to him? Should we not throw ourselves on him, knowing that apart from him we can do nothing?"[6]

The apostle Paul prays a fascinating prayer in Ephesians. It's a prayer for Christians. It's a prayer for their inner lives. It's a prayer for a powerful work of the Spirit in their lives. But consider the focus and purpose of this request for the Spirit's power. Paul prays that through the Spirit they will be strengthened with power in their inner beings, that Christ will dwell in their hearts through faith, and that they will "be filled to the measure of all the fullness of God." And what is the end result of all this? A greater awareness of the depth of God's love for them (Ephesians 3:14–19, NIV).

The phrases Paul uses are different ways of describing the same thing. He is praying that the Holy Spirit will work in the inner lives of his Christian friends so they will be brought into a deeper union with Jesus, a greater awareness of his presence with them, and a fuller knowledge of his love for them. He doesn't want God to be an impersonal truth, a vague idea or philosophy.

Isn't this what we need more than anything else—to know that God truly loves us? Isn't this the only thing that can ultimately sustain us when we experience suffering and doubt and discouragement? when we feel alone in the world? when our child has cancer? The power we need in those moments is the power to believe that everything Jesus did two millennia ago really is for us.

This is what the Spirit does in God's people. He works in our hearts, in our affections and emotions. *The Spirit mediates the presence of Jesus Christ to us.* The Spirit is why Christians can say when we gather, "Jesus is with us right now" (see Matthew 18:20).

The Spirit shows us that Jesus is with us and loves us. He takes us from being people who know theoretically that God is our Father to being people who know experientially in our hearts that we are his children—people who can cry "Abba! Father!" to God (Galatians 4:6). This isn't something we can write down in easy steps. It's not a neat formula. It's the wonderful, myste-rious work of God's Spirit in our hearts.

Do you see how important this is? Without the work of his Spirit in our hearts and minds, the truth of Scripture will be just words on a page. Paul understood that. Before his prayer for the Ephesians, he spent three chapters expounding some of the richest doctrinal truths about God's plan of salva-tion known to mankind. But he knew that apart from the Spirit, his words would be nothing more than lifeless facts, dead orthodoxy.

It's not enough that we simply know truth. God wants us to feel it, to believe it, and to apprehend it in the deepest, most personal way. He wants us to be able to say, "The cross is for me. The empty tomb is for me. For-giveness and adoption and redemption are mine because I am united with Jesus Christ! Jesus loves me! Jesus is with me!"

This is living truth. It is impassioned orthodoxy—truth set on fire in our hearts.

Sound doctrine is so important. But we can never settle for merely know-ing doctrine. God has given us his Holy Spirit, and he invites us to ask to be continually filled with his Spirit afresh so that doctrine becomes the living story of God's great love for us. So that it melts our hearts. So that this truth sets us on fire with love for the Savior who loved us first. The glorious truth of God's love for us in the giving of his Son isn't something we can grasp through mere knowledge or bigger books. We need the power of God's Holy Spirit to give us "strength to comprehend" how big and wide and deep God's love for us is (Ephesians 3:18–19).

———

Do you know what Jesus spent extended time teaching his disciples in the hours leading up to his arrest and crucifixion? He spent those final moments teaching them about the Holy Spirit (John 14–16). What does that tell us, as followers of Jesus, about how important it is to learn about the person and work of the Spirit? Jesus called the Spirit another Helper or Counselor. Jesus had fulfilled this role during his earthly ministry, but soon he would send another Helper. The Greek word he used was *paraclete,* which refers to one who advocates for, defends, counsels, encourages, comforts, and helps. What a powerful summary of the Spirit's work in our lives.

And what is the ultimate aim of the Spirit's encouragement, comfort, and help? To enable us to know and see the glory of the Savior. The Holy Spirit is all about glorifying Jesus. To glorify something is to exalt it, to show it to be wonderful and worthy and good. When Jesus told his disciples about the Holy Spirit the night before his death, he said of the Spirit, "He will glorify me" (John 16:14).

J. I. Packer taught me that understanding this is the key to understanding the Holy Spirit's work. Packer says that the Holy Spirit in his "Jesus glorifying" work is like a spotlight behind us that shines forward and throws an illuminating light on Jesus. The Spirit's goal is to show us Jesus in all his perfection, holiness, and mercy. As we read Scripture, as we meditate on Christ, the Spirit cuts through the darkness of our sin-dulled minds and lights up the person and work of Jesus.

The Holy Spirit isn't interested in drawing attention to himself. His role is to point away from himself and to Jesus. Packer writes, "The Spirit's message to us is never, 'Look at me; listen to me; come to me; get to know me,' but always, 'Look at *him,* and see his glory; listen to *him,* and hear his word; go to *him,* and have life; get to know *him,* and taste his gift of joy and peace.'"[7]

The point of a spotlight is not to stand in front of it and stare into its bright light (that would blind you). A spotlight is useful only when it's pointed at others, enabling us to see them more clearly. And that's what the

Spirit does. That's the most loving, powerful thing he can do in our lives—help us to see and treasure Jesus Christ.

You know the Spirit is working if you're more amazed by Jesus, more desirous to serve and obey him, more ready to tell other people about him, more ready to serve the church he loves.

THE INVISIBLE
MADE VISIBLE

"God's plan has always been a group plan—
he reveals himself through his people."

I HEARD A STORY on the radio about a summer camp for atheist middle-school children. Some guy decided that it wasn't fair for religious kids to have all the fun camps and programs while atheist kids got nothing. So he started a camp. I found this fascinating. It was a place where students could play and swim, do crafts, and sit around campfires talking about evolution and how ludicrous religion is. I wondered what you had to do to get into trouble at that camp. Maybe sneak a peak at a Bible or whisper about the merits of Intelligent Design theory? I don't know.

One part of the story featured a few of the atheist kids railing against religion. One girl was pretty fired up. She said something like, "And if there is a God, why doesn't he come out and show himself? Why doesn't he just appear and say, 'Hello, I'm God. Believe in me!' Why doesn't he do that? It doesn't make any sense."

I laughed because I could relate to her question. Sometimes I wish God would do that. Once a year he could hold a big rally for the whole world, with television coverage, satellite links, and streaming Internet, and come out and—*boom!*—just do something really massive. Maybe turn a well-known, nasty, angry atheist into a donkey or something. Of course he could change him back at the end if he wanted. But it would need to be impressive so everybody would say, "Wow! There is a God. I want to sign up."

But when I really think about it, I know this idea is silly. Partly because I know that unless God opens people's spiritual eyes, they wouldn't believe even if he did this every week. Jesus said that if people don't accept the testimony of God's Word, even having someone come back from the dead wouldn't convince them to believe (Luke 16:31). And that's true. Jesus came back from the dead, but that wasn't enough for his enemies or even some of his friends. Some still doubted (Matthew 28:17).

And besides, what kind of stories would we have to tell in heaven if God just showed up and made everybody believe?

Imagine those conversations.

"So when did God save you?"

"Oh, it was the year he came out and turned Christopher Hitchens into a turtle."

"Snapping turtle, wasn't it?"

"Oh, right. That was clever. Yep, that's when I believed."

That's not a conversation that leads to worship. That's not a story that makes you shake your head in amazement. God is too great a storyteller to settle for something so plain.

Instead, he's chosen to write a story in human history that will, at the end of time, leave the universe speechless. It's the story of his great rescue mission in Jesus. The story of how he redeemed—made new—all that human sin had ruined.

But this is the incredible part. God is writing his story through his people. Through his children. Through his church. Through us.

So God doesn't come out on a big stage once a year to prove himself to the world. He does something so much riskier and more daring and, on the face of it, so preposterous that it makes you bite your lip—he makes *us* the show. He proves himself and displays himself through his church.

———

Most Christians neglect the doctrine of the church. That's not really surprising. This subject by necessity involves people. Real, annoying, infuriating, obnoxious, stubborn people, whose preferences and styles and smells can bring soaring theological ruminations crashing to the ground.

You can study the doctrine of justification and think only about our perfect Savior and his cross. But if you think about the church, chances are you'll start thinking about a specific group of people, a specific pastor, a specific denomination, and all the specific mistakes, deficiencies, and problems that go with them. And this is where a lot of us get tripped up. We don't hear what God has to say about the church because his voice is drowned out by the noise of our own experiences, perceptions, and disillusionment.

Pushing past all this can be difficult. But we have to try. We need to care about the church for own spiritual good and for the sake of the world that needs us to be the church. But an even simpler motivation for caring is because God does. Every metaphor used in Scripture to describe the church shows how deeply God cares. He calls the church his *bride* (Ephesians 5:25–32). He calls it his *household* or *family* (2:19). He says we are his *temple* in which he dwells by his Spirit (2:21–22). He says we are his *body* (1:22–23).

How can we claim to know and love Jesus and yet be indifferent toward his bride, his temple, his family, his own body? Can I say that I love Jesus but hate the wife he cherishes? Can I say I enjoy spending time with him but refuse to enter his house? Can I claim friendship with Jesus but think his body is repulsive? It's not possible.

———

For the first two decades of my life, I didn't give much thought to the "us" aspect of the Christian faith. I viewed faith in a very individualistic way. It was about *me* and *my* Jesus. I didn't consider Christianity's corporate or group nature.

Of course I *went* to church. That's what Christians do—we have meetings. But it was just tradition. It was a habit like sleeping, breathing, and all the other things we can do without thinking. In my more cynical moments, I viewed church suspiciously, as a way for pastors to give themselves jobs and exert power. But, really, I didn't give it much thought. So while church attendance played a big part in my life growing up, the church didn't have much of my heart.

I treated the church like a gas station. Everybody needs a gas station, right? You stop in (usually when you're in hurry) to get filled up. You go to the one that's most convenient for you. You get what you need, then you move on. I stopped by the church for the spiritual fuel that comes from worship, teaching, and relationships with other Christians. But then I hit the road and got back to my own plans—my own destination.

I think that describes a good number of Christians today, and they are abandoning the church. Some drop out completely. Others attend meetings but lack a real commitment and engagement in any one church. This leads to the church-hopping syndrome. I know a guy who used to go to one church for the singing and then drive to another church for the sermon. He had this timed so perfectly that he could stop by McDonald's in between for coffee and a breakfast sandwich. I think the only thing he missed was the offering, in both churches.

So why is this happening? If we're the body of Christ, why are so many body parts not showing up to play their part? No doubt some are burned out or disillusioned by the corruption or poor leadership they've seen. Others feel that the church is cumbersome and that there are more effective ways to get things done.

But my guess is that a vast majority of Christians who have lost their vision for the church are like I was: they've never taken the time to study what the Bible says about God's purpose and plan for the church. Instead, they're living their lives guided by their feelings or experience. They're pragmatic, so they're focused more on what "works" than on what Scripture dictates. They're consumers who approach church asking, "What's in it for me?"

But what if we saw that the church is more than a human program, more than what we disparagingly refer to as organized religion? What if we saw that it originated in the heart and mind of God himself and that his plan began before the dawn of human history and stretches into eternity? What if we learned that the church was so precious to Jesus that he was willing to shed his own blood to obtain it? What if the church is the means by which God has chosen to accomplish his purpose for us and for the world? And what if it is irreplaceable?

If we could see this, then we'd realize that rejecting the church is rejecting God himself.

God's plan for glorifying himself in the world has always been a group plan. He has always planned to redeem a *people*. And he's always revealed himself to the world through a nation. That was the past perfection in the first pages of the book of Genesis. That is the future described in the closing pages of Revelation—God dwelling among his people.

I'm not sure how I went so long without seeing this. Part of my problem was that I read my Bible as a collection of stories about isolated, outstanding individuals. But when you look more closely, you realize that while the Bible does tell the story of individuals such as Abraham, Sarah, Joseph, Moses, Ruth, and David, their stories and the significance of their lives are always directly tied to what God is doing in the family and the nation of which they're a part.

The history of the Jewish nation in the Old Testament is a preview of God's ultimate purpose to save a people for himself through Jesus. Down through the centuries God kept hinting at and pointing toward the coming of Christ and the establishment of his eternal kingdom to which people of every tribe and tongue would belong.

When God called Abraham, he promised him that one day his family would be a great nation. He said that through Abraham's descendants all the nations of the world would be blessed (Genesis 12:2–3). God was announcing the worldwide nature of his purpose in Christ.

Hundreds of years later God used Moses to rescue Abraham's descendants, the Israelites, from slavery in Egypt. God demonstrated his saving power and led them out of bondage toward the Promised Land. Through a weak and insignificant people, God displayed his power to the nations.

God gathered the people of Israel at the foot of Mount Sinai and spoke to them in a thundering voice (Exodus 19–20). He announced that if they obeyed his commandments and were faithful to the covenant he made with them, they would be his "treasured possession among all peoples," a "kingdom of priests," and a "holy nation" before him (Exodus 19:5–6).

Deuteronomy 9:10 calls the day when God spoke to the people "the day of the assembly." In Hebrew the word *assembly* is *qahal,* which is sometimes translated *congregation.* The Greek version of this word, *ekklesia,* is the basis of our word *church.* John Frame points out that this was, in an important sense, the beginning of the church. "It was on this day," he writes, "that the nation of Israel became, by covenant, God's holy nation, distinguished from all the other nations of the world."[1]

This amazes me. An unseen, eternal God chose to join himself to a ragtag group of humans. He set them apart as his special people and gave them the privilege of representing him to the world.

If you lived in the days of Moses and wanted to know what God was like, you wouldn't find the answer in the temples of Egypt or the sorcery of the Canaanites. The only way to glimpse the living God was to go to the desert, to an unimpressive group of nomads called the Israelites. In their worship, in their obedience to God's laws, in their rituals and commitment to holiness, the character of God was displayed.

The same thing can be said of the church today. Frame notes that thousands of years later, after the coming of Jesus Christ, the apostle Peter would use the words of Exodus 19:4–6 about Israel to describe Christians in the New Testament church. First Peter 2:9 says, "But you are a chosen race, a royal priesthood, a holy nation, a people for his own possession, that you may proclaim the excellencies of him who called you out of darkness into his marvelous light."

What is the church? It is the fulfillment of God's promises to Abraham to bless all the nations of the world. The church, comprised of men and women from every nationality and ethnicity, is now God's chosen people in the world. The church is how God makes himself known in the world.

———

Back when I lived in Oregon and was just learning to care about theology, one of the first set of sermons I listened to by C. J. Mahaney concerned God's purpose for the church. I was twenty years old, and that was the first time I was confronted with a biblical, century-spanning, world-shaking vision of the church. I loved Jesus and wanted to accomplish great things for God, but I still treated the church like a gas station. In my mind the real action and spiritual excitement were somewhere else.

Then I listened to that sermon series. It was called *Passion for the Church.* I remember thinking that was the oddest pairing of words. In my mind passion and church had no connection. It might as well have been called *Passion for the Laundromat.* But for some reason I listened.

C.J. preached from the book of Ephesians, a book that's been described as the apostle Paul's masterpiece on the church. He showed that, in the church, God was creating a whole new humanity—those who were reconciled to him and to each other (Ephesians 2:13–16). He showed from Matthew 16:18 that the church was the only institution Jesus had promised to sustain forever. The church was what God was using to teach Christians to know and obey him and to advance his mission around the world.

C.J. read a quote by John Stott that stopped me in my tracks: "If the church is central to God's purpose, as seen in both history and the gospel, it must surely also be central to our lives. How can we take lightly what God takes so seriously? How dare we push to the circumference what God has placed at the centre?"[2]

I couldn't shake that question. How could I take lightly what God took so seriously? How could I be so nonchalant, so belittling about the church that Acts 20:28 says Jesus "obtained with his own blood"?

For the first time I began to realize that God's purpose for the Christian's involvement in the church was radically different from my gas-station approach. The church wasn't merely a place to swing by for a fill-up. The journey of the Christian faith was supposed to be made *with* other believers.

The church isn't a gas station, I realized. It's the bus I'm supposed to be traveling on.

———

Some people throw the word *church* around as if anytime two Christians are in the same room, they are a church. So exactly what makes a church a church? I've heard performers at Christian concerts say, "We're gonna have church in here tonight!" as though church were merely a matter of Christians singing certain songs together. Christians will describe their campus ministry or neighborhood Bible study or even online group as a church. All these groups can be good and wonderfully encouraging, but that doesn't make them churches.

Since the Reformation, protestant Christians have agreed that a church requires two essential elements: the right preaching of God's Word and the right practice of baptism and communion.[3] These two marks of a true church tell us several important things about the church's character and purpose.

First, we learn that the church is to be a congregation of people who are submitted to the truth and authority of the Bible to teach, train, reprove, and correct them (2 Timothy 3:16). And the right teaching of the Word means presenting the good news of Jesus's substitutionary death and resurrection for sinners as its central message (1 Corinthians 15:1–3). Thus the church is built on a specific message, not just any random idea or philosophy.

Second, the priority of baptism and communion reemphasizes the necessity of the church being a *defined* community fixated on the gospel of Jesus Christ. Both are ways for God's people to act out and remember who we are and what we have through faith in Jesus's death and resurrection for us. And both distinguish who is and who is not part of God's people.

Baptism is the entry point into the church. It symbolizes a Christian's death to sin, resurrection with Jesus to new life, and entry into God's family (Matthew 28:19). It occurs one time, when a person first believes.

Communion is repeated many times throughout a Christian's life. Jesus instructed his followers to partake of the bread and the cup in remembrance of his broken body and blood poured out in his atoning death on the cross (1 Corinthians 11:23–26). As members of a local church eat and drink together, they proclaim Jesus's death as the source of their salvation. And they say to each other and the watching world, "We're still here. We're still pressing forward in faith. We're connected to Jesus and to each other because he died for our sins and made us God's children."

The New Testament is filled with practical instruction about what local churches are supposed to be and do. We see that churches are organized under the leadership of men who meet clearly defined character qualifications. They must manage their own families well and practice and teach healthy doctrine (1 Timothy 3; Titus 1:5–9). These qualities are important because a primary purpose of the church is to teach and train Christians to know and obey God. The church is also the place where Christians receive care and nurture from other believers. In the local church Christians put into practice the Bible's commands to love, serve, honor, pray for, and encourage one another (John 13:34; Galatians 5:13; Romans 12:10; James 5:16; 1 Thessalonians 5:11).

Does it matter that we belong to a specific local church? Evidently it does. This is illustrated in passages of Scripture that encourage Christians to honor and obey the leaders in their local church (Hebrews 13:17), to accept the discipline of the community (Matthew 18:15–19; Galatians 6:1), and not to neglect gathering with other believers (Hebrews 10:25).

What all this adds up to is that the New Testament assumes believers will participate in a local church where they can be baptized, partake of communion, be taught God's Word, worship, use their gifts to serve, be cared for spiritually by qualified leaders, be held accountable by a loving community, and bear witness to nonbelievers of Jesus's saving death. Christians are to join an assembly not just for their own spiritual health but so that the world around them can clearly see the reality of Jesus Christ.

———

Getting on the bus of God's plan for the church involved a more dramatic change of course for me than it does for most people. I ended up moving across the country to be part of C.J.'s church. I curtailed my conference speaking schedule so I could throw myself into the life of the church. I stopped publishing my magazine so I could work as an intern in the youth ministry and be trained as a pastor.

Looking back, I realize that my internship wasn't just training for ministry. It was an internship in understanding what church life is all about. In many ways it was a jarring experience. I learned that life in a local church wasn't anything like putting on a conference. On the conference circuit it was relatively easy to sweep into a city for a weekend, look impressive to people who didn't know me, and sound good as I taught a message I'd given a hundred times before.

Being a pastor in a local church was totally different. I didn't look impressive when people saw me day in and day out. And it wasn't enough to have a few inspiring messages. I needed to search God's Word and help people apply it to real-life situations and challenges. I had to learn how Jesus's death and resurrection made a difference in the dark valleys of pain—things I didn't have to face when I jumped from one city to another doing conferences.

Life in the local church was harder and less glamorous. But it was also sweeter and more rewarding than anything I'd been part of before. I saw the gospel change people. Not just tears and promises of change at altar calls, but sustained, true change in individuals and families.

I saw the body of Christ living and breathing and moving. I saw the love of Jesus made real as members wept with one another at the death of a child, as they carried one another in times of need, as they nurtured one another in times of temptation and doubt. As the well-worn saying goes, the church isn't a building or a meeting—it's people. But you never get to actually see this if your involvement is limited to meetings in one building. The real beauty of people being a church in a local community is only seen when you hang around long enough to watch them loving and serving one another through good times and bad.

Although I lost the adulation that comes with being a visiting speaker and author, I gained something so much better. I gained friends who really knew me—my strengths and my weaknesses. I gained brothers and sisters who were willing to challenge me when I was proud and comfort me when I was discouraged.

For the first time I realized that growing as a Christian wasn't something I could do on my own. Progress as a disciple required relationships and community. Studying the Bible on my own and even hearing good preaching weren't enough by themselves. I needed relationships in the church to practice what I learned. And I needed relationships in the church to help me see all the ways I wasn't practicing what I claimed to believe. I had no idea how inaccurately I saw myself. I didn't have blind spots; I had blind patches. Or, maybe more accurately, blind acres.

I'm a proud man. And I'd like to pretend that whatever maturity I have is the result of my wisdom, good breeding, and superior spiritual effort. But I can trace every example of growth and change in my life to the help of fellow Christians. And most often they were Christians in my local church. That's not surprising, is it? The people who know us best are the ones who can help us the most. It's impossible to calculate all that I've gained from their examples, their loving correction, their encouragement and prayers for me.

I learned that God's purpose for me is inextricably tied to his purpose for his people. My faith isn't all about me. It isn't only about my story and my journey. Being a Christian is about *us* belonging to God and to each other and then together fulfilling God's mission in the world.

———

What is God's mission for his church? "The task of the church," writes J. I. Packer, "is to make the invisible kingdom visible through faithful Christian living and witness-bearing."[4]

I love that statement. The church makes the invisible kingdom visible. The world can't see God. They can't see his reign in our hearts. But we join our lives together in the church so they can see him. They see him when we obey his commands. When we love one another. When we preach his Word and proclaim his gospel. When we do good works and serve the poor and the outcast. On earth everything we do—our worship, our building of Christian community, our service, our work—is to be done with an eye to spreading the fame and glory of Jesus Christ so the nations might know and worship him with us.

In John 20:21, Jesus said to his disciples, "As the Father has sent me, even so I am sending you." And in his final words before he ascended into heaven, Jesus gave all his followers an assignment that we call the Great Commission:

> All authority in heaven and on earth has been given to me. Go there-
> fore and make disciples of all nations, baptizing them in the name of

the Father and of the Son and of the Holy Spirit, teaching them to observe all that I have commanded you. And behold, I am with you always, to the end of the age. (Matthew 28:18–20)

The purpose of Christian community in the church is not only our joy and spiritual growth. The purpose is also mission—displaying and advancing God's reign and rule in the world.

I'll be honest. The mission Jesus has given us scares me. I'm much more comfortable being called out of the world than I am being sent into it. As a pastor I can devote myself to the concerns of the church, spend most of my time with other Christians, and shut myself off in the safety of church life like a hamster in a plastic rolling ball.

But that impulse to wall myself off from the world isn't always motivated by a love for holiness. Too often I separate myself from the world because I'm afraid or just plain lazy. Unbelieving people think I'm weird. They're different from me, and different can be uncomfortable.

In those moments I have to remind myself: it's not enough for me to be holy. When Jesus left, he didn't say, "Stay on this hill and be holy." He told his followers to be holy and to go share the gospel with the world. For the church to be faithful, we need both a concern for holiness and a heart to reach the world. Each of us has to continually evaluate our motives, our lifestyle choices, and our efforts to befriend people who don't know Jesus.

I once heard John Piper share the story of being invited as a young boy to attend a movie with his classmates. His very godly but very conservative parents frowned on movie watching. But while his mother would have preferred he not go, she didn't forbid him. Instead she explained her own convictions and let him make the choice. "Do what you think is right," she told him. "We have standards, Son, but they have to come from the inside." Reflecting on the story, Piper said, "There's a world of difference between separation and consecration. The issue is not separating rules but consecrated hearts."[5]

There's a lot of wisdom for the church in those words as we wrestle with questions about engaging and influencing a godless culture. To consecrate something means to set it apart for God's use. True consecration is an inward reality, not a matter of physical proximity or outward regulation.

There's no contradiction between consecration and evangelistic mission. If our hearts are consecrated, we can live in the darkest culture and powerfully shine forth the truth of the gospel. If our hearts are not consecrated, no amount of separation or man-made rules will keep us from the influence of worldliness (1 John 2:15–17). It will be in us no matter how high we build the walls around ourselves.

Jesus said that Christians are to be like salt and light in the world (Matthew 5:13–16). John Stott writes, "So Jesus calls his disciples to exert a double influence on the secular community, a negative influence by arresting its decay and a positive influence by bringing light into its darkness. For it is one thing to stop the spread of evil; it is another to promote the spread of truth, beauty and goodness."[6] The church is called to engage the world around us with countercultural lives and countercultural truth from God's Word—to arrest the decay brought about by human rebellion and spreading the life-giving light of God's truth.

Notice that both analogies Jesus uses assume contact. Salt is a natural preservative. It halts decay. But it won't work if it's diluted. And it has no effect if it's isolated. Salt has to come into contact. So it is with the church. We have to be in the world, engaging and influencing every aspect of culture with the truth of the gospel.

In the same way Jesus doesn't call his people to be just a city. We're to be a city on a hill that shines forth light to a dark world. "Flight into the invisible is a denial of the call," writes Dietrich Bonhoeffer. "A community of Jesus which seeks to hide itself has ceased to follow him."[7]

If we would obey Jesus, we must go into the world. I've been challenged by the example of other churches to study my local community with the evangelistic intentionality of a missionary. To ask questions like "If I were a missionary to another nation, how would I view my life? What decisions would I make about where I live or how much I need to live on? Where would I spend my time so I could form friendships with unbelieving people? What would I seek to learn about the culture so I could befriend and clearly communicate the gospel? What are the idols and false gods people are worshiping?"

Ask these questions, and then apply them to your current location. The mission field is right in front of you. Imagine how this kind of evangelistic urgency could be used by God to touch your campus, workplace, neighborhood, and community.

———

God's people can't reach the world if we hide. And we can't reach the world unless we're distinct from the world. We need to recapture the connection between holiness and mission. God calls his people to be distinct and holy, not so we can feel morally superior to our sinful neighbors. He calls us to be holy so that our neighbors will see the transforming power of the crucified, risen Jesus Christ.

It's not enough simply to go to the world. In Genesis, Abraham's nephew Lot went to the city of Sodom. Scripture states that Lot was a righteous man (2 Peter 2:7). But he lost his family to the sinful culture of the city. When God visited it in judgment, none of Lot's extended family and none of his neighbors would leave with him. Even after fire rained down on Sodom, Lot's wife looked back with longing eyes on the city and was punished (Genesis 19).

The world needs a church that will engage it, go to it. But how will we go to the world? Lot went to the world, but the world reshaped him. Jonah was a missionary, but he preached to Nineveh without love or compassion. He burned with rage when God showed the city mercy (Jonah 4:1).

Jesus is our model of love-motivated mission. Jesus wept over the sin of Jerusalem (Matthew 23:37–39). He stopped for the blind, the lame, and the outcasts. He ate with sinners. He scandalized the religious by befriending prostitutes and tax collectors. He went to the world with love and a saving message that countered everything the world stood for. He was willing to suffer and die at the hands of the people he came to save.

It was love that motivated God to send his Son on a mission of salvation (John 3:16). The same must be true of us. Only the great commandments to love God with heart, soul, mind, and strength and to love our neighbor as we love ourselves can push us outside ourselves and our narrow self-interests (Mark 12:28–34). Only this love can compel us to lay down our lives caring for the poor, marginalized, and oppressed of the world.

Only this love will give us the sustained courage to go into the world to speak the foolish, unwanted, yet saving message of a crucified Messiah. Love has to fuel mission. We can't go to the world because we want their approval; we can't go for power or to prove ourselves right. Mission has to be the overflow of a love for God that aches to see others experiencing his grace, love, and compassion for people who are lost and destined for hell.

Admittedly, the mission Jesus has given us would be easier if we didn't have to love, if we didn't have to care. It would be so much easier if we could either hate the world or just not care.

When I read about the violent, radical strain of Islam that has led to terrorism, I'm repulsed by it. But I can also see its appeal. There's something very straightforward, very doable about the assignment to hate the modern world, fight it, and try to blow it up. That's a relatively simple job description. I could do that. Blow myself up and then die and go to heaven.

But Jesus asks something much harder of his followers—something that takes much more courage and sacrifice. It's a mission that requires divine empowerment. He tells us to die to ourselves and live for him. He tells us to lay down our lives in the service of people who often despise us. He tells us to fully engage in a world that wants to seduce us and that hates us when we resist. He sends his church to plead with a culture that loves its sin.

Jesus asks us to die. But this is a sort of slow death. It's not a death that takes away life but a death that gives others life. It's the death of taking up a cross and walking in the footsteps of our crucified Savior. It's suffering for the message of the gospel. It's dying to popularity and being a church that stands for righteousness. This is something much more painful and terrifying than a split-second decision to press a button and become a human bomb. But it is the way of Jesus, and it leads to everlasting life.

What's your definition of success for the church? Numbers? Political power? The acceptance of Christianity in popular culture? We all carry around some concept of what it would look like if the church were really making progress.

Each year a Christian magazine publishes a list of the one hundred biggest churches as well as the one hundred fastest-growing churches in

America. Now, there's nothing wrong with this idea, and I'm sure it's of service to many people. But I had to stop reading that particular issue because I found it wasn't good for me. I started to feel like I was ogling other churches across the country. I felt like I was lusting after success and numbers and acclaim and that it was distorting my motivation for being a pastor. So I put the magazine aside.

When I find myself discouraged about the church, I have to stop and think about God's definition of success. It helps me to remember what Jesus taught about the nature of his kingdom and how it would grow. Jesus said the kingdom was like the tiniest of seeds that grows into the largest of plants (Luke 13:18–19). At first it doesn't look impressive. Nobody cares about it. But over time and so slowly you hardly notice, it grows and expands.

For Christians who want to see God's kingdom come with convincing, awe-inspiring power, a tiny, slow-growing seed can be something of a letdown. Have you ever sat and tried to watch a plant grow? That's how it can feel with God's kingdom. It's growing, but you can perceive it only over long stretches of time.

Jesus said the kingdom was like yeast used to make bread (Luke 13:20–21). Yeast is small and seemingly insignificant in quantity compared to the other ingredients, yet when it's worked into the dough, it causes the whole loaf to rise. It fundamentally changes the composition of the whole.

The kingdom of God isn't impressive to human eyes. It's outnumbered. In some ways it seems to be swallowed up by the world around it. But ever so slowly it's permeating the world around it and effecting change in ways no one anticipates.

The advance of God's kingdom takes time. And contact. The yeast does nothing sitting in a bowl removed from and unmixed with the dough. People of God's kingdom accomplish nothing when we're separated and have no contact with the world around us.

Jesus told another story about seeds being planted in different kinds of soil (Matthew 13:1–23). Most of the seeds didn't grow. They were eaten, trampled, or choked, or they withered. But a few grew and produced a great harvest. Growth and advance in God's kingdom should be expected amid seeming setbacks, even failure. Sometimes God draws big crowds. But not always. Maybe not often.

Jesus said that the kingdom was like a banquet held by a king that no one respectable or successful wanted to attend (Luke 14:15–24). All the beautiful people turned down the invitation and made up excuses for their absence. So the king sent his servants into the streets and gathered in the lowlifes, the poor and uneducated and overlooked of the world. It wouldn't make a very good ad campaign, but that's your basic description of the church. It's a huge party for losers. Losers who realize that only Jesus can save them.

I think when Christians talk about reaching the culture, we sometimes don't want to reach it for the sake of God as much as for ourselves. We want to win for winning's sake. We want acceptance because we're tired of looking foolish. We want success as the world defines it. We want a loser-free church that is hip and sophisticated.

But none of this squares with what Jesus told us about his kingdom. He didn't tell us to aim for numbers or adoring crowds or cultural acceptance. He told us just to love him, love each other, and love the world by telling them about him.

I want to learn to be faithful to the two Great Commandments and the Great Commission and leave the results to God. I want to reach the world because I really love God and I really love my neighbor.

I'd like to be part of a church that makes God's list of the most faithful.

Paul says that "through the church" God is making known the truths he had kept hidden for centuries. He says heaven itself leans down to watch in wonder the "manifold wisdom of God" on display in the church (Ephesians 3:9–11).

This part of God's plan leaves me speechless. He chooses to include us. With our flaws—with all our weaknesses, petty jealousies, blind spots, and ignorance—he lets us play a part in his story.

Why are we still here? Why hasn't he brought us home? Why has he given us a mission that seems so hard? so impossible? Because he wants to give us stories to tell around the campfires of heaven. Stories of how he empowered us when we thought we couldn't go on. Stories of how he enabled us to love in the face of opposition, hatred, and even death. Stories of how he used our weak and feeble voices to announce the saving message of the gospel. Stories of how he saved people we thought were beyond saving. Stories of how he orchestrated the crashing chaos of world history so people from every nation and tribe and tongue would be represented in his family on the final day. Stories of how our ineffective churches still managed to put his glory on display.

11

HUMBLE ORTHODOXY

"Here's what deflates my arrogance faster than
anything else: trying to live the truth I have."

A FEW YEARS AGO I was in Seattle with an old friend who had written a
popular book about his personal reflections and experiences with the Christian faith. He began telling me about the letters he was getting from readers.
He said the harshest ones were from people who presented themselves as
"caring about doctrine." Their e-mails were vitriolic, pointing out the theological errors and inconsistencies of what he had written.

My friend isn't a pastor or Bible scholar. He's a poet and a storyteller.
That's part of what makes his writing appealing. Honestly, he did get some
things wrong in his book. I think he knows that. But I saw how hard it was
for him to admit that when the information was coming from people whose
words and attitudes were ugly.

As we've learned, *orthodoxy* means right thinking about God. It's teaching and belief based on the established, proven, cherished truths of the faith.
And *doctrine* is simply Christian teaching. But one of the problems with the
words *orthodoxy* and *doctrine* is that they're usually brought up when someone is being reprimanded. So they've gotten something of a bad reputation,

like an older sibling who is always peeking around the corner, trying to catch you doing something wrong.

I think every generation of Christians faces the temptation to buck orthodoxy for just this reason. Even if we know something is true and right, we don't like others telling us we have to believe it. And if youthful pride weren't enough, the temptation to abandon orthodoxy really intensifies when its advocates are unlikable and meanspirited.

I don't know any other way to say this: sometimes it seems like a lot of the people who care about orthodoxy are jerks.

But why? Does good doctrine necessarily lead to being argumentative, annoying, and arrogant?

———

We've reached the end of this book. If you're new to the Christian faith, some of the Christian beliefs we've explored may have been unfamiliar to you. Or if you've studied doctrine before, perhaps the chapters were mostly a review. But whether our theological knowledge is great or small, we all need to ask a vital question: what will we *do* with the knowledge of God that we have?

Will it lead us to an ever-growing desire to know and love the Lord? Will it practically affect the way we think and live? Will we have the courage to hold on to the truth even when it isn't popular? And how will we express our beliefs? With humility—or with pride?

I don't want to be like the people who wrote angry letters to my friend. At the same time, I don't want to be like well-intentioned people I know who are careless, almost unconcerned about Christian truths. They'd never make others feel uncomfortable about their beliefs, but that's because they believe hardly anything themselves.

Do we have to choose between a zeal for truth and kindness? Does embracing deeply held beliefs require that we let go of humility?

Most people want to choose between the two, but the Bible doesn't give us that option. It tells us that we need both. We need conviction, and we need gentleness. We need orthodoxy, and we need humility.

———

He was young and afraid. What business did he have being a pastor? He wondered sometimes. How could he lead a church being torn by opposition? He wanted to be bold. He wanted to be fearless. He prayed that God would make him so. But he felt so isolated, so completely alone. And then the letter came. Its message must have hit him like a blow to the stomach, knocking the air out of him.

His friend, mentor, and father in the faith was writing to say good-bye. The end was near.

Today we call the letter 2 Timothy. We read it as one of the twenty-seven books of the New Testament. We see crisply printed text divided into four chapters with neatly numbered verses and descriptive subheadings. We read it as someone else's story in a faraway place and time.

But I wonder what it was like for Timothy to read the letter. For him it wasn't someone else's story. It was *his* story. It wasn't long-past history. Timothy read it in the uncertain, terrifying present. "For I am already being poured out as a drink offering," the apostle Paul wrote. "And the time of my departure has come" (4:6).

This time Paul wasn't going to be released from prison. He was going to be executed.

Few things clear away the cobwebs in your mind like the words of a godly man who knows he is about to die. In 2 Timothy, Paul is looking back on a life that will soon be over. He is looking ahead to the unknown future of the fledgling church, which must now struggle on without his guidance. No wonder there is such urgency and emotion in his words.

And what does he choose for his final message? Paul's driving concern is the preservation of the gospel—the heart of Christian orthodoxy. For Paul this isn't about proving someone else wrong, winning an argument, or adding people to his little club. For Paul, orthodoxy makes the difference between life and death, heaven and hell. Whether or not it is faithfully communicated determines if the world will know the saving truth about Jesus Christ.

Paul urges Timothy to stand unashamed on the truth about Jesus's life, suffering, and bodily resurrection. "Remember Jesus Christ, risen from the dead, the offspring of David, as preached in my gospel," he wrote (2:8).

You might think that telling a Christian to "remember Jesus" borders on the unnecessary. Can Christians really forget him? Paul knew they could. And even worse, he knew that they could claim allegiance to Jesus but lose sight of the real meaning of his life and death.

The true message of the gospel was under attack. False teachers parading as Christians had denied it, distorted it, and twisted it to serve their own selfish desires. Paul compared their teaching to gangrene—a disease that rots human flesh into a guacamole-colored open sore and is often remedied by amputation (2:17–18). For Paul the analogy was no exaggeration. A distorted gospel rots the soul.

The only antidote for Timothy, Paul said, was to keep teaching the orthodox truths of the faith that had been passed down to him. "Follow the pattern of the sound words that you have heard from me, in the faith and love that are in Christ Jesus," Paul urged. "By the Holy Spirit who dwells within us, guard the good deposit entrusted to you" (1:13–14).

Some people think of orthodoxy as something lifeless and restrictive—

a paint-by-numbers guide that stifles creativity. But Paul saw it as a treasure. It wasn't a canvas for self-expression. It was a "good deposit," something so precious it needed to be guarded and protected.

Now it was Timothy's job to put on display the beauty of this treasure, to preserve it, and to pass it on unaltered to those who would follow. "What you have heard from me," Paul wrote, "in the presence of many witnesses entrust to faithful men who will be able to teach others also" (2:2).

Reading 2 Timothy reminds me of the sad reality of falsehood and lies. I wish I lived in a world where beliefs were like different flavors of ice cream— no wrong answers, just different options. But that's not the world we live in. We live in a world of truths and lies. We live in a world in which God's true revelation and the smooth words of charlatans and false prophets compete for our attention. A world where there is murder, genocide, and the worship of idols. A world where teachers and writers offer empty hope in human achievement and material possessions (3:1–9). A world filled with evil and an Evil One who is bent on distorting and destroying the truth and those who believe it (1 Peter 5:8).

Love for God and love for neighbor require opposing falsehood. There is nothing more unloving than to be silent in the face of lies that will ruin another person. Sometimes love demands that we say, "This philosophy, no matter how plausible or popular, is not true. This person, no matter how likable, gifted, or well-intentioned, is teaching something that contradicts God's Word; therefore, it is untrue."

Paul modeled this type of love-infused courage—courage that was willing to contend for God's unchanging truth that has once and for all been "delivered to the saints" (Jude 3).

You and I need to be willing to contend for truth. But there's a fine line between contending for truth and being contentious. I think this is why, in his final instruction to Timothy, the old apostle goes out of his way to tell Timothy that even though orthodoxy is important, it's not enough by itself.

Truth matters, but so does our attitude. We have to live and speak and interact with others in a spirit of humility. Paul wrote:

> Have nothing to do with foolish, ignorant controversies; you know that they breed quarrels. And the Lord's servant must not be quarrelsome but kind to everyone, able to teach, patiently enduring evil, correcting his opponents with gentleness. God may perhaps grant them repentance leading to a knowledge of the truth, and they may come to their senses and escape from the snare of the devil, after being captured by him to do his will. (2 Timothy 2:23–26)

I find these words amazing in light of Paul's circumstances. He's about to die. He sees false teachers working to destroy the church. He has been betrayed and abandoned. You would expect him to say, "Nuke the heretics, and don't worry about civilian casualties!" But he doesn't. Instead he says, "Don't be a jerk."

Don't be quarrelsome.

Don't get sidetracked on secondary issues.

Be kind.

Be patient.

When other people are evil, endure it while trusting in God.

When you need to correct someone, do it with gentleness.

Even when Paul was opposing false teachers—the enemies of orthodoxy—he hoped that his correction would bring them to their senses. Maybe he pictured himself standing by as Stephen was murdered (Acts 7:54–60). On that day no one could have imagined that Saul, the destroyer of the church, would become Paul, the defender of the church and an apostle of Christ Jesus. But the risen Lord had rescued him and commissioned him to announce the gospel across the world.

Paul had been shown grace by the Lord. So he did the same toward others, even opponents. He genuinely cared about people who disagreed with him. Even when he fiercely opposed them, he didn't just want to beat them in an argument; he wanted to win them to the truth.

My friend Eric says that what Christians need today is humble orthodoxy. I like that phrase. I think it's a good description of what Paul was telling Timothy to practice. Christians need to have a strong commitment to sound doctrine. We need to be courageous in our stand for biblical truth. But we also need to be gracious in our words and interaction with other people.

Eric says that a lot of Christians today are turned off by orthodoxy because they've never seen it held humbly. I think that's true. Many Christians, especially younger ones, are running from orthodoxy, not so much because of doctrine, but because of the arrogance and divisiveness they associate with those who promote it.

So why do people who care about orthodoxy and doctrine often have a harsh streak? Why is there so much arrogant orthodoxy in the church? The Bible says that " 'knowledge' puffs up, but love builds up" (1 Corinthians 8:1). Ever since the first man and woman in the garden turned from God to gain the sweet, forbidden knowledge offered by the serpent, there has been an inclination in every human heart to pursue knowledge to inflate the self rather than to glorify God.

In his book *The Reason for God,* Tim Keller says that all sin is attempting to find a sense of identity and meaning apart from God. "So, according to the Bible," he writes, "the primary way to define sin is not just the doing of bad things, but the making of good things into *ultimate* things."[1]

Applied to the topic at hand, Keller's point is that if we make a good thing like right theology ultimate—if being right becomes more important to us than God—then our theology is not really about God anymore; it's about us. It becomes the source of our sense of worth and identity. And if theology becomes about us, then we'll despise and demonize those who oppose us.[2]

Knowledge about God that doesn't translate into exalting him in our words, thoughts, and actions will soon become self-exaltation. And then we'll attack anyone who threatens our tiny Kingdom of Self.

If we stand before the awesome knowledge of God's character and our first thought isn't *I am small and unworthy to know the Creator of the universe,* then we should be concerned. Too many of us catch a glimpse of him and think, *Look at me, taking this all in. Think of all the poor fools who have never seen this. God, you're certainly lucky to have me beholding you.*

———

It's regrettable that human sin can distort sound teaching just as it can mess up anything else that's good in the world. But should this cause us to abandon the pursuit and defense of biblical truth?

Paul didn't think so. He spent his last moments of life urging Timothy to hold to the truth about Jesus. And the problems of pride and turf wars wouldn't go away even if we tried to avoid orthodoxy. We'd just find something else to throw at each other. We'd find something else to be proud about.

The solution to arrogant orthodoxy is not less orthodoxy; it's more. If we truly know and embrace orthodoxy, it should humble us. When we know the truth about God—his power, his greatness, his holiness, his mercy—it doesn't leave us boasting; it leaves us amazed. It doesn't lead to a preoccupation with being right but to amazement that we have been rescued.

Genuine orthodoxy—the heart of which is the death of God's Son for undeserving sinners—is the most humbling, human-pride-smashing message in the world. And if we truly know the gospel of grace, it will create in us a heart of humility and grace toward others. Francis Schaeffer, a Christian writer and thinker from the twentieth century, modeled this kind of profound compassion. He genuinely loved people. And even as he analyzed and critiqued the culture, he did so "with a tear in his eye."[3]

That is humble orthodoxy. It's standing for truth with a tear in our eye. It's telling a friend living in sexual sin that we love her even as we tell her that her sexual activity is disobedient to God. It's remembering that angry, unkind opponents of the gospel are human beings created in the image of God who need the same mercy he has shown us. It's remembering that when we're arrogant and self-righteous in the way we represent orthodoxy, we're actually contradicting with our lives what we claim to believe.

But while we shouldn't be mean and spiteful in representing biblical truth, neither should we apologize for believing that God has been clear in his Word. The humility we need in our theology is first and foremost a humility before God. As pastor Mark Dever puts it, "Humble theology [is] theology which submits itself to the truth of God's Word."[4] This is a good reminder for me. Because I think it's possible for me, or anyone for that matter, to overreact to arrogant orthodoxy with a brand of squishy theology that believes others are arrogant if they think the Bible teaches anything clearly.

But truth can be known. And what the Bible teaches should be obeyed. Just because we can't know God exhaustively doesn't mean we can't know him truly (Psalm 19:7–10; John 17:17). Just because there is mystery in God's Word doesn't mean we can pretend God hasn't spoken clearly in the Bible.

"Christian humility," Dever writes, "is to simply accept whatever God has revealed in His Word. Humility is following God's Word wherever it goes, as far as it goes, *not* either going beyond it or stopping short of it.... The humility we want in our churches is to read the Bible and believe it.... It is not humble to be hesitant where God has been clear and plain."[5]

I won't pretend that I've arrived at humble orthodoxy. When I gain a bit of theological knowledge, I all too frequently can get puffed up with pride. But I'll tell you what deflates my arrogance and self-righteousness faster than anything else: trying to live whatever truth I have.

Do you want to keep your orthodoxy humble? Try to live it. Don't spend all your time theorizing about it, debating about it, or blogging about it. Spend more energy living the truth you know than worrying about what the next guy does or doesn't know. Don't measure yourself by what you know. Measure yourself by your practice of what you know.

Do I know something of the doctrine of God? Can I list his attributes of sovereignty, omnipotence, and love? Then I should live that truth and stop worrying and complaining and being anxious.

Do I know something of the doctrine of justification? Can I tell you that I'm justified by grace alone through faith alone in Christ alone? Good. Then I should live that truth by repenting of my worthless efforts to earn God's approval. I should weep over my self-righteousness when I think and act toward others as if I'm anything but the recipient of pure, unmerited grace.

Do I know something about the doctrine of sanctification? Do I know the priority of holiness and the reality of remaining sin in my life? Then why attack or look down on another Christian who seems less sanctified? I have enough areas where I need to grow to keep me busy. I should pray for more of the Holy Spirit's power to enable *me* to grow in obedience.

Here's a useful exercise. Go back over the doctrines we've studied in this book, and think about the real-world, real-life implications of each truth for your life. What would it look like to live the truth of each one? What would change about your relationships, your words, your attitudes, and your actions?

I think this is what Paul was telling Timothy to do when he said, "Watch your life and doctrine closely. Persevere in them, because if you do, you will save both yourself and your hearers" (1 Timothy 4:16, NIV). It's not enough to get our doctrine straight. Life and doctrine can't be separated. Our lives either put the beauty of God's truth on display, or they obscure it.

———

It helps me to remember that one day in heaven there will be only one right person.

I'm sorry, but it won't be you. Or me.

It will be God.

Everybody else in heaven will be wrong in a million different ways about a million different things. The Bible tells us that only those who trusted in Jesus Christ, who turned from sin and believed in him, will be in God's presence. But on a host of secondary matters, we'll all discover how much we got wrong.

Maybe some people picture heaven as a place where all the "right" people celebrate that they made it. But I don't think that's true. I think it will be a place of beautiful humility.

The funny thing is, I'm really looking forward to this aspect of heaven. I can't wait for that crystal-clear awareness of all the opinions and attitudes and ideas and strategies that I had in this life that were quite simply wrong.

No one will be proud. No one will be bragging. We all will want to talk about how wrong we were about so many things and how kind God was to us. I can imagine someone saying, "Seriously, I am the most unworthy person here."

And then someone else will say, "No, friend, it took more grace for me to be here. You need to hear my story."

And we'll say, "No offense, King David, but we've already heard your story. Let somebody else share." (Of course we'll let him share again later.)

At the end of every conversation, we'll agree that when we were back on the old earth, we really had no idea how unmerited that grace really is. We called it grace, but we didn't really think it was totally grace. We thought we'd added just a tad of something good. That we had earned just a bit. We'll realize to our shame that to differing degrees we trusted in our intellect, our morality, the rightness of our doctrine, and our religious performance when all along it was completely grace.

"For by grace you have been saved through faith. And this is not your own doing; it is the gift of God, not a result of works, so that no one may boast" (Ephesians 2:8–9).

Every one of us will have a lot to apologize for.

I estimate that somewhere near the first ten thousand years of heaven will be taken up with the redeemed people of God apologizing to each other for all the ways we judged each other, jostled for position, were proud and divisive and arrogant toward each other. (Of course this is just an estimate; it could be the first twenty thousand years.)

I imagine Paul telling Barnabas he's sorry for splitting up the team over Mark. And admitting to Mark how he should have been more willing to give him another chance. And then all the Christians from first-century Corinth will tell Paul how bad they feel about what a complete pain they were for him.

All the people in churches who split over silly things like organ music will come together and hug each other. The Baptists and Presbyterians will get together, and one side will have to admit to the other side that they were wrong about baptism. And then the side that was right will say they're sorry for their pride and all the snide comments they made. And then there will be no more sides, and the whole thing will be forgotten.

Because of course we'll all be happy to forgive each other. And we'll keep saying, "But God used it for good. We couldn't see it then, but he was at work even in our weakness and sin."

In the meantime, we should strive to hold our beliefs with a charity and kindness that won't embarrass us in heaven.

The air of heaven will blow away the fog that so often clouds our vision in this life. In eternity we'll see the silliness of self-righteousness and quarreling over the nonessentials. But we'll also see with piercing clarity just how essential the essentials really are. We'll see just how precious the truths of the gospel really are.

We will look into each other's eyes, and we won't be able to stop saying, "It was all true! It was all true!" Every word. Every promise.

We'll see that the Cross really conquered death and hell and washed away our sins. We'll see the everlasting reward of believing in Jesus and the eternal hell of rejecting him. We'll look back on our lives and see that God never did forsake us. Not even for a split second. That he was with us every moment—even the darkest moments of despair and seeming hopelessness. We will know in a deeper way than we can now imagine that God truly worked *all* things together for our good. And we'll see that Jesus really did go to prepare a place for us, just as he said.

And everything we did for the sake of Jesus will be so worth it. Every time we stood for truth and looked foolish. Every time we shared the gospel. Every act of service. Every sacrifice.

We will meet men and women from every nation of the old earth who gave their lives in the cause of the gospel—martyrs who died rather than abandon the unchanging truths of the faith. We'll meet people who lost homes and family and whose bodies were whipped and tortured and burned because they refused to renounce the name of Jesus. And we will honor them, and all will see that what they lost and suffered was nothing in comparison to what they gained.

No one will say, "I wish I'd believed less. I wish I'd cared less about the gospel."

———

Jesus said that people who come to him and hear his words and put them into practice are like a man building a house who dug down deep and laid the foundation on rock. When a flood came and a torrent broke against the house, it couldn't be shaken (Luke 6:46–49, NIV).

As we go about our daily lives—eating, sleeping, studying, working our jobs, falling in love, starting families, and raising children—we all believe specific things about what matters in life, about what our purpose is in this world. In one way or another we all believe something about God.

Our lives are like houses. And each one is built on some foundation of belief. The question is whether what we believe is true—whether it will withstand the flood of suffering in this life, the torrent of death, and the final judgment before our Creator.

Jesus said that an unshakable foundation for life is found only in knowing him, in believing his words and living by his truth. The most important question any of us can ask is, Am I building my life on who Jesus is and what he has done? Is my life built on the rock of a true knowledge of God?

Being grounded on that rock doesn't make you or me better than anyone else. It should make us aware of how dependent we are. It should humble us. The only thing that enables us to stand firm is Jesus and his words. The only thing that enables us to know and dwell with God is the solid rock of the Savior.

The message of Christian orthodoxy isn't that I'm right and someone else is wrong. It's that I am wrong and yet God is filled with grace. I am wrong, and yet God has made a way for me to be forgiven and accepted and loved for eternity. I am wrong, and yet God gave his Son, Jesus, to die in my place and receive my punishment. I am wrong, but through faith in Jesus, I can be made right before a holy God.

This is the gospel. This is the truth that all Christian doctrine celebrates. This is the truth that every follower of Jesus Christ is called to cherish and preserve. Even die for. It is the only truth on which we can build our lives and rest our eternal hope.

A REFLECTION
AND DISCUSSION GUIDE
FOR *DUG DOWN DEEP*

You can use this guide, written by Thomas Womack, to help you sort out and deepen your thoughts and reactions to what you read, chapter by chapter, in *Dug Down Deep.* It's meant for your personal study or—even better—for a group setting, with others who are motivated to sincerely engage with the message of the book. We don't expect you to use every question; choose the ones that best fit your needs. Our hope is that these questions will spark lively and insightful discussion as you explore what it means to build your life on truths that last.

Chapter 1, "My Rumspringa"
1. On page 5 of this opening chapter, Josh recalls years past when he "didn't know or fear God"; he was void of "any driving desire to know him." How closely does that description match any period in your life? If you remember such a time, what other phrases would accurately describe your life in those days?
2. In his twenties, recognizing his "spiritual deficiencies," Josh played the blame game (pages 5–6). If you've ever done the same regarding your spiritual shortcomings, who did you blame, and why?
3. "I wasn't listening," Josh says (page 6) about the sermons he heard in his teenage years. From what you know of his story, why was that true? What caused it?

4. In the church where he now serves as a pastor, Josh sees young adults who remind him of himself in high school—"church kids who know so much about Christian religion and yet so little about God" (page 6). If you were to get acquainted with some of those young adults, what would you want to ask them or say to them?

5. Josh's friend Curtis talks about today's "me-ology"—so many people thinking only of themselves (page 10). How extensively do you see that happening in our culture? Do you see it much in the people you know best? How about in yourself?

6. In various ways Josh emphasizes that how we view God has a forceful impact on every aspect of our lives (see especially pages 10–11). It's a sweeping assertion. How do you react to it? Do you find yourself easily agreeing with him or not? What questions does this bring to mind?

7. On page 11, Josh makes his key point in this chapter: "We're all theologians. The question is whether what we know about God is true." Realistically and practically, how does a person determine whether his or her beliefs about God are accurate? How can people identify any personal misconceptions about God?

8. At the top of page 13, Josh quotes these words from God: "Stand by the roads, and look, and ask for the ancient paths, where the good way is; and walk in it, and find rest for your souls" (from Jeremiah 6:16 in the Bible). What was your response to reading those words? Reflecting further on them, what do you find appealing or troubling or intriguing in those words?

9. "Every new generation of Christians," Josh says (page 15), "has to ask the question, what are we actually choosing when we

choose to be Christians?" How would you answer that question? How might others answer it?

10. Ultimately, Josh says, "it has to be about a person—the historical and living person of Jesus Christ" (page 15). What's the significance of using both these words: *historical* and *living*?

11. Josh talks here about the words *theology, doctrine,* and *orthodoxy.* How comfortable are you with using those terms as Josh defines them?

12. Look back at page 4. Josh wondered about the Amish teens who, after their rumspringa, decided to return to traditional Amish life. Instead of pursuing God, were they choosing "just a safe and simple way of life"? When can "safe and simple" be a good choice for life? When can it be a bad choice?

Chapter 2, "In Which I Learn to Dig"

1. Chapter 2 opens with the parable Jesus told about two builders. Josh mentions in particular (on page 18) the question Jesus asked as he started this story: "Why do you call me Lord but don't do what I say?" Josh adds, "That question makes me uncomfortable because I can't pretend I don't understand it. And I feel that he's talking to me." What's your response to that question from Jesus?

2. "It's possible," Josh says (page 19), "to base our confidence and trust—the very footing of our lives—on what is insecure and faulty. On shifting sand." By contrast, imagine someone who "built" his or her life on a truly stable foundation. What would that person's life look like, in your opinion? How would you describe it?

3. At the bottom of page 19, Josh defines what "being a Christian means." Look back at what he states there. Which parts of his description would most closely match your life? Which parts less obviously describe you?

4. For understanding the Bible's teachings, Josh commends the kind of effort that includes "thinking and reading and grappling with sometimes challenging truths" (page 20). What helps you the most to become mentally engaged in something to that degree?

5. "But the hardest work of all," Josh goes on to say, "is putting the truth into practice.... Truth requires action." Do you think that last statement is accurate? To what extent do you agree with it? Are some aspects of truth meant only for our minds and hearts?

6. On pages 21–29, Josh describes his experience of positive spiritual growth in the years after high school. How would you characterize what was going on in his mind and heart and life?

7. What events and experiences in this part of Josh's story are similar to what has happened (or is happening now) in your spiritual journey?

8. What aspects of Josh's personal story in this chapter are the most different from your experience?

9. Josh emphasizes (on page 30) that being personally drawn to Jesus in our hearts must be "the first and final motivation" as we explore the Bible's teachings. But he adds, "We can't know him and relate to him in the right way without doctrine" (page 31). Does a statement like that seem to make Jesus more attractive or less attractive? Why?

10. Josh further defines doctrine (on page 31) as "the meaning of the story God is writing in the world. It's the explanation of what he's done and why he's done it and why it matters to you and me." For you personally, what are the most important things you sense and know already about "the story God is writing in the world"?

11. Tragic suffering is Josh's theme on pages 32–33. When such hardship comes our way, he says, "firsthand knowledge of God's character and love is the only thing that can hold us." Throughout history many believers in God have said much the same thing about their suffering. But other people have pointed to such tragedies as an indication of God's lack of love or power—or even as evidence for his nonexistence. What explanation can you give for such opposite reactions to suffering?

12. When someone lives out biblical doctrine "with joy and humility," the result, Josh observes, is "beautiful" (page 33). He says it can also bring something into *your* life that's "good and beautiful" and "firm and trustworthy." To what extent do you believe this can be true for you?

Chapter 3, "Near but Not in My Pocket"

1. When you look in a mirror to check your appearance, what's your typical expression? Describe your "mirror face" in a few words or phrases.

2. Josh suggests that "our overwhelming self-centeredness" causes us special difficulty in learning more about God. Do you think that's true for most of us? Why or why not?

3. Because of our self-centeredness, we often end up seeing God "in our own image," Josh says (page 39). What examples of this have you recognized in yourself or in your friends?

4. Josh discusses the "Divine Butler" and "Cosmic Therapist" images of God (pages 40–41) and says these concepts mirror to some degree how he has viewed God. For young people especially, what would be particularly attractive about these perceptions of God?

5. On pages 41–42, Josh summarizes things the Bible tells us about God—things that reveal him to be "utterly and wonderfully different" from us. What would be the value and benefit to someone who clearly recognizes this distinctiveness about God?

6. Reflect again on that listing of some of God's attributes on pages 41–42. Which help you the most to understand who God is and what he's like?

7. Keeping in mind Josh's story from his single days (on pages 43–44), describe some significant details in your background and circumstances that you're sure God was always in control of.

8. Are you ever tempted to take God's love for granted? In what specific ways do you think God wants us to recognize and appreciate his love?

9. Josh discusses (on pages 46–48) how God is "God-centered" and how this concept unsettled him deeply at first. Why can this be difficult for us to accept?

10. Josh explains on pages 49–50 that "God is both *transcendent* and *immanent*." How would you express in your own words these seemingly opposite concepts?

11. Of God's myriad qualities, which ones seem most awesome and amazing to you?

12. How clearly and strongly do you sense that God is personally inviting you to know him better?

Chapter 4, "Ripping, Burning, Eating"

1. "Does Scripture have the authority to tell us how to live?" Josh asks (page 55). What answers would your friends give to that question? If you pressed the issue with them, what reasons would they likely give for their answers? What do you think has influenced their perspectives?

2. Has your view of the Bible evolved over time? If so, what are some of the ways you've looked at the Bible in the past?

3. "The Bible presents itself," Josh observes, "as a living communication from a personal God to the human race—more specifically to *you*" (page 55). What do you think he means by "living communication"?

4. Josh describes the Bible as "the foundation of every...Christian belief" (page 56). In what specific ways is the Bible the foundation of your beliefs about God? What other foundations are there for your beliefs, practically speaking?

5. Josh also states that apart from the Bible ("God's Word"), "there is no genuine spirituality" (page 57). Many people in our culture today would disagree with that statement. But from Josh's perspective, why is it a true declaration? And how true and applicable is it for you?

6. Recalling his own perceptions from childhood, Josh cites the "fairly common" view of the Bible as "a bunch of disconnected stories sprinkled with wise advice and capped off with the inspirational life of Jesus" (page 58). How closely does that match your impressions of the Bible, past or present?

7. Josh speaks of the Bible's "story line…from start to finish" (page 58). He also quotes at length a description of this story line as given in the introduction to a children's book by Sally Lloyd-Jones. Look again at her words (quoted on pages 59–60). What elements in her description are most compelling to you?

8. From your perspective, why would it be particularly beneficial and enjoyable to recognize the Bible as a single, unified story?

9. Josh says that God's purpose behind all the Bible's stories and teachings is *relationship*—with us! (See page 61.) In what meaningful ways have you sensed that purpose coming from the Bible's pages?

10. Josh is confident that the Bible is fully trustworthy as God's Word (see pages 61–63). How valid are his stated reasons for such confidence?

11. What do you think it means to really "hear" God in the Bible, as Josh says in this chapter?

12. Josh emphasizes how much God has revealed to us in Scripture. Then he says, "The question is, will we listen? Will we obey when we don't like what the Bible has to say?" (page 65). What influences and convictions will determine your answers to that?

13. Josh describes the Scriptures by using three key terms on pages 68–69: *inerrancy, clarity,* and *sufficiency.* How do these terms relate uniquely to the Bible? Try expressing what they mean in your own words.

14. Think again of those three concepts explained on pages 68–69. Why would each be important in determining the authority the Bible has in a person's life?

15. Josh mentions (on pages 69–71) the prophet Jeremiah's experience of "eating" God's words. Does such an expression seem strange—or a good fit? How are those terms appropriate for describing our intake of Scripture?

16. "The Bible is the story of what God has done for us," Josh says (page 72). How convinced are you that the Bible is the story of what God has done—and will do—for *you* personally? What questions do you have in your mind and heart about this?

Chapter 5, "God with a Bellybutton"

1. What do your friends think of Jesus? How do they view him?

2. What would you say are the most common ways that our culture views Jesus?

3. What has influenced your perspective of Jesus?

4. To learn more about Jesus from the Bible, Josh speaks of exploring (a) the *person* of Christ and (b) the *work* of Christ. These two approaches "are meant to be kept together," Josh says. "You can't grasp the significance of either without the other" (page 76). Would the same be true for studying any great person from history? Or is Jesus different in that regard?

5. Josh gives a brief biography of Jesus on pages 76–78. Was any of this new information for you? Which aspects of his biography do you view as most significant?

6. "Jesus Christ is the most famous, most powerful, most controversial and revolutionary figure in all human history," Josh says (page 78). Do you think this will always be true or not? What historical figures or current celebrities might eclipse the fame and influence of Jesus in the future, in your opinion?

7. Josh says that the question *Who is Jesus?* "divides the human race" (page 78). In what ways do you think that is true?

8. On pages 78–79, Josh mentions a few "false teachings" about Jesus that have sprung up over the centuries. Do any of these still get traction today? In what ways might some of them have particular appeal today?

9. Josh describes Jesus as being "fully God and fully man in one person forever" (page 80). Why would that be significant? Why would it be important to grasp?

10. On pages 80–82, Josh cites a number of scriptures to support the conclusion that Jesus is "truly God." For you, which of these scriptures are the most helpful and the most influential in understanding Jesus? Which are the most remarkable and interesting? And what questions do they raise?

11. Josh says that God becoming man—in the form of Jesus—"is, without question, the greatest miracle recorded in Scripture" (page 82). In your own opinion, why is it so miraculous?

12. On pages 83–84, Josh again cites a number of scriptures, this time to support the concept that Jesus is "fully man." Which of these help you the most in understanding Jesus? Which are the most intriguing and interesting to you? What questions do they raise?

13. Josh mentions our common tendency to want to "experience" Jesus but not to study Jesus (page 85). Can you relate? Why do you think this tendency is widespread?

14. Ultimately, Josh says, a "feeling-driven approach to Jesus…produces the opposite of what we actually want." Citing the influence of his friend C.J., Josh goes on to say, "If you want to feel deeply, you have to think deeply.… True emotion—emotion

that is reliable and doesn't lead us astray—is always a response to reality, to truth" (page 86). Which truths about Jesus trigger the strongest emotions for you?

15. "Jesus never asks us how we feel about him," Josh states. "He calls us to believe in him, to trust in him" (page 86). What's your response to that?

16. On page 86, Josh transitions from the person of Jesus to the work of Jesus. How would you summarize this work, as Josh presents it on page 87? And what's so significant about this work?

17. The discussion goes cosmic on page 88 as Josh gets into God's highest purpose for the universe he's created. Again, how would you summarize this purpose as presented here? And how would you explain the significance of it?

18. Josh speaks of God's plan for dealing with mankind's sin (on pages 89–90). As Josh unfolds it here, what is crucial about the role Jesus plays in that plan?

19. Have you ever shared Josh's desire to go back in time to meet the man Jesus in person? If so, what prompted that desire in you?

20. Do you agree with what Josh says in the last paragraph of this chapter? Can you honestly say the same thing, word for word, about yourself? Why or why not?

Chapter 6, "A Way to Be Good Again"

1. At the beginning of this chapter, Josh tells the story of his dream and what led up to it. In what ways can you identify with Josh's experiences?

2. "Why did he have to die? What did Jesus accomplish through his death on the cross? What was happening as he hung there

between heaven and earth? And what effect does his death have on you and me today? What does it change?" Josh asks those deep questions at the top of page 98. After reading this chapter, what do you see as the best answers to them?

3. On page 99, Josh describes a vivid memory of when, as a young teenager, he realized, *I don't understand why Jesus had to die.* Can you recall a specific moment when you came to the same realization? If so, how did it affect you?

4. Why is the death of Jesus so huge in the historic meaning of Christianity? And what questions, if any, does this raise for you?

5. What is the meaning of the word *atonement* in this chapter? What does he mean by it, as far as you can tell? (See especially pages 98 and 102.)

6. On pages 100–101, Josh brings in "the Trinitarian nature of God" and why knowing about it is necessary for understanding what Jesus has done for us. How would you state in your own words the connection between the Trinitarian nature of God and Jesus's sacrifice for us?

7. Why does Josh say it's wrong to view Jesus on the cross as a "victim" (page 101)?

8. As Josh explains it on pages 102–4, what should each human being understand about his or her sinfulness and guilt? Do you accept and agree with the line of reasoning Josh presents here? What questions does it raise for you?

9. "We all want to think of ourselves as basically good people," Josh says. "But we can believe that illusion only because we forget most of our past decisions and actions and thoughts" (page 106). How accurately does that describe you?

10. On pages 106–8, Josh explores the sacrificial nature of the death of Jesus. It reflects "the principle of atonement through substitutionary death" (page 106). How would you explain in your own words what Josh is talking about on these pages?

11. Amir's story from Khaled Hosseini's novel *The Kite Runner* prompts this question from Josh: "Can any of us ever atone for our past wrongs like this?" (page 110). How would you answer that question? And how do you respond to Amir's story?

12. On pages 111–12, Josh explains the theological doctrines of *penal substitution* and *propitiation*. What does he mean by these concepts? How helpful are they in understanding what Jesus has done, and in what way?

13. Josh closes this chapter with Jenny's story (pages 113–15). In what ways can you relate to Jenny?

14. What does this chapter's key phrase *a way to be good again* mean for you? What do you *want* it to mean? As you're aware of how you're responding in your mind and heart to the message of this chapter, try expressing your reflections and thoughts in a prayer to God.

Chapter 7, "How Jesus Saved Gregg Eugene Harris"

1. Do you have friends or acquaintances who are like Gregg Eugene Harris in some way? How are they like him? Are *you* like him in any way?

2. Why do you think the words of the "two Jesus freaks" had such an impact on Gregg, as described on page 118?

3. In your opinion, how appropriate and relevant are the phrases "living water" and "good news" in describing what Jesus has done? (Josh uses them on page 119.)

4. What do you see as the most important factors that shaped Gregg's childhood? How do they compare with the most important influences in your background?

5. From your perspective, what seems to be our culture's general understanding of what it means to "get saved"?

6. In your own words, how would you define God's grace?

7. On pages 125–26, Josh cites a number of scriptures to support the conclusion that we're all incapable of doing anything to bring about our salvation. Which of these scriptures are the most helpful for you on this topic? And what questions do they raise?

8. On page 126, Josh mentions a phrase Jesus used: "the poor in spirit." Josh explains it as "people who know they can't save themselves, people who realize their spiritual poverty and help-lessness." To what extent does that describe the way you view yourself?

9. Josh says on page 126 that because God does all the work of making salvation possible for us, then "*no one* is beyond hope.... It means God can save anyone." Do you agree with his conclusion? Does it seem unfair in any way? Why or why not?

10. On pages 129–31, Josh writes about the doctrine of *regeneration,* or being "born again." As Josh outlines it, what does this involve?

11. Have you ever shared Gregg's desire to make yourself into a "good Christian" or even a "great Christian"? If so, what prompted this desire? How did you act on it? And how did it work out?

12. Josh speaks (on page 133) of a "heavenly calling" and says that it "distinguishes all genuine Christians." If Josh is right about that, what does that fact say about your own life?

13. Have you ever felt God "chasing" you, as Gregg did? If so, describe that experience.

14. On pages 136–37, Josh speaks of repentance and faith as being "two sides of the same coin." What does he mean by that? As you understand it, what is repentance? What is faith?

15. Two more theological terms pop up on pages 138–40—*justification* and *adoption*. What does he mean by them? How well do you understand them?

16. What surprises you most in Gregg Harris's story?

17. Josh closes this chapter by reflecting on "how mighty God's salvation really is" (page 142). Have you thought about that before? As you see it, what's so "mighty" about the way God saves people?

Chapter 8, "Changed, Changing, to Be Changed"

1. After talking about "Dave," the guy whose story was featured in the radio program, Josh asks (on pages 148–49), "Can you relate to Dave's story?... Have you ever wondered why you still want to sin?... Does God really change people?" How would you answer those questions?

2. Josh introduces the theological concept of *sanctification* on page 149. What does he want us to understand about this term? How could you illustrate the process of sanctification to explain it to someone else?

3. "I think it's safe to say that no doctrine is more practical than sanctification," Josh states (page 150). What's practical about it?

4. Josh offers "a big question" on page 151: "Why is this process of changing so stinking hard? Why is it so painful? Why do

Christians still struggle with sin?" What help does Josh offer for answering those questions in the pages that follow?

5. Josh's key terms on page 153 are *already* and *not yet.* What's the significance of these words as they relate to this chapter's topic?

6. This chapter's title—"Changed, Changing, to Be Changed"— reflects the three-part process that Josh explains on pages 153–54. How would you explain these three stages in your own words?

7. How do you understand the concept of *indwelling sin* (or *remaining sin*), as Josh describes it on page 154? (See also pages 164–65.)

8. Do the drawings and captions further your understanding of what Josh is trying to communicate? What specific help do they offer? What further questions do they prompt?

9. Which of those nine illustrated points (pages 155–63) are the hardest for you to fully grasp?

10. "We aren't equally holy," Josh writes (on page 165). "While one Christian is not more justified than another, some Christians are more like Jesus than others." If that's true, so what? What difference would it make to you?

11. Josh then quotes this scripture: "Work out your own salvation with fear and trembling, for it is God who works in you, both to will and to work for his good pleasure" (Philippians 2:12–13). What would obeying that scripture mean for you? How would you go about it?

12. Josh says that our culture "has effectively pretended away sin" (page 166). Have you recognized this cultural tendency as well? In what ways do you see it?

13. As evidence for how we make light of sin, Josh points to the typical ways we apologize. We "pretend, blame, and excuse all sin away" (page 167). How have you observed this to be true, in your life and in others around you?

14. Keeping in mind the things Josh talks about in this chapter, what do you think is required to have a constructive, honest view of the sin in your life?

15. How convinced are you that God wants you to overcome the sin in your life? To the best of your understanding, how does God want you to do this?

16. In the matter of obedience to God and holiness in our lives, Josh says this: "Christian growth…has to be defined by becoming like Jesus. It has to be rooted in relationship to him. And it has to be built on real, Bible-rooted conviction" (page 170). What exactly does such conviction involve? Where does it come from?

17. "The Christian life is about putting on new behavior," Josh writes, "clothing ourselves with Jesus himself" (page 171). Earlier in the same paragraph he says, "Becoming like Jesus isn't just a matter of not doing wrong. It's a matter of actively 'doing' righteousness. It's pursuing obedience." If this is what God is looking for in the lives of his children, then what kinds of questions should Christians ask themselves about their actions and behavior?

18. In your prayers do you often address God as "Father"? Why or why not?

19. What kind of Father is God to you? How does he help you understand more deeply that you're his child?

20. Josh ends the chapter by stating that "sanctification is work. But it's good work. It's work enabled by the Holy Spirit. It's the privilege of the redeemed. It's the great honor of God's adopted children to work to be like their Father." What does that "good work" include for you in the immediate future?

Chapter 9, "I Believe in the Holy Spirit"

1. What are the most important beliefs you've formed about the Holy Spirit? Where did these beliefs come from?

2. In the opening pages of this chapter, Josh acknowledges that topics related to the Holy Spirit have been part of a decades-old controversy among many churches, leaving some people "with mainly negative impressions. This isn't a healthy state of affairs," Josh concludes. "Whenever we live some part of our faith in reaction to anything other than God's Word, we become unbalanced and misguided. We shouldn't neglect the person and work of the Holy Spirit just because other people have misrepresented him." He goes on to say that choosing "to give careful thought and attention to the Holy Spirit" is "a decision to be a faithful disciple of Jesus Christ and a student of God's Word." Think about that. Is this a choice and decision that *you* want to make? If so, what is your motivation?

3. After reading Josh's discussion on pages 179–80, how would you explain the Holy Spirit's role in the Trinity?

4. According to the story from his past that Josh relates on pages 181–82, what prompted him to seek a better understanding of the Holy Spirit? What were the crucial elements in his experience? And how do these relate to your experiences and desires to better understand the Holy Spirit?

5. Josh says that in looking back on his experiences in those years, he had "a very narrow understanding of how and why the Holy Spirit works in people's lives" (page 183). What seemed to be narrow about it? How did it need to broaden and expand?

6. From his discussion on pages 184–86, how would you characterize Josh's beliefs and convictions and attitudes about such spiritual gifts as tongues, prophecy, and healing?

7. On page 186, Josh speaks of the Holy Spirit as "a gift that infinitely surpasses" the greatest prayer request you could ever make to God. Why is the Holy Spirit such a surpassingly great gift to us?

8. Josh says on page 187 that "there is no such thing as normal or nonsupernatural Christian living. Every day of faith is a day of the supernatural work of the Spirit in our lives." What encouragement do you find in that statement? What other reactions do you have to it?

9. How do you respond to Dan Wallace's story that Josh relates on pages 188–89? Can you identify with him in any way? Why or why not?

10. Josh says that the Holy Spirit "works in our hearts, in our affections and emotions," and that he "mediates the presence of Jesus Christ to us" (page 190). It is, he says, "wonderful, mysterious work" (page 191). To what extent can you say that the Holy Spirit has done this work in your heart?

11. Josh closes this chapter by emphasizing that "the ultimate aim of the Spirit's encouragement, comfort, and help" is "to enable us to know and see the glory of the Savior" (page 192). How would you explain Josh's point in your own words?

Chapter 10, "The Invisible Made Visible"

1. Josh mentions hearing on the radio about an atheist child who wondered why God didn't "just appear and say, 'Hello, I'm God. Believe in me!'" Josh said he laughed because he could relate to her question. But then he realized that if God did something like that, it would be "silly." Do you agree? What would be silly about it?

2. This chapter's title refers to God's people—his children, Christians, the church. It's through them, Josh says, that God "proves himself and displays himself" (page 197). Why do you think God chose such a strategy?

3. Josh says this is a hard concept for us to appreciate because of our frequent disillusionment and disappointment with God's people. "Pushing past all this can be difficult. But we have to try" (page 197). Why, from Josh's perspective, do we "have to try"? And to what extent do you agree with him?

4. At the bottom of page 197, Josh mentions several words used in Scripture for the church. How do these words demonstrate God's care for his people?

5. On pages 198–99, Josh relates how he viewed his faith "in a very individualistic way" for twenty years, without much regard for the church. He suggests that his experience "describes a good number of Christians today, and they are abandoning the church." Notice again his thoughts on the reason for this: "My guess is that a vast majority of Christians who have lost their vision for the church are like I was: they've never taken the time to study what the Bible says about God's purpose and plan for the church. Instead, they're living their lives guided by their feelings or experience. They're pragmatic, so they're focused

more on what 'works' than on what Scripture dictates. They're consumers who approach church asking, 'What's in it for me?'" To what extent does that describe your attitude or your friends' attitudes toward church?

6. On pages 199–201, Josh relates the biblical big picture of how Christians together fulfill God's ancient promises to the forefathers of Israel. "The church," he writes, "comprised of men and women from every nationality and ethnicity, is now God's chosen people in the world. The church is how God makes himself known in the world" (page 201). What responsibilities do you think go along with this "chosen people" status for believers today?

7. Josh talks about his growing realization that "the journey of the Christian faith was supposed to be made *with* other believers" (page 203). Why would this be true about our spiritual journey? Why can't we progress just as well on our own?

8. "So exactly what makes a church a church?" Josh asks (page 203). How does he answer that question? What are the essentials?

9. Another question from Josh: "Does it matter that we belong to a specific local church?" What's the best answer to this?

10. Josh describes on pages 205–7 how he first threw himself into the life of a local church and the surprising things he discovered. What seem to be the most critical lessons he learned?

11. Josh says, "I can trace every example of growth and change in my life to the help of fellow Christians" (206–7). Is the same true for you, spiritually speaking? Do you expect it to be a true statement about you in the future?

12. Another Josh question: "What is God's mission for his church?" (page 207). How would you answer that? What does God want to accomplish through his church?

13. On page 208, Josh admits to being scared by the mission Jesus has given his church. What are his reasons for this fear? How logical are they, in your opinion? To what degree do you share those fears?

14. Also on page 208, Josh speaks of "a heart to reach the world," while on the following page he mentions having a "consecrated" heart, one that's inwardly set "apart for God's use." Are these ultimately the same thing? Why or why not?

15. Josh reminds us, "Jesus said that Christians are to be like salt and light in the world" (page 209). What does that mean to you?

16. Are you willing to think of yourself as a "missionary" for Christ to the people in your community? If that were true about you, toss yourself the questions Josh poses on page 210: "What decisions would I make about where I live or how much I need to live on? Where would I spend my time so I could form friendships with unbelieving people? What would I seek to learn about the culture so I could befriend and clearly communicate the gospel? What are the idols and false gods people are worshiping?"

17. Josh urges a "love-motivated mission" for the church, fueled by the love of God: "Only this love can compel us to lay down our lives caring for the poor, marginalized, and oppressed of the world. Only this love will give us the sustained courage to go into the world to speak the foolish, unwanted, yet saving message of a crucified Messiah.... Mission has to be the overflow of a love for God that aches to see others experiencing his grace, love, and compassion for people who are lost and destined for hell" (page 211). Think about your experience of God's love through Jesus. What is that love compelling you to do? What is it about this love that draws you into serving others?

18. The message Josh gives on page 212 is difficult. Listen to it again: "Jesus asks something much harder of his followers— something that takes much more courage and sacrifice. It's a mission that requires divine empowerment. He tells us to die to ourselves and live for him. He tells us to lay down our lives in the service of people who often despise us. He tells us to fully engage in a world that wants to seduce us and that hates us when we resist. He sends his church to plead with a culture that loves its sin. Jesus asks us to die." In order to commit your life to this kind of "slow death" for the sake of Jesus and his good news of salvation for the world, what will have to be true in your heart and mind?

19. On pages 212–14, Josh seeks out God's definition of success for the church. Do you agree with the conclusion he reaches? How much does that conclusion match what "success" means to you?

20. After reading this chapter, what do you most want to hear from God and to talk with him about? Allow your thoughts and requests and questions to come together in brief sentences of prayer to God.

Chapter 11, "Humble Orthodoxy"

1. Josh observes, "Sometimes it seems like a lot of the people who care about orthodoxy are jerks" (page 218). Has that been your impression? What experiences prompted your answer?

2. "We all need to ask a vital question," Josh says. "What will we *do* with the knowledge of God that we have?" (page 218). The answer, of course, will take our entire lifetimes to unfold. But what will the answer look like for you in the immediate future?

3. Josh says we need both conviction and gentleness, both orthodoxy and humility (see pages 218–19). How are you growing
   in these areas? What are you learning about them? How is this
   changing you?

4. In this chapter Josh draws our attention to the book of the
   Bible known as 2 Timothy, "the words of a godly man who
   knows he is about to die" (pages 219–20). That godly man was
   Paul. What is the essence of these final words from Paul to
   Timothy, as Josh relates them in this chapter?

5. Josh reminds us, "We live in a world of truths and lies." And he
   says, "There is nothing more unloving than to be silent in the
   face of lies that will ruin another person" (page 221). What lies
   in and from our culture do you need to be aware of and ready
   to expose and confront?

6. "Truth matters," says Josh, "but so does our attitude. We have
   to live and speak and interact with others in a spirit of humility" (page 222). What can help you maintain this kind of
   humility?

7. Josh mentions the "inclination in every human heart to pursue
   knowledge to inflate the self rather than to glorify God" (page
   224). What can you do to stay aware of this prideful tendency
   and to guard against it?

8. "The solution to arrogant orthodoxy is not less orthodoxy; it's
   more" (page 225). What does Josh mean by that? If he's right,
   what response from you could be wisely appropriate?

9. Josh reminds himself and us that "the humility we need in our
   theology is first and foremost a humility before God" (page
   225). What is it about God and about you that makes that
   statement particularly true?

10. We're urged again on page 226 to put truth into action. "Try to live it. Don't spend all your time theorizing about it, debating about it, or blogging about it. Spend more energy living the truth you know than worrying about what the next guy does or doesn't know. Don't measure yourself by what you know. Measure yourself by your practice of what you know." On that score, how are you measuring up?

11. "Here's a useful exercise," Josh suggests (on page 227). "Go back over the doctrines we've studied in this book, and think about the real-world, real-life implications of each truth for your life. What would it look like to live the truth of each one? What would change about your relationships, your words, your attitudes, and your actions?" Try following that suggestion for at least one or two of chapters 3–10 in this book, after first identifying and reviewing the key topic in each chapter. If you can, set aside time to do this for all those chapters.

12. Read again, on page 230, Josh's description of our anticipated experience in eternity. What are you looking forward to the most?

13. On this chapter's last page, we come to this paragraph: "Jesus said that an unshakable foundation for life is found only in knowing him, in believing his words and living by his truth. The most important question any of us can ask is, Am I building my life on who Jesus is and what he has done? Is my life built on the rock of a true knowledge of God?" In an unhurried way, talk about this with God your Father, and express to him what's happening in your heart and mind.

ACKNOWLEDGMENTS

A SPECIAL THANKS TO…

Steve and Ken and the team at WaterBrook Multnomah and Random House for their support.

Moby Dick's House of Kabob for feeding me and to Whole Foods and the Kentland's Starbucks for space to write.

Bob and Sharron for making that morning on the beach possible.

The good people of Covenant Life, who make pastoring such a joy. Thank you for the way you support me, encourage me, and pray for me.

All the pastors of Covenant Life for allowing me to invest the time needed to complete this book. Thank you, Kenneth, Grant, and Corby, for all that you carried and led during that time.

All those who read the book and gave me suggestions: Robin, Ken, Greg, Heather, Amy, Josh, Brian, Isaac, and Jeff.

C.J. for the irreplaceable part you played in this story.

Eric for the vision of humble orthodoxy and for prodding me to write.

Justin, who encouraged me three years ago at Together for the Gospel to "write a boring book." Well, here it is, bro! And you were kind enough to read and critique every page. Thank you, Lane, for your gracious support.

John for urging me in Al's basement to turn the humble orthodoxy message into a book.

Mark for lunch and help with the table of contents.

My T5G boys (Collin, Justin, Tullian, and Greg), who listened to me talk endlessly about my writing voice, titles, and blurbs. May God answer our prayers in Asheville.

My editor, David, for allowing me to experiment, for giving me space to write differently, and for always having a vision for the message of this book. To Carol for the line edit.

My assistant, Katherine, for making do without meetings and for so passionately believing in this book.

All the people who prayed for me while I wrote, including my Facebook and Twitter friends. I'm particularly grateful to Mom, Tim, Meg, Linda, Raul, Elsabeth, Trisha, the Covenant Life staff, the Berry family, Donna, and Deborah for consistently telling me that you were praying.

Grandma Harris for trusting Jesus all these years.

My dad for late-night interviews and for letting me share your story.

My children—Emma, Joshua Quinn, and Mary Kate—for being excited about this book, talking to me about titles, celebrating every finished chapter, and asking which one was my favorite.

My sweet wife, Shannon, the love of my life. Thank you for serving me, putting up with me, and caring for our kids day in and day out. Thank you for letting me read you chapters even when you were tired. The book is done, sweetheart! I'm ready to clean the basement and go camping now.

My mom, who went to be with Jesus the summer after this book was first published. You taught me to read, taught me to write, and were my first editor. Most important, you pointed me to the Savior and prayed for me when I strayed. I love you and miss you so much.

NOTES

Chapter 1: My Rumspringa

1. Velda, quoted in "The Devil's Playground," *21C Magazine,* www.21cmagazine.com/issue1/devils_playground.html.

2. Tom Shachtman, *Rumspringa: To Be or Not to Be Amish* (New York: North Point, 2006), 251.

Chapter 2: In Which I Learn to Dig

1. J. Gresham Machen, *Christianity and Liberalism* (New York: Macmillan, 1923), 29.

Chapter 3: Near but Not in My Pocket

1. Christian Smith with Melinda Lundquist Denton, *Soul Searching: The Religious and Spiritual Lives of American Teenagers* (New York: Oxford University Press, 2005), 163–65.

2. J. I. Packer, *Knowing God* (Downers Grove, IL: InterVarsity, 1973), 83.

3. J. I. Packer, *Concise Theology: A Guide to Historic Christian Beliefs* (Wheaton, IL: Tyndale, 1993), 27.

4. Wayne Grudem, *Bible Doctrine: Essential Teachings of the Christian Faith* (Grand Rapids: Zondervan, 1999), 72.

5. R. C. Sproul, *The Holiness of God* (Wheaton, IL: Tyndale, 2000), 38.

6. I borrowed the microscope-telescope analogy from John Piper's sermon "Passion for the Supremacy of God, Part 1," delivered at

Passion 1997, Desiring God, www.desiringgod.org/Resource
Library/ConferenceMessages/ByDate/1997/1906_Passion_for_the
_Supremacy_of_God_Part_1/.

Chapter 4: Ripping, Burning, Eating

1. A. J. Jacobs, *The Year of Living Biblically: One Man's Humble Quest to Follow the Bible as Literally as Possible* (New York: Simon and Schuster, 2007), 4.
2. Jacobs, *The Year of Living Biblically,* 9.
3. Sally Lloyd-Jones, *The Jesus Storybook Bible: Every Story Whispers His Name* (Grand Rapids: Zonderkidz, 2007), 14–17.
4. J. I. Packer, *God Has Spoken: Revelation and the Bible* (Downers Grove, IL: InterVarsity, 1979), 50–52.
5. Sinclair B. Ferguson, *Handle with Care! A Guide to Using the Bible* (London: Hodder and Stoughton, 1982), 22.
6. Ferguson, *Handle with Care!* 28.
7. Wayne Grudem, *Bible Doctrine: Essential Teachings of the Christian Faith* (Grand Rapids: Zondervan, 1999), 41.
8. For further study I suggest reading the chapters on Scripture in a good systematic theology such as Wayne Grudem's *Bible Doctrine.* Or study J. I. Packer's book *"Fundamentalism" and the Word of God,* which lays out a comprehensive statement on the doctrine of Scripture. R. C. Sproul's excellent book *Knowing Scripture* will give you practical tools for interpreting and studying the Bible. And if you wrestle with questions about the reliability of Scripture, read Paul Barnett's *Is the New Testament Reliable?* It's not wrong to have questions. But it is wrong to leave questions unanswered and wallow in doubt when strong, reliable answers are available.

Chapter 5: God with a Bellybutton

1. C. S. Lewis, *Mere Christianity* (New York: Macmillan, 1960), 40–41.
2. The information on the wrong views of Christ's nature is drawn from Wayne Grudem, *Bible Doctrine: Essential Teachings of the Christian Faith* (Grand Rapids: Zondervan, 1999), 241–44.
3. The Chalcedonian Creed states: "We then, following the holy Fathers, all with one consent, teach men to confess one and the same Son, our Lord Jesus Christ, the same perfect in Godhead and also perfect in manhood; truly God and truly man, of a reasonable soul and body; consubstantial with the Father according to the Godhead, and consubstantial with us according to the Manhood; in all things like unto us, without sin; begotten before all ages of the Father according to the Godhead, and in these latter days, for us and for our salvation, born of the Virgin Mary, the Mother of God, according to the Manhood; one and the same Christ, Son, Lord, Only-begotten, to be acknowledged in two natures, inconfusedly, unchangeably, indivisibly, inseparably; the distinction of natures being by no means taken away by the union, but rather the property of each nature being preserved, and concurring in one Person and one Subsistence, not parted or divided into two persons, but one and the same Son, and only begotten, God the Word, the Lord Jesus Christ, as the prophets from the beginning have declared concerning him, and the Lord Jesus Christ himself has taught us, and the Creed of the holy Fathers handed down to us." Taken from "Ancient Creeds," www.monergism.com/thethreshold/articles/onsite/ancientcreeds.html.
4. John M. Frame, *Salvation Belongs to the Lord: An Introduction to Systematic Theology* (Phillipsburg, NJ: P and R Publishing, 2006), 131.
5. Frame, *Salvation Belongs to the Lord,* 130.

6. J. Gresham Machen, *Christianity and Liberalism* (New York: Macmillan, 1923), 96.

7. Machen, *Christianity and Liberalism*, 97.

8. Machen, *Christianity and Liberalism*, 103.

Chapter 6: A Way to Be Good Again

1. J. I. Packer, *Concise Theology: A Guide to Historic Christian Beliefs* (Wheaton, IL: Tyndale, 1993), 134.

2. John R. W. Stott, *The Cross of Christ* (Downers Grove, IL: InterVarsity, 1986), 68.

3. Stott, *The Cross of Christ*, 103.

4. The original version of the story "The Room" (first published in *New Attitude* magazine, April 1995), along with information that clears up questions about its authorship, can be accessed at JoshHarris.com, www.joshharris.com/the_room.php.

5. Marilyn Elias, "A Mind Haunted from Within," *USA Today*, May 8, 2008, Section D, 1–2.

6. Khaled Hosseini, *The Kite Runner* (New York: Riverhead, 2007), 1.

7. Hosseini, *The Kite Runner*, 2.

8. Stott, *The Cross of Christ*, 175.

9. One example of the Muslim version of the story is on www.the modernreligion.com/room.html.

Chapter 7: How Jesus Saved Gregg Eugene Harris

1. Jerry Bridges, from a sermon on Ephesians 4:7–13 titled "Gifts of Grace to Build the Church" given at Covenant Life, Gaithersburg, MD, on November 23, 2008, www.covlife.org/resources.

2. John Phillips, "San Francisco," copyright © 1967, MCA Music Publishing.

3. John M. Frame, *Salvation Belongs to the Lord: An Introduction to Systematic Theology* (Phillipsburg, NJ: P and R Publishing, 2006), 185.

4. Jerry Bridges, *The Discipline of Grace: God's Role and Our Role in the Pursuit of Holiness* (Colorado Springs: NavPress, 1994), 51.

5. J. I Packer, *Knowing God* (Downers Grove, IL: InterVarsity, 1973), 200.

6. Sinclair B. Ferguson, *Children of the Living God* (Colorado Springs: NavPress, 1987), xi.

Chapter 8: Changed, Changing, to Be Changed

1. "The Ten Commandments," *This American Life,* episode 332, www.thisamericanlife.org/Radio_Episode.aspx?sched=1246.

2. Wayne Grudem, *Bible Doctrine: Essential Teachings of the Christian Faith* (Grand Rapids: Zondervan, 1999), 493.

3. Ted Haggard, "In God They Trust: NBC's Tom Brokaw Goes Inside the World of Christian Evangelicals," October 28, 2005, MSNBC .com, www.msnbc.msn.com/id/9804232/.

4. Robert Murray McCheyne, quoted in John Piper, Justin Taylor, eds., *Suffering and the Sovereignty of God* (Wheaton, IL: Crossway, 2006), 212.

5. Martin Luther, the first of The Ninety-Five Theses written in 1517, quoted in Bruce Demarest, *The Cross and Salvation: The Doctrine of God,* ed. John S. Feinberg (Wheaton, IL: Crossway, 2006), 270.

6. Timothy Keller, "All of Life Is Repentance," www.pcabakersfield .com/articles/all_of_life_is_repentance.pdf.

Chapter 9: I Believe in the Holy Spirit

1. For an example of how misguided this teaching is see 2 Corinthians 12:7–10, where we learn that an ailment Paul faced had nothing to

do with his sin or unbelief. In fact, it was God's purpose to glorify himself through Paul's weakness.

2. John M. Frame, *Salvation Belongs to the Lord: An Introduction to Systematic Theology* (Phillipsburg, NJ: P and R Publishing, 2006), 159.

3. J. I. Packer, *Keep in Step with the Spirit: Finding Fullness in Our Walk with God* (Grand Rapids: Baker, 2005), 11.

4. Daniel B. Wallace and M. James Sawyer, eds., *Who's Afraid of the Holy Spirit? An Investigation into the Ministry of the Spirit of God Today* (Dallas: Biblical Studies Press, 2005), 7.

5. Wallace and Sawyer, *Who's Afraid of the Holy Spirit?* 8.

6. Wallace and Sawyer, *Who's Afraid of the Holy Spirit?* 9.

7. Packer, *Keep in Step with the Spirit,* 57.

Chapter 10: The Invisible Made Visible

1. John M. Frame, *Salvation Belongs to the Lord: An Introduction to Systematic Theology* (Phillipsburg, NJ: P and R Publishing, 2006), 234.

2. John R. W. Stott, *The Message of Ephesians: God's New Society* (Downers Grove, IL: InterVarsity, 1979), 129.

3. Wayne Grudem, quoting John Calvin: "Wherever we see the Word of God purely preached and heard, and the sacraments administered according to Christ's institution, there, it is not to be doubted, a church of God exists." *Bible Doctrine: Essential Teachings of the Christian Faith* (Grand Rapids: Zondervan, 1999), 369.

4. J. I. Packer, *Concise Theology: A Guide to Historic Christian Beliefs* (Wheaton, IL: Tyndale, 1993), 194.

5. John Piper, "Evangelist Bill Piper: Fundamentalist Full of Grace and Joy" (sermon, 2008 Desiring God Conference for Pastors, February 5, 2008), www.desiringgod.org/ResourceLibrary/Biographies/2594 _Evangelist_Bill_Piper_Fundamentalist_Full_of_Grace_and_Joy/.

6. John R. W. Stott, *The Message of the Sermon on the Mount* (Downers Grove, IL: InterVarsity, 1985), 64–65.

7. Dietrich Bonhoeffer, quoted in Stott, *The Message of the Sermon on the Mount*, 62.

Chapter 11: Humble Orthodoxy

1. Timothy Keller, *The Reason for God: Belief in an Age of Skepticism* (New York: Dutton, 2008), 162.

2. I've adapted a quote by Keller in which he addresses the issue of politics: "If we get our very identity, our sense of worth, from our political position, then politics is not really about politics, it is about *us*. Through our cause we are getting a self, our worth. That means we *must* despise and demonize the opposition" (Keller, *The Reason for God*, 168).

3. D. A. Carson, *The Gagging of God: Christianity Confronts Pluralism* (Grand Rapids: Zondervan, 1996), 439.

4. Mark Dever, "Humble Dogmatism," Together for the Gospel, www.t4g.org/2006/02/humble-dogmatism/.

5. Dever, "Humble Dogmatism."

RECOMMENDED READING
FOR FURTHER STUDY

If reading *Dug Down Deep* has created an appetite in you for further study of Christian theology and doctrine, here are some books I recommend that relate to the content of each chapter. Keep digging!

Chapters 1 and 2 on the Importance of Christian Doctrine
Bible Doctrine: Essential Teachings of the Christian Faith by Wayne Grudem
Concise Theology: A Guide to Historic Christian Beliefs by J. I. Packer
Doctrine: What Christians Should Believe by Mark Driscoll and Gerry Breshears

Chapter 3 on the Doctrine of God
The Holiness of God by R. C. Sproul
Knowing God by J. I. Packer
The Pleasures of God: Meditations on God's Delight in Being God by John Piper

Chapter 4 on the Doctrine of Scripture
Ancient Word, Changing Worlds: The Doctrine of Scripture in a Modern Age by Stephen J. Nichols and Eric T. Brandt
"Fundamentalism" and the Word of God: Some Evangelical Principles by J. I. Packer
Knowing Scripture by R. C. Sproul

What Does God Want of Us Anyway? A Quick Overview of the Whole Bible
by Mark Dever

Chapter 5 on the Doctrine of the Person and Work of Christ

For Us and for Our Salvation: The Doctrine of Christ in the Early Church
by Stephen J. Nichols

Putting Jesus in His Place: The Case for the Deity of Christ by Robert M.
Bowman Jr. and J. Ed Komoszewski

Seeing and Savoring Jesus Christ by John Piper

Chapter 6 on the Doctrine of the Atonement

The Cross of Christ by John R. W. Stott

In My Place Condemned He Stood: Celebrating the Glory of the Atonement
by J. I. Packer and Mark Dever

It Is Well: Expositions on Substitutionary Atonement by Mark Dever and
Michael Lawrence

Chapter 7 on the Doctrine of Salvation

Do I Know God? Finding Certainty in Life's Most Important Relationship
by Tullian Tchividjian

*The Gospel for Real Life: Turn to the Liberating Power of the Cross…Every
Day* by Jerry Bridges

What Is the Gospel? by Greg Gilbert

Chapter 8 on the Doctrine of Sanctification

The Enemy Within: Straight Talk About the Power and Defeat of Sin by Kris
Lundgaard

Holiness: Its Nature, Hindrances, Difficulties and Roots by J. C. Ryle

Instruments in the Redeemer's Hands: People in Need of Change Helping People in Need of Change by Paul David Tripp

You Can Change: God's Transforming Power for Our Sinful Behavior and Negative Emotions by Tim Chester

Chapter 9 on the Doctrine of the Holy Spirit

Engaging with the Holy Spirit: Real Questions, Practical Answers by Graham A. Cole

Keep in Step with the Spirit: Finding Fullness in Our Walk with God by J. I. Packer

Showing the Spirit: A Theological Exposition of 1 Corinthians, 12–14 by D. A. Carson

Chapter 10 on the Doctrine of the Church

What Is a Healthy Church? by Mark Dever

What Is a Healthy Church Member? by Thabiti M. Anyabwile

Why Church Matters by Joshua Harris

Why We Love the Church: In Praise of Institutions and Organized Religion by Kevin DeYoung and Ted Kluck

Chapter 11 on the Importance of Sound Doctrine and Humility

Bible Doctrine: Essential Teachings of the Christian Faith by Wayne Grudem

Don't Stop Believing: Why Living Like Jesus Is Not Enough by Michael E. Wittmer

Salvation Belongs to the Lord: An Introduction to Systematic Theology by John M. Frame

ABOUT THE AUTHOR

JOSHUA HARRIS is the lead pastor of Covenant Life Church in Gaithersburg, Maryland. A gifted speaker with a passion for making theological truth easy to understand, Joshua is perhaps best known for his runaway bestseller, *I Kissed Dating Goodbye*, which he wrote at the age of twenty-one. His later books include *Boy Meets Girl*, *Not Even a Hint*, and *Why Church Matters*. He and his wife, Shannon, have three children.

www.joshharris.com
twitter.com/harrisjosh
www.facebook.com/joshharris.fanpage

More Books By
Joshua Harris

I Kissed Dating Goodbye shows what it means to entrust your love life to God. Joshua Harris shares his story of giving up recreational dating and discovering that God has something even better—a life of sincere love, true purity, and purposeful singleness.

Boy Meets Girl presents a healthy, joyous alternative to recreational dating—biblical courtship. It's romance chaperoned by wisdom, cared for by community, and directed by God's Word. Harris reveals how it worked for him and his wife, and includes inspiring stories from others who've learned to keep God at the center of their relationship.

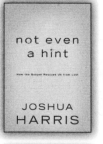

Lust isn't just a guy problem—it's a human problem. In this "PG-rated" book—straightforward without being graphic—Harris shares his own struggles, speaks to those entrenched in lust or just flirting with temptation, and unveils how the gospel frees us to live holy lives.

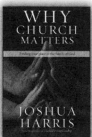

We are a generation of consumers, independent and critical. We attend church, but we don't want to settle down and truly invest ourselves. In *Why Church Matters* Harris shows how vital the church is for our growth and for God's mission in the world.

Read an excerpt at WaterBrookMultnomah.com